Spy
Mysteries
Unveiled

COLONEL VERNON HINCHLEY

Spy
Mysteries
Unveiled

DODD, MEAD & COMPANY

NEW YORK

Preface

FEW SUBJECTS in all history have been so maltreated by writers as espionage. Since it is concerned with *secret* service, it never advertises: even if an outstanding case should come into the open—even into open court—full details are seldom revealed. This is reasonable enough: if the evidence should show how a spy was caught, then his successor could avoid capture.

Yet people—very respectable people—have as avid an interest in spies as they have in murderers. With so little factual information available, the temptation to journalists and authors is to dramatise and romanticise. Every woman spy is by definition glamorous—but none of those I have met caused me to miss a single heart-beat. There are no ordinary agents—they are nearly all 'master-spies': the others are 'spy-masters': all cases are 'sensational.'

It is the popular imaginative treatment of spy cases which has prompted me to write this book. I think I can claim in all modesty to know as much about spies and counter-spies as the next man, and my experience has been practical, not imaginative. In some chapters I have presented classic cases from new angles: in many I have included information in my possession

5

but not covered by the Official Secrets Act. In others I have reconstructed particular cases, also from a fresh and factual viewpoint: I have tried to complete some unfinished records, advancing solutions to some famous mysteries of espionage. To disarm possible criticism in advance, I ought to emphasise one feature of my reconstructions. It will be quite obvious that I was not present at all the conversations repeated. With some I may have happened to know one or more of the participants: in others I have merely made elementary deductions—if I know the *effect* of the conversation it is not too difficult to reconstruct its pattern.

My records will probably arouse different feelings among my readers: surprise—even astonishment: anger: incredulity. There is an old cliché about fact being stranger than fiction. In espionage this is almost always true. It may not be as dramatic, sentimental, or bloodthirsty, but it can indeed be *very* much stranger—and even more sensational!

V.H.

London, 1963

Contents

ONE

Gary Powers—Spy Pilot

"I CAN'T UNDERSTAND IT," said the American general. "How did the Russians shoot down the U-2?"

"Maybe they've got a new rocket——"

"We should have heard *something* about it—Russia isn't a completely closed book. We've been overflying Russia for four years. Their MIGs couldn't fly as high as the U-2, and their rockets couldn't reach it. Then how in hell did they shoot Powers down?"

"That's the 64,000-dollar question," said his chief of staff.

135 Lubianka Street, Moscow, looks like an ordinary block of offices. It *is* a block of offices, but they are by no means ordinary. This is The Centre, as Communist spies call it—the headquarters of The Net, the vast espionage organisation built up by the Russians.

It was late at night, in April, 1960, when the visitor from the Kremlin arrived: Granitov, one of Khrushchev's personal assistants. He made for the room of a Director of Regional Espionage named Malinski, who greeted his caller courteously.

"We are alone?" asked Granitov, his tone full of meaning.

"Yes. One moment." Malinski locked the door, and instructed

9

the office telephone exchange that he was not to be troubled with calls. "Now, what can I do for you?"

"I should say that I am here direct from the Kremlin," Granitov began.

Malinski immediately began to think with some apprehension of his past mistakes and failures, but Granitov's next words reassured him.

"I have put up a certain suggestion in high quarters, and it has been approved. Now I need your services—yours. That is why I have come direct to you, and not to Comrade Skelepin."

"I am honoured. You have only to tell me what I can do."

"You are in charge of the Central-South Asia section? Good. But we must begin at home. For nearly four years American spy planes have been flying over Soviet territory——"

"Yes, I know that. It is an affront—a typical capitalist affront. I read an account in the Air Corps journal about three years ago. These American aircraft fly very high, I understand?"

"*Too* high. Our defences—fighters and rockets—can't get near them. Imagine, they are taking photographs of Russia from seven miles up!"

"And they are good photographs, too," Malinski nodded. "You know that our American section has some copies—'borrowed' from the Pentagon by one of our agents."

"Yes. But at the moment I am not interested in photographs. It is important that one of these U-2 aircraft should be brought down—quickly."

"But—but what can I do——"

"The Defence Ministry offer no hope. That is why I come to you. Your area includes India, Pakistan and Afghanistan, does it not?"

"Yes—and Persia."

"You must drop everything else and leave for Afghanistan tonight. The Army will provide the aircraft. I will outline the plan, but you will have to fill in all the details. One of these American aircraft *must* be shot down!"

"Am I permitted to ask why?" Malinski queried.

"I don't see why not. Comrade Nikita intends to wreck the forthcoming Summit Conference."

"What? But I thought he wanted it!"

"He did. But America and Britain have made it quite clear that they will stand firm over Berlin—Nikita's first objective. Now Nikita cannot risk a failure—there are too many Stalinists waiting for him to fail——"

"I have often wondered why he does not eliminate them."

"He will! But in the meantime he wants to bring down a U-2 on Russian soil——"

"I have it! He will use the incident to smash the Summit Conference!"

"Yes. And he will gain the world's sympathy. And at the same time he will discredit Eisenhower, who has not kept the promises he made at Camp David. Now let us look at maps . . . ."

Next day Malinski, after taking every precaution, got in touch with his resident agent in Kabul, the Afghan capital.

"I need a technician—he should be an expert on aircraft. He must be a Pathan—and have relatives in Pakistan. And he must be reliable—friendly to Russia."

"A Pathan! They don't make the best mechanics. But I'll look around. How long can you give me?"

"Until tomorrow morning."

"What? Hell!"

"I'll meet you here at twelve noon—bring the man with you."

Mohammed Ghazni Khan slipped over the Pakistan frontier with ease. No boundary among these wild mountains could ever be patrolled adequately. And the Pathans straddled the boundary. Mohammed Ghazni Khan might have no near blood-relative in Pakistan, but he had thousands of distant cousins, men of his own tribe. He was making for an old family friend, who lived in Peshawar.

None of his colleagues would have recognised him in his

dirty cotton clothes. In his squadron he was esteemed a very smart officer, one of the best jet pilots in the Afghan air force. He flew a MIG—and had been trained in Russia. Now he passed as a humble tribesman of the North-west Frontier Territory, passing without comment through the Pathan country.

A bus carried him from a village near the Khyber Pass to Peshawar. There his friend received him cordially.

"Now you see what I want," said Mohammed Ghazni Khan, after the inevitable coffee. "I want a man who works at the airport—the military section of it—in fact, the American section of the military section."

"But our people are only employed there on menial jobs," his friend Moulay Khan protested. "Cleaners—porters—things like that. The Americans see to all the aircraft."

"I am quite willing to be a cleaner or a porter."

"What! You, the son of my friend, father of a hundred sons, owner of a thousand camels!"

"Find me a cleaner who will let me take his place. He will not lose by it, I promise you."

"Very well, I will try. I will go into the shanty town where such people live. I will take a boy with me, and send him for you when I have found the man you want."

Evidently the task was not too difficult—the boy was back within two hours. He led the way to the outskirts of Peshawar. Here was a district of crude huts and rough shanties: many of the people occupying them had come here in 1947, as refugees from the shocking Hindu-Moslem strife preceding and following independence.

"Here is your man, Mohammed," said Moulay Khan. "He is sick, so will be glad of the rest. But I have told him that you will pay over his wages."

"So I will—and a hundred rupees a week more."

"And you will hand the job back to him when you have finished?"

"Of course I will."

In the East it is not unusual for one man to hand over his job to another—or even to sell it to him! A foreman of a squad of unskilled workers is interested only in the number engaged, not in individuals.

So Mohammed Ghazni Khan was accepted at the Peshawar airport. His job was to help to keep the runways clear of sand blown over by the wind. Not a very exciting task. And, at first sight, not a good background for a saboteur or spy.

Yet he had surmounted his first difficulty—he had gained admission to the airport.

But not to the American section. This consisted of a large hangar and a parking apron, both guarded by military police.

Mohammed was well qualified: a skilled pilot, speaking good English, and with plenty of courage and initiative. Perhaps all he needed was time—but that, he understood, was the one thing lacking. The alternative was clear—he must be prepared to take risks.

Moulay Khan was willing to help. The Pathan's loyalty is to his tribe rather than to his country, and Russia and America were two distant places almost meaningless to the local people. Few Pathans can resist a financial inducement.

It was Moulay Khan who in fact directed much of the detailed work involved in the plot. One of his men, a waiter in the officers' mess, came in with a story about a transport due in from Turkey. As Mohammed Ghazni Khan knew that the American Double Ten squadron, which carried out aerial espionage, was based in Turkey, he was of course interested in the news—and asked for more.

Service men from the Western countries seldom keep their mouths shut. They have been brought up in the tradition of free speech. True, they are often warned, and may even curb their tongues when on leave or pass. But in their own messes, talking to their friends, what need is there for restriction? Waiters and servants are akin to Chesterton's mentally Invisible Man. Besides, they have all passed the standard Security tests.

But not security against bribery. By judicious expenditure

of rupees, Mohammed Ghazni Khan was able to fit several more fragments into the jigsaw puzzle. The U-2 on the apron had just been prepared for a very long flight. Its pilot was among the party being flown in from Turkey. Even his name had been mentioned—Captain Gary Powers.

Mohammed Ghazni Khan understood only his own part of the task, which is good espionage practice. If caught and tortured, he could give little away. And within forty-eight hours he would be gone—back to Afghanistan.

The American sector of the airfield was sealed off, but what are a few strands of wire to a determined man? The U-2 aircraft was under individual guard. A military policeman stood by it or circled round it, relieved every two hours.

Mohammed Ghazni Khan had picked up these details by distant observation through night glasses. For that matter, the concrete apron was well lighted. He noticed another trifle— the relief always took place on the starboard side of the aircraft, away from the entrance to the cockpit. This decided his plan.

He waited until 2 A.M. The man on duty and his relief chatted for a couple of minutes. There is nothing more boring than guard duty, and their enthusiasm had long before flagged.

In that two minutes the barefooted Afghan had climbed into the cockpit. There was not too much room. In front of him was the complicated instrument panel of the aircraft. By his side and behind him were more instruments—radar, radio, cameras and others which he could not identify.

That did not matter. His objective was the altimeter, the delicate instrument which indicated the height at which the aircraft flew. He had curled himself up on the floor of the cockpit. Now, an inch at a time, he twisted his body around so that his hands could reach the altimeter. He knew exactly what to do—he had practised it well before leaving Kabul. He carried a tiny torch, but would not need it—he could do the job in the dark.

The plastic face of the altimeter was fastened to the instrument by four small screws, one at each corner. Using his fingers as his eyes, Ghazni Khan unscrewed the one at the top right-hand corner.

The second part of his task was as simple. He carried a number of screws exactly like the one he had removed—the Russian in Kabul had given them to him. He inserted one of them in the vacant hole. That was all.

Now he had to wait, in absolute stillness, for nearly two hours. His own part in the scheme was accomplished. What was it all about? He knew that the inserted screw was highly magnetised. That is to say, it would affect the accuracy of the altimeter, by attracting its steel needle. The altimeter of course worked on the aneroid principle, reacting to the pressure of the atmosphere. As this lowered, the needle would swing to the right, showing a rise in height as marked on the numbered indicator. What would happen now that a powerful magnet had been inserted? Presumably the needle would still swing to the right but, attracted by the magnet, it would swing farther than it should have done.

Captain Gary Powers was no stranger to the U-2, that amazing aircraft built for flight at exceptionally high altitudes. He had flown many sorties along the Turkish-Russian frontier, reporting on weather conditions and radar defences.

This was a different task, but he was quite confident. He did not pretend to understand the many pieces of complicated apparatus he carried, but that was unnecessary. His flight plan was complete in every detail. He had to switch this on at one spot, that at another.

The flight was as uneventful as he had been assured it would be. The Russians knew he was there—three MIG fighters had vainly attempted to reach him. But now, near Sverdlovsk, came disaster. To quote his own words: "Quite unexpectedly I heard a kind of hollow explosion and saw an orange flash. Perhaps the plane was not hit directly, and the explosion took place *near* the plane." It appeared obvious that the fatal weapon was a rocket—no MIG was anywhere near at the time. The aircraft hurtled earthwards, but Powers was able to bale out.

Powers's equipment included a poisoned needle, but no one could blame his failure to use it. He was captured, tried and sentenced to ten years' imprisonment. And Mr Khrushchev made good use of the incident to shatter the Summit Conference —and did indeed gain some sympathy in non-Communist countries in his complaint against American spying from the sky. He did not think it worth while to mention that Communist pilots had been doing the same thing over Western Europe for years.

Since the shooting down of the U-2 had been so useful to him, it was scarcely surprising that Khrushchev had agreed to Powers's exchange for a Russian agent when he had served less than two years of his sentence.

After the trial of Powers, one of the senior Soviet officers who had been engaged on it was talking to his brother, who was a member of the Communist Presidium.

"As I see it, from foreign newspapers, the Americans are not so concerned about Powers as about the fact that we shot down his aircraft at 68,000 feet."

"Yes, that is so. They don't believe that we've got a rocket which can do it."

"But we have?"

"No."

"What?"

"I wish we had."

"But—but what happened, then? In the trial Powers said that he was flying at 68,000 feet when his aircraft was hit."

"He *thought* he was flying at 68,000 feet. His altimeter wasn't very reliable. Workmanship in the capitalist states is often faulty, I gather. The people's hearts are not in their jobs."

TWO

George Blake—Double Spy

WHEN HE LAST APPEARED IN PUBLIC, George Blake had a faint smile on his lips.

He was standing in the Old Bailey dock on the 3rd of May, 1961. He had just heard the Judge sentence him to forty-two years in prison—one of the longest sentences ever passed in a British court. It might seem that he had little to smile about. Yet he knew the full details of his case—then hidden from the general public.

That little smile was the last of many mysteries in the strange career of George Blake.

Actually, his name was not Blake, and he had no drop of British blood in his veins. His father, whose name was Behar, was born in Cairo of mixed Turkish-Spanish-Jewish origin. Later Egypt became a British protectorate, so he ranked as a 'British protected person.' In the first World War he served in the British Army, was promoted to captain, and was decorated for gallantry. In 1919 he married a Dutch girl, Catherine Beijdervellen, of a well-known Protestant family of Rotterdam. Behar was of the Jewish faith, but his son was brought up as a Lutheran.

17

George, born in Rotterdam in 1922, was the eldest of three children of the marriage.

Albert Behar died in 1933, and ten-year-old George was sent to Cairo, where he lived until he was sixteen. He returned to his mother in Holland shortly before the war.

When war came, Mrs Blake and the two younger children fled to England. George stayed behind to complete his education. Then came the German bombers, blasting the city of Rotterdam, and the hopes of young George.

So George Behar, using the pseudonym Pieter de Vries, joined the Dutch Resistance. He was intelligent and fearless in fighting the German Occupation forces. Once the Gestapo caught him, but he managed to escape.

But there followed a disaster which may have had long-term effects on his career. The whole of the British sabotage organisation in Holland was betrayed to the Germans. He was one of the few agents who evaded arrest. He continued his activities, at times working with the Communist Underground movement, which often acted independently of other Resistance groups.

After more successful exploits at the risk of his life, Behar earned such a reputation for skill and daring that he was recruited for the British Secret Service, a much more selective and more secret department than the war-time sabotage organisation known as S.O.E.

At that stage Behar was a brilliant but self-taught beginner at espionage. He was too useful for his life to be risked through some amateurish mistake in tactics. So he was told to come to England for training. He made his way across France and Spain and thence by sea.

During this first visit to his adopted country Behar passed with top marks through the arduous technical courses of a professional spy. He was commissioned in the R.N.V.R. and for the remainder of the war worked as a Naval Intelligence officer. It was at this time that he obtained British citizenship, and took the name of Blake.

After the war he was posted to the British Zone of occupied Germany. The British Secret Service acts on the practical principle: set a spy to catch a spy. His opponents were now not the Germans but the Russians, whose agents were active in the British Zone.

What could have been his reactions at this stage? He had earlier conceived a good deal of respect for Communist organisation and efficiency during his war-time activities against the Germans. He may have admired their methods whilst detesting their ideals, but, whatever his beliefs, he seemed to be strongly anti-Communist. He appeared to be the keenest spy-catcher of his hand-picked group. Yet he does not seem to have caught any Russian spies. Perhaps he was just unlucky!

The time came for him to be released from the R.N.V.R. He returned to England, and as a civilian was sent with a Government grant to Cambridge to study Russian. When he was sufficiently proficient he was offered a post in the Foreign Office.

This appointment was very unusual. As a rule the British Foreign Office selects its staff with great care. Candidates for positions of any responsibility must be British-born sons of British-born parents. Yet the young man who now became a Vice-Consul was a mixture of Jew, Dutchman, Spaniard and Turk, reared in Holland and partly educated in Egypt—a twenty-five-year-old who had never set foot on British soil until he was about twenty.

What had happened to all the Security checks? Had someone grown careless? Had strings been pulled? Or was some faceless master-mind grooming Blake for one of the most daring Intelligence coups of the century?

If this last supposition be correct, it would have been realised that if anything went wrong, questions would be asked about Blake's appointment. But it would also have been realised that in that event he could be discredited and disowned—an occupational hazard of the ruthless Intelligence game.

So far I have kept to the facts as previously revealed. It is now essential to fill a vital gap by recording an important incident and an interview—though obviously I cannot guarantee its word-for-word accuracy.

The Foreign Office has its own Intelligence service. Naturally it is concerned not with guns or bombs, but with political trends in foreign countries. Blake's qualifications as a linguist prompted his allocation to the Intelligence Branch.

The time of the interview is a sunny spring morning in 1948. The place is a sound-proof room in an old-fashioned house within a half-mile of Whitehall. At a big desk sits a shrewd old gentleman whose name is never mentioned, even by his own staff. Let us dub him "K," which is near enough to what he was called at Cabinet meetings. He is glancing keenly at young George Blake.

"Now that China's going Communist, my boy," says "K," "British foreign policy has got to be re-assessed. It seems possible that Mao Tse-tung may retain his independence. But if Russia gets a political stranglehold on China, the West will face a combination of two of the greatest countries in the world —a combination which in time will be irresistible."

"I understand, sir," nods Blake.

"Certain negotiations have taken place. An interim decision has been reached. Top-secret memoranda exist and copies are filed in the Kremlin and in Mao's headquarters. Britain must have copies of the memoranda, so that we may know where we stand."

"Not an easy job, sir."

"Practically bloody impossible," says "K." "I'm giving you the assignment."

"Thank you, sir. I take it as a compliment. When do I start for Moscow?"

"You don't. Russian counter-espionage has had thirty years to perfect its methods. The Chinese are newcomers to the game, so you'll begin from that side. I'm arranging for you to be posted to Seoul in Korea. As Vice-Consul on special duties.

You can have plenty of money but not much time. Recruit some top-grade agents. Report to me when you think you're ready to pull the job off. Now go and have a spot of leave, and learn how to handle a pair of chopsticks."

War overtook Blake before he had his secret pipe-lines organised. Two years are not enough for the organisation of a widespread espionage network.

In June, 1950, Seoul was captured by North Korean forces. A mob, crazy for loot, surrounded the British Legation. But George Blake went out, alone but unafraid, and persuaded them to disperse. It was not easy. It was little short of heroic.

Yet it was only a few days before Communist troops entered the Legation and made prisoners of the staff and British subjects who had taken refuge within it. With a crowd of missionaries, nuns and captured soldiers, they were taken North on a grim death-march through snow and slush. Weak and underfed, if they fell from exhaustion brutal guards shot them out of hand. Beatings with rifle-butts were a daily occurrence. Such experiences were scarcely calculated to win converts to Communism.

A year later, at a camp at Hadjang, the standard attempts at indoctrination began. The date is important—it was August, 1951—for one of the espionage charges made later against Blake was in respect of that period.

Students of the Blake case agree that many mysteries could be solved if only we knew exactly what happened in the bleak interrogation room of Hadjang camp, among the drifting North Korean snows. Did this tough, intelligent, almost heroic young man suddenly crack in what seems an incredible manner? Or did he bring off an Intelligence coup so brilliant that he had to be broken to conceal its full effects? Let the facts speak for themselves.

After some amateurish attempts at indoctrination by North Korean officers, an expert took over. He was a Russian Intelligence officer known as Major Kuzmitch, but that was not his real name. He was highly intelligent and efficient at his difficult task. He was tall, handsome, fair-haired, and could be rather charming—when he liked. The prisoners nicknamed him "Blondie."

Blake had a series of sessions with Major Kuzmitch; years later, fellow-prisoners were questioned as to Blake's manner after these sessions. They report that although he did not disclose much about what had been said on both sides, Blake's strong anti-Communist views did not appear to have altered in the slightest.

Questioned as to Major Kuzmitch's method of approach, other prisoners said that to draw them out he pretended to see certain good points in the Western way of life. We can imagine that he had some interesting discussions with so intelligent a victim as George Blake.

We can also imagine that Blake must have thought back to his interview with old "K" on a sunny morning three years previously. He had failed, so far, in his assignment. He had been starved, beaten and degraded by his Communist captors. He was young and ambitious—eager to come out on top in the murderous mental jungle warfare of Secret Service. Were the brain-washing sessions a brilliant success—not for Major Kuzmitch but for Blake?

Let us suppose that Blake, with his ten-year experience of Communist mentality, did not merely resist conversion to Communism *but converted Major Kuzmitch!*

Let us suppose that, pressing home his success, Blake promised Major Kuzmitch asylum in the West if he would prove himself by what is known in Intelligence circles as 'working his passage.' Let us further suppose that—unable to complete his vital assignment himself—Blake sent Major Kuzmitch back into Communist China to ferret out that vital information about Sino-Russian relations which would influence the framing of British foreign policy for the next decade.

The suggestion seems incredible. It seems almost as incredible, in fact, as that Blake himself should suddenly become a

Communist. For if Major Kuzmitch had acted as Blake directed and somehow obtained the vital information, his life would not have been worth a kopek in Russia. He would have had to escape abroad—make his secret way to a Western country, hand over his information and ask for sanctuary.

And that is precisely what Major Kuzmitch did! By the time Blake was back in England, making his sensational report to "K," Major Kuzmitch had got to the United States. His arrival was kept secret, according to official reports, "because of certain information he was able to provide." I emphasise by repetition this astonishing fact—that Kuzmitch, not Blake, defected to the opposing side.

The Korean war ended and Blake returned to England early in 1953. Fellow-prisoners were unanimous as to his courage and physical fortitude whilst he was being beaten and insulted by Communists who hoped to convert him. They said he never wavered.

And these witnesses were not gullible types. They included Sir Vyvyan Holt, British Minister in Seoul, who said that his life had been saved by Blake's tireless nursing. They included Philip Deane, correspondent of the London *Observer*, Commissioner Lord of the Salvation Army, and M. Jean Meadmore, the French Consul-General.

During Blake's trial, the Attorney-General said that "his philosophical and political views underwent a change, and in the autumn of 1951 he held the strong conviction that the Communist system was the better one and deserved to triumph." He must have been misinformed. The savage treatment of Blake in Korea was scarcely calculated to convert him to Communism!

After a few months' leave, Blake was sent back to Occupied Berlin, this time as an officer of the British Secret Service Department known as M.I.6.

We have now reached the period when, according to Blake's 'confession,' all the secret documents which passed through his hands were shown to his Russian Secret Service contacts. This

monstrous betrayal of the country to which Blake owed so
much is alleged to have included details of the personnel of the
British Secret Service in Germany and the Middle East. If, as
was implied, Russia thus learned all about our espionage
organisations, here was material for a series of sensational spy
trials which would have made that of Captain Gary Powers
appear trivial in comparison.

It would have been an opportunity which the Russians
would never have neglected—*if* it had been available. *But the
records show that no such trials took place!* So the Russians did
not get a list of British spies from Blake—if they had, they could
never have resisted such a wonderful opportunity for propaganda
trials.

What, then, did happen? It is quite obvious that Blake was
not converted to Communism in Korea. Whatever did happen
must have occurred in Berlin. We approach, indeed, the important incident—or, rather, series of incidents—to which
earlier reference has been made.

In Berlin Blake, as a matter of course, used local agents.
One of them lived in East Berlin, and from time to time
supplied valuable economic information about East Germany.
So far as could be checked, it was accurate, and Blake gave full
support to his agent.

But one evening he took a risk. He had bought two tickets
for an East German theatre, and he sent one of them to his
agent. This man would then pass on his report to Blake while
the theatre was in darkness.

Instead, however, he whispered, "Follow me home!" Blake
trusted the man, who had been a competent and well-paid
agent, and duly followed him. To his chagrin, he found that he
had been led into a trap—the East German police awaited him.
What was even more disconcerting, he discovered that his
agent was in Russian pay!

Blake was taken to the Russian spy headquarters in what had
once been St Antonius's Hospital. There a Soviet officer put

the case very plainly. Blake was a spy: he was in Russian hands —and was likely to be for at least ten years. But there *was* an alternative. If he cared to spy for the Russians . . .

Blake made up his mind at once. His usefulness as a British agent was gravely impaired—he would never be able to venture into East Berlin again, and would doubtless be carefully watched even in West Berlin. Yet a good deal could be saved from the wreck. He could provide the Russians with misleading information. At the same time the Russians would 'inspire' him with information also intended to be misleading. Yet if you *know* that you are being 'inspired,' it is at least useful to learn what your opponents want you to believe. Then you can make a reasonable guess at the truth. The British would know that Blake was being 'inspired.' The Russians would not.

Blake duly reported what had happened to old "K," who approved his decision. So now Blake was launched on a new career—as a double spy.

The time came—as it inevitably does in the career of even the most brilliant double spy—when the Russians began to notice that the information Blake supplied was not always accurate. True, it consisted almost entirely of official documents which he handed over to be photographed. Many of these concerned British policy—which could of course be ill-advised.

When Blake was withdrawn from Germany and sent to the Lebanon, the Russians had not lost faith in him, and promptly re-established contact.

Yet, as I have said, the life of a double spy has a definite time limit. Thanks to Blake, the Russians had been misled over British policy in the Middle East. But if the plan was extended, it was bound to fail. But now his career was suddenly disrupted by the arrest of one of his sub-agents.

Horst Eitner was a German ex-soldier without a job until he met General Gehlen, a German Intelligence chief whose anti-Communist network was eventually taken over by the Americans. At first he did well, but his financial demands were too high, and he was dismissed. He was then enlisted by the British in Berlin, and worked under Blake. Again, he made a good beginning, but in September, 1960, the West German Secret Service discovered that he was a double agent, working primarily for the Russians! Arrested, he appealed to Blake to give evidence in his favour—and Blake made no reply. Thereupon Eitner denounced Blake, also as a Russian agent.

This was no news, of course. But it did indicate that Blake's period of service as a double spy must come to an abrupt end. At the same time his activities must be 'covered' by a plausible story. So he was ordered back from Beirut to London. (If he *had* been a Russian spy, would a clever man like Blake have meekly obeyed the summons, knowing what awaited him? He would have promptly joined Burgess and Maclean in Moscow.)

It was especially important that the Russians should accept as genuine some 'official' reports about Kuwait and the Trucial sheikdoms. Thus Blake had to be offered up as a sacrifice. His trial, and the savage sentence of forty-two years' imprisonment, would surely convince the Russians that he had indeed been a faithful agent—for them.

But where is Blake today? Is he sewing mailbags in a British jail? Or is he settled in Canada, under another name, with a reasonable capital behind him—the reward for a supreme act of self-sacrifice for Britain?

We shall see. The time will come when the full story can be revealed—and it is doubtful if we shall have to wait until the year 2003 to hear it.

THREE

Burgess and Maclean

No CASE IN MODERN TIMES attracted more attention than that of Burgess and Maclean. None has been more subjected to the process of dramatisation referred to in my introduction. Today even official American reports refer to Burgess and Maclean as nuclear spies, whereas in fact they had no technical knowledge whatsoever. Indeed, I hope to demonstrate that probably they were not spies at all! This especially applies to Burgess.

The case of Dr Bruno Pontecorvo is similar in some respects. An Italian and a clever physicist, he was engaged by Britain in nuclear research. There are those who complain that we should not employ foreigners, only British. But the number of British scientists in this particular field and of Pontecorvo's class was very limited, and we considered ourselves lucky to gain his services.

But, as usual, we did not pay him according to his ability. His salary was but a fraction of the earnings of some callow and husky-voiced youth developed into a pop singer by an enterprising manager. This left the way open for Russia, and offered a double advantage—at one stroke the Russians could weaken our nuclear team and strengthen their own. Pontecorvo had no national loyalty to Britain: he worked for a salary. The Russians did not waste time in trying to make a Communist of him: they were uninterested in his political beliefs, if any. They simply offered him nearly three times more pay than he was getting in England!

But although his account of the current state of British nuclear development would doubtless be of great interest to the Russians, there was no evidence that he had *previously* been acting as a spy while working in England. Thus there is no comparison between his case and that of Dr Fuchs.

Burgess and Maclean were not international hirelings. Both came of respected families which had served their country well—the father of Burgess was a distinguished sailor, while Maclean's was esteemed as leader of the Liberal Party in the House of Commons.

Many young men, themselves of ample means, were affected by the misery produced by the slump of the nineteen-thirties. Burgess and Maclean were among them—individually, for they had never been close friends. In the controversies of the time they decided that Communism was the only solution to the world's economic problem: so did many others. Youth is prone to idealism, and the Communist creed can be presented attractively, though experience of crudities and cruelties of its Russian form usually damp earlier enthusiasm. Both men were actually Communist Party members, for a year or so only.

Burgess was a very clever young man, but his life was undisciplined. He was a homosexual and a drunkard. Parties at his flat were wild—and exclusively male. More than once he was in trouble for driving a car while under the influence of drink.

During the war he served with the B.B.C., and then at the headquarters of the S.O.E.—the department which organised sabotage and Resistance operations. Later, he joined the Foreign Office. All his service was in a junior capacity, where he had little access to secret information.

His conduct was unsatisfactory. His private life could not be kept secret, and his seniors were concerned about his drunken bouts and his homosexuality. He never disguised his Left-wing sentiments, and boldly criticised Government policy—especially towards Russia. He was constantly 'odd man out' among his colleagues, and emphatically opposed their opinions. In 1950 he received a formal reprimand for indiscreet talk—which of itself suggests that he was no spy: the first essential of espionage is a close mouth. Just before he fled the country he had been belatedly asked to resign. Had he refused, his dismissal would have followed automatically.

Maclean, on the other hand, was highly regarded by his superiors. He received regular promotions, and attained a senior rank. But he was a psychopath, a 'split personality.' For weeks he would do excellent work: then would follow a spell of drunkenness and violence—there was one especially vicious outbreak in Cairo, but the kindly Foreign Office treated it as a nervous breakdown—and sent him to a psychiatrist. He was a neurotic pervert, and his sexual life was peculiar. He was married, with a family, but when he was drunk he became a homosexual.

Burgess and Maclean were peculiar characters, and it is amazing that they should have been employed in a department of such delicacy. But by May, 1951, trouble was at hand. In 1949 the Foreign Office received information that the Russians had possession of the contents of a secret document. A security check began—any one of 6000 people might have been implicated. The check took two years. Then the suspects had been gradually narrowed down to two or three—and one of them was Maclean.

The case did not indicate any great Security checks. Until then both Burgess and Maclean had passed them all. But even in my earliest years in espionage it was a steadfast principle that no one should ever be employed on work demanding secrecy if he were (*a*) a drunkard, and therefore liable to talk too much, or (*b*) a homosexual, and therefore open to blackmail.

There was yet another incident which must have perturbed

the Foreign Office. Some member of the staff had obviously warned Burgess and Maclean that trouble was approaching, rapidly.

They decided to decamp. But the subsequent story of their flight was marked by one very peculiar feature.

The Foreign Office has long been noted for its reticence. Not until *four years after* the case broke did it issue a report. This consisted of a formal synopsis of information already published in the Press. Paragraph 13 gave an interesting account of the flight of Burgess and Maclean. It read:

"Immediately the flight was known, all possible action was taken in the United Kingdom, and the French and other Continental security authorities were asked to trace the whereabouts of the fugitives and if possible to intercept them. All British Consulates in Western Europe were alerted, and special efforts were made to discover whether the fugitives had crossed the French frontiers on May 26 or 27. As a result of these and other enquiries, it was established that Maclean and Burgess together left Tatsfield by car for Southampton in the late evening of Friday, May 25, arrived at Southampton at midnight, caught the s.s. *Falaise* for St Malo, and disembarked at that port at 11.45 the following morning, leaving suitcases and some of their clothing on board. They were not seen on the train from St Malo to Paris, and it has been reported that two men, believed to be Maclean and Burgess, took a taxi to Rennes and there got the 1.18 P.M. train to Paris. Nothing more was seen of them."

This paragraph is indeed interesting—if only because it scarcely contains a word of truth!

(*a*) The French Security authorities say that they were not notified until six days after the flight of the two men.

(*b*) The authorities were asked if possible to "intercept" the fugitives. But the report also states quite accurately that Burgess "was under no obligation to report his movements."

Both men were British citizens: no charge had been made against them: they were free to travel as they willed.

(c) "Leaving suitcases and some of their clothing on board. . . . They were not seen on the train . . . "

They were not on the train. Indeed, *they were not even on the boat!*

A friend of mine knew Maclean—though he knew nothing of his drunken or homosexual proclivities; they both happened to be members of the same motoring club. My friend did not know Burgess.

My friend and another man were travelling to St Malo on the *Falaise* on the night of May the 25th, 1951. The cabin allocated to them was stuffy and noisy, and they asked the purser if he could give them another and better one.

"We are completely booked up. But a steward has reported that one reserved cabin has not been occupied—the luggage is there, but no passengers. I'll put a call over the loudspeakers. Come back in ten minutes, will you?"

They heard the public announcement. "Will Mr Mitchell and Mr Burgess kindly claim their cabin at once, please."

They did not come forward. A steward conducted my friend and his companion to the cabin, and removed the luggage of the two men. On one bag was the name, not Mitchell, but Donald Maclean. My friend was naturally intrigued; he looked over the ship, especially in its bars. There was no trace of his acquaintance Maclean. And when the passengers disembarked next morning he watched them carefully—Maclean was not among them.

My friend, a man of impeccable probity and meticulous attention to detail, was quite certain that Maclean was not on board. Neither he nor Burgess had approached their cabin during the night. Their luggage was not claimed.

Small wonder, then, that the French police failed to trace the movements of the fugitives. Yet Burgess and Maclean *did* flee

the country at that time—almost certainly during the night of
May the 25th–26th. How?

It is only fair to say that Burgess's story follows the Foreign
Office account in its essentials. He claims that his own flight was
unpremeditated. On his return from America he found Maclean
perturbed by the signs that he was under suspicion: he had
decided to flee to Moscow, and asked Burgess to join him. But
Burgess had planned a holiday in France, and made up his
mind only at the very last moment.

He says that they travelled in the *Falaise*, went by train from
Rennes to Paris and then on to Berne, and by air to Prague,
where they got visas and a flight to Moscow. He claims that the
Russians knew nothing of their coming. There is nothing
impossible in his story, but several incidents could suggest
the reverse of what he implies. He had hired a car, drove it to
Southampton, and left it on the dockside. "I thought that,
even if I didn't go with Donald, the car might come in useful."

This is a feeble argument. The abandoned car *could* have
been a deliberate plant, to distract attention from the actual
flight.

Britain is a comparatively small island, but its air space is vast.
Huge squadrons of detective aircraft might police it, and still
miss occasional intruders—or escapers. In more than one case
of ordinary crime, much less espionage, the criminals have
entered or left England illicitly by private aircraft.

Further, charter flights from small airfields or even from
open country are not always as closely supervised as regular
traffic. Again, criminals have been known to use this means of
escape.

(To quote one example: in the notorious Chalk-pit murder
case, which involved Thomas John Ley, former New South
Wales Minister of Justice, a reluctant witness admitted during
the Old Bailey trial that he was in Switzerland one morning,
in Ley's Kensington flat in the afternoon, and back in Switzerland the same evening! He used a modern smuggling route: he
flew to an isolated spot near the South Coast by charter plane,

was met by a fast car which took him to London, and returned
by the same route.)

It is possible that this is the method used by Burgess and
Maclean, with Russian connivance or assistance. It is quite
certain that they attained their objective, Russia. I put the
point to Guy Burgess when I encountered him in Moscow a
few years ago. Unfortunately he was too drunk to give a
comprehensible reply.

Some years after their flight the Russians produced the
two men at a Press conference in Moscow. This was not very
informative. Burgess was employed in the Foreign Literature
Publishing House, recommending English books for trans-
lation into Russian: Maclean is adviser for another Soviet
publishing house which publishes foreign books in their
original languages and Russian books in foreign languages. The
episode was apparently ended. But the important question
remains: were they Russian spies before their flight?

Public and Press have roundly condemned them. Among our
Allies reactions were even more emphatic—their defection was
described in such exaggerated terms that it was declared to have
swayed the American decision to deny the British the use of
Pacific testing ranges for nuclear weapons. When I was with a
mission in the U.S.A. I found a great reluctance to pass on
any confidential information—after all, I might be another
Burgess or Maclean. But this caution was quite unjustified.

When Mr Macmillan visited Moscow in 1959, Burgess con-
trived to have a message sent to him. The man was anxious to
return home to England: would the Prime Minister guarantee
his immunity? The Prime Minister naturally refused to do
anything of the kind, and left the note unanswered.

Now suppose you were the Director of Public Prosecutions
and Burgess did come home, *what charge would you prefer
against him?*

The obvious answer is espionage. But it is part of the duty of
the D.P.P. to recommend prosecution only if there is evidence

sufficient to provide reasonable grounds to the charge. The evidence available in this case is very flimsy indeed.

In the case of Maclean, there is the fact that enquiries among 6000 staff had narrowed suspicion down to a handful. But suspicion is not evidence.

More important—and certainly contributing more to the exaggerations in the case—was the information conveyed by Petrov, a Russian agent who defected in Australia. Much of his story concerned his own work, and was readily acceptable—it could to a certain extent be proved. Nevertheless, his description of Burgess and Maclean as "long-term spies" was derived from conversations with a friend, another Russian agent named Kislytrin, who told him that they had supplied information to Russia over a long period. But what the soldier said is also not evidence. Hearsay is, very properly, inadmissible in a British court.

The Russians are no amateurs in espionage. Their spy-masters were quite unlikely to engage drunkards and sex perverts: and the conduct of Burgess is all against the theory that he was a Russian spy. Had he been, he would never have attracted attention to himself by his violent opposition to the Establishment. Nor would he have resigned, or laid himself open to dismissal, from a situation so favourable to a spy. Instead, he would have striven to earn the confidence of his superior officers so as to obtain access to secret information.

And surely the idea of two 'spies' being called for over a ship's loudspeaker system is the height of the ludicrous!

There may be suspicion, but there is no *proof*, that Burgess and Maclean ever did any spying before their flight. Once they had sought asylum in Russia, their hosts would of course extract from them a good deal of interesting and useful information about Anglo-American relations—but not about details of nuclear technology, for they had none. This would indeed constitute a breach of the Official Secrets Act, for which the two men could be punished. But this offence would also have to be proved—and the Russians would scarcely be likely to give confirmatory evidence. The inevitable conclusion is that Burgess and Maclean were not spies, but renegades.

If you disagree with my view, you might like to become an assistant to the D.P.P. and formulate a spy charge which would stand up to the cross-examination of a defending counsel!

I wrote this chapter before the muddled events of April the 18th, 1962, but see no reason to alter a word of it.

An official announcement said that a superintendent of the Special Branch had obtained warrants for the arrest of Burgess and Maclean.

"There are grounds for supposing that Donald Maclean and Guy Burgess may be contemplating leaving, or may have left, the U.S.S.R. for some other territory.

"In order that they may be arrested should they come, in transit or otherwise, within the jurisdiction of our courts, warrants have been applied for and issued for offences against Section One of the Official Secrets Act, 1911."

The inevitable spate of rumours swept the country. Newspapers spent thousands of pounds as correspondents watched airports and docks. All for nothing—Burgess and Maclean did not make the journey. They never intended to do so.

The reluctance of Maclean to return is understandable. The suspicions of 1951 may have been strengthened by subsequent investigation. Or he may have been apprehensive about what might emerge from a keen police interrogation. (In cases like those of Fuchs and Blake, no real evidence was available until they had been questioned.)

A visit by Burgess was more probable. He was very fond of his mother, who was ill in London. If he were indeed clear of espionage, as seems possible, he had only to face interrogation on the question of violation of the Official Secrets Act—for which there would be no confirmation from Russia. And he could have argued to himself that the British Government would be reluctant to recommence the laundry of dirty linen now of considerable age.

The whole affair appears to have been sparked off by a mis-understanding following a conversation in Moscow. Burgess was due for a holiday. Where should he go? The Black Sea? Very pleasant, but he had been there several times already. What about this new riviera being developed in Bulgaria? Cuba was said to be very interesting.

This was the information which reached British sources. Now conditions in a suspicion-and-secrecy-ridden country like Russia are peculiar; even a visit to Bulgaria *might* be the pre-liminary to another and longer journey. Hence the official action. In the event, however, Burgess went to Yalta, not Bulgaria. Maclean announced correctly that he had never had the slightest intention of leaving Russia.

Some of the Press reports now make amusing reading. The two men were actually on the way to Amsterdam by air; they had been expelled by the Russians, who wanted them to be tried so as to revive American suspicions of British security. Or Burgess and Maclean were being exchanged for Lonsdale, the Russian head of the Portland spy ring. Alternatively, they had made a bargain with M.I.5. In return for a mild sentence they would now reveal all they knew about Russia. The ingenuity or ingenuousness of the suggestions was quite intriguing.

On the day of the official announcement I was asked to broad-cast a commentary on the case. I had no hesitation, despite the many conflicting reports, in describing the announcement as a deterrent. The Government could have been seriously embarrassed by a trial. The case itself had done quite enough harm in disturbing Anglo-American relations—and the Prime Minister was due to leave for Washington a few days later! No wonder that the Government decided that it would be better for all concerned if the two renegades remained in their adopted country; they were scarcely likely to leave it once they knew definitely that they would be arrested and tried the moment they reached any place where the writ of British law runs.

Burgess's own explanation was quite fantastic. He threw the blame for the rumour on the Dutch, intent on minimising the return to Russia of Alexei Golub, who had earlier defected to Holland; this was absurd. He claimed that the trial of the members of the Committee of 100 showed that he himself would be tried in private. And he inferred that the Government had 'panicked' lest, if he did return to England, he would be compelled in self-defence to denounce other homosexuals still in the Foreign Office!

FOUR

The Unmasking of Dr Fuchs

THE MOST REMARKABLE FEATURE of the Fuchs case was its ending.

Fuchs had joined the Communist Party as a student, not because of a belief in Marxism, but because he disliked the Nazis. When he fled to England he might have broken with the Communists, but they had decided to keep an eye on him. The Russian Secret Service is long-sighted. More than once they have picked out a young man and 'developed' him, not because he was a Communist—often he was not—but because he was clever and likely to achieve a position of importance.

For a time Fuchs was not troubled. But when he began to work with the British atomic-energy-research team, the Russians were delighted. Here was an unique source of information. In their wildest dreams the Russian spy-masters could scarcely have thought of having a spy so usefully placed.

When, in 1943, he was posted to work in America, the Russians transferred him to the local spy ring. His immediate chief was Anatole Yakolev, who was nominally employed in the Soviet Consulate in New York. As was the custom, Yakolev did not meet his agents personally. His 'cut-out' man was

Harry Gold, who collected information from Fuchs; the latter
was at that time working at the Los Alamos plant in New
Mexico.

After Fuchs returned to England his conscience began to
trouble him. Britain had sheltered him when he was a hapless
refugee from Nazi tyranny, had given him British citizenship,
and provided him with well-paid and fascinating work: true, he
had unique qualifications to perform it. And he had rewarded
British generosity by turning traitor. For some years he had
been supplying vital secret information to the Russians. He
came to the conclusion that he "could not go on."

The Russians had provided for this possibility. They had
pressed money on him, so now they were in a position to blackmail him. "Do as we say, or we will denounce you to the
British." But his conscience was now very active, stimulated by
the kindness of his British friends. He began to miss appointments with his cut-out: his information was less regular and far
less important.

The Russians look well ahead, but are over-organised. They
insist on controlling even local details from Moscow. And these
local details were not always accurate. Once Fuchs was instructed to identify himself to the cut-out by carrying five
books bound with string supported by two fingers of one hand.
In the other hand he was to carry two books. His contact would
carry a copy of Bennett Cerf's *Stop me if you have heard this*.

This arrangement was grossly over-planned, but might have
succeeded. But maybe it was as well that Fuchs decided not to
keep the appointment. He was to have met his contact "at a
stop on the British Underground called Paddington Crescent,
possibly Teddington Crescent." Fuchs might have spent the
rest of his life looking for such a station, for it does not exist—
under either of its names.

The Russians were highly concerned when they noted
the obvious signs of Fuchs's declining enthusiasm. As a spy he
was uniquely situated: no one could possibly replace him.
The information he had passed over was of immense value,

and had contributed strongly to Russia's early mastery of the atomic bomb. It would be disastrous if Fuchs were now to desert.

Every pressure was applied—persuasion and threats. But whatever enthusiasm he had had for Communism had now evaporated, and the time came when Moscow had to recognise that they had lost their most valuable spy. An unwilling agent is useless: it would be impossible to depend on his information —and, if pressed too hard, he might go over to the other side. The British might 'turn him round' so that he would deliberately supply the Russians with false information.

Regretfully, therefore, they wrote him off as a spy. But they did not propose to deny themselves his services. First-class nuclear physicists were rare. They could not force him to spy, so they decided that he would work not for Britain and U.S.A. but for Russia. So Fuchs received a peremptory order. He was to go to Russia: arrangements for his journey were being made.

And Fuchs refused to go!

"What?" cried the West European Director in The Centre at Moscow—the headquarters of the Intelligence Service. "He refuses, you say?"

"Yes."

"You have tried——"

"I have tried everything. He is obdurate."

"But why?"

"Oh, you know how sentimental these Germans can be. Somebody has been nice to him—so he is stricken with remorse for what he has done."

"The fool!"

"He says that he decided to retire months ago."

"The fool! He will see that no one ever retires from our job."

"What do you propose to do? Have him liquidated by OS2?"

"No. Let the British liquidate him."

"What?"

"If he will neither spy for us nor work with us, he is useless. Very well, we will hand him over to his friends. Let's see what his precious sentimental conscience will make of that. Work out a plan for my approval. Not a direct denunciation— let the British and Americans think that they have been clever enough to catch him. They will be delighted—but Fuchs will not!"

Egg Brownjohn (the name is assumed) of the F.B.I. did not resemble an egg in the slightest—he had a well-formed, athletic body. There were times when he wished that his parents had not christened him Egbert. In his day he had been an active gang-buster in Chicago. Now from an office, he directed the operations of others.

He was studying a report from the American Commission which had investigated the explosion of the Russian atomic bomb. Its conclusions were emphatic: the Russians *must* have had access to American nuclear secrets. Attached to the report was a note from J. Edgar Hoover. Egg was to drop all other assignments and concentrate on this: the report in itself suggested the branches of research which had obviously been tapped. All past and present employees must be checked— quickly.

Egg sighed as he called his staff together. They had plenty to work on—their records were remarkably complete. True, every person who had ever worked in a nuclear plant had been passed for Security by the F.B.I. "Forget that," Egg ordered. "Somebody must have ducked. Find him."

The F.B.I. is not deterred by the size of a task—this one involved the checking of hundreds of men—their private lives as well as their work. A vast machine swung into action. Unlike the Mounties, the F.B.I. may not always get their man, but if they fail it is not for lack of trying.

The Russian agent in New York, Korev, was perturbed. He

too did his planning from an office: his official position was that
of a translator on the United Nations staff.

His first effort to obey the orders from Moscow had failed.
It had seemed to be such a good idea, but it had failed.

There was a time when it was not unduly expensive to bribe
a policeman, but today such possibilities are rare. Korev,
however, had one or two policemen on his payroll—they had no
idea that they were aiding a Russian spy.

One patrolled a sooty district of Brooklyn. His orders were
simple. He was given an old envelope, with some scribbled
words on it. If ever he were called to a fatal accident, he was to
slip the envelope into the victim's pocket. There it would of
course be found by the police.

Days passed, and no death came his way. Then he was
attracted by the screams of a landlady of a lonely rooming-
house. One of her lodgers had hanged himself in a lavatory.
The policeman duly slipped the envelope into the man's
pocket before calling his precinct office. He proposed to do no
more.

Unfortunately the plan did not work out, for it was a very
obvious case of suicide—the man had left a letter for the
coroner giving a full explanation. Why, then, should the petty
contents of his pockets attract attention?

Korev had made the mistake of a suspicious man who believes
everyone else is suspicious. He did not realise that there is
but small contact between an ordinary street cop and the
spy-catchers of the F.B.I. The envelope, with the rest of the
meagre contents of the man's pockets, was destroyed after the
inquest.

At any moment a reprimand might come from Moscow—
why had he not obeyed his orders? He must do something more
dramatic. As so often happens in such circumstances, he
descended to melodrama.

He decided to act in Washington. A woman rang up the
F.B.I.—not the police—and demanded to speak to Mr Hoover.
The switchboard girl transferred her to a man whose task it was

to deal diplomatically with cranks. The woman began to talk almost incoherently about men who were trying to 'get' her. Suddenly she screamed, and the line went dead.

It might be a hoax, but in duty bound the officer followed it up. The call had come from a public call-box, and here blood was found to be splashed on the wall and floor. A copy of the *Washington Post* lay on the shelf beside the directory, and the sharp-eyed G-man noticed some pencilled writing in one of the margins. It was not very clear, but at last he deciphered it— a list of six names.

Four of them appeared to be Russian. Unusual elsewhere, foreign names are not uncommon in U.S.A., which during the last hundred years had received forty million immigrants. But four Russian-sounding names out of six was a very large proportion. The F.B.I. decided to investigate, and in due course the copy of the *Washington Post* found itself on Egg Brownjohn's table.

By this time he was well into his process of elimination. Hundreds of people had been checked. There remained dozens of others—mostly men who had now left the atomic service, and who had not yet been traced. By the instinct which the good policeman often has, Egg put the six names alongside the list of those as yet unchecked. The six all appeared in that list!

It could be a coincidence. The branch of the F.B.I. which had dealt with the woman's telephone call had suspected a hoax. But when Egg discovered that the four Russian names were those of members of the Soviet Embassy staff who had now returned to Russia, he was confident that this was no hoax.

The Washington police were using every known method of tracing the woman, but without success. Egg himself proposed to trail the two non-Russians.

The first trail was brief—the man was dead. Yet there was a tenuous connection with the atomic leakage—he had once been questioned about a small piece of nuclear equipment missing from a laboratory. He had been able to convince the interrogators that he knew nothing about this.

The sixth man had last worked in Los Alamos, New Mexico. Egg took a sergeant with him and made his way thither.

His enquiries were, however, fruitless. His quarry was only vaguely remembered—he had left the plant five years before. His record was excellent: he was a first-rate nuclear physicist. Subsequent information was negative: he had been very reticent, and had moved but little in such social circles as then existed. He was "the sort of man you never noticed."

In the meantime the F.B.I. sergeant was busy in Santa Fé. Using the well-established police methods of photographs and patience, he traced a hotel at which his quarry had stayed. And there a sharp-eyed chambermaid provided a fragment of information.

She remembered the man. He had looked so lonely—he needed mothering. His linen was not in good shape, and he had asked her to do some mending. Maybe it was the size of his tip which prompted her memory.

Otherwise he was commonplace enough. The sergeant was a keen interrogator, and at last the girl recalled one trivial detail. He had put his shirts into a drawer, and she had taken them out to look over them. Then a piece of cardboard had fallen out. It was part of one side of a "Jello" package, and had been cut in an unusual shape. She drew it, to the best of her recollection. One end was square, the other shaped like a letter L.

That was all, but the sergeant was happy as he reported to his chief. For the cardboard suggested a favourite Russian-spy method of identification. Two agents would be given a piece of paper or cardboard which had been cut or torn into two pieces. When they met, if the two fragments fitted together then the agents could go ahead with confidence, certain that they had encountered their colleague.

It was only a trifle, but it did justify the F.B.I. in notifying

Scotland Yard that a nuclear physicist named Dr Klaus Fuchs might repay investigation.

The Special Branch of Scotland Yard did not tarry.

The Canadian spy case had broken in 1945. When Igor Gouzenko defected in Ottawa, he carried over with him incontrovertible evidence of a Canadian spy ring directed from the Russian Embassy. The suspects were rounded up: most were amateurs, and careless: their own papers revealed interesting information. In all, hundreds of names were collected. It was soon apparent, however, that the spies had jotted down the names of acquaintances who *might* be able to provide information.

Among the members of the spy ring was Dr Allan Nunn May, a brilliant British nuclear scientist. And one of the names he had jotted down was that of Dr Klaus Fuchs.

After returning from Los Alamos to England, Fuchs was appointed to Harwell Atomic Research Establishment and put in charge of the theoretical physics division. It has been suggested in certain quarters that M.I.5 were careless in permitting such promotion to a man with Fuchs's background.

What actually happened behind the scenes was that the resident Security Officer at Harwell, Wing Commander Arnold, requested an immediate investigation of Fuchs, as a result of which he was under observation for nearly six months. But we have seen that his troubled conscience had caused him to keep clear of his former Soviet contacts. So the 're-vetting' report could only be noted: "Nothing known against."

Towards the end of 1949 Fuchs was in a state of mind that only an experienced psychiatrist could have disentangled. He had betrayed the country which had given him sanctuary and had become a paid Soviet agent. Then he had changed his mind and broken with his Russian contacts. That left him in fear of punishment by Britain if his espionage were discovered; and in fear of what the Soviet punishment squads might do in revenge for his defection. Whatever happened, he was bound to suffer.

And the situation was made more complicated by the fact that Fuchs had become attached to Harwell after his fashion. He liked his colleagues and had been elected chairman of the staff association. It would have taken little at that time to impel him to go to W/C Arnold, confess everything, and throw himself on Britain's mercy.

Then something happened which may or may not have been arranged by some cynical mind in Moscow. A vacancy arose for a professor of theology at Leipzig University. The post was filled by a Quaker—the man Fuchs loved, he said, more than anyone in the world—his own father. And if it ever now leaked out that Fuchs had voluntarily betrayed his former Soviet paymasters, the future of his father, living under the Communist régime of East Germany, would be grim indeed.

Fuchs was on the verge of a breakdown. His hair became unkempt and he went unshaven for days at a time. Mouldy nibbled sandwiches turned up among his papers. Week-old cups of scummy forgotten tea stood in odd corners of his office.

In December, 1949, Fuchs was visited by a friendly man—Jim Skardon of M.I.5. The conversation began with reminiscences of Fuchs's political activities before he fled from Germany. Then quite casually Skardon asked: "Were you in touch with a Russian agent in America? And did you give him details of your work?"

Fuchs hesitated. And we must remember that he had had one of the finest mathematical brains in Britain, quick, clear and accurate. "Er—I don't think so," he murmured. It was an astonishingly feeble answer. It led eventually to a complete confession.

Officers of M.I.5. have no powers of arrest. That is the job of Scotland Yard's Special Branch. So after the Prime Minister and the Attorney-General had considered the case, Fuchs was invited to London. There he was met by Commander Leonard Burt, head of the Special Branch, and arrested. Fuchs sat down as if he had been struck. "You realise what this will mean to

Harwell," he muttered. It was an indication of the twisted loyalties that had been writhing within his mind for so long.

His trial and conviction are matters of history, and he was given the maximum sentence—fourteen years' penal servitude. During that weary time he had no idea that he had been deliberately betrayed by his own employers. Since on his release he went to work in East Germany, it may be that he does not know it yet.

FIVE

"I knew 'Buster' Crabb!"

I AM A LANDSMAN, and have never had more than the most casual contacts with Naval Intelligence. But one case intrigued me—as it did millions of other people. So I made my way to Portsmouth, to seek out a naval friend. I guessed that I would find him in a quiet Pompey hotel where naval types gather. I am tolerated there as a poor pongo—that disrespectful Navy term for a soldier.

"Yes, I knew 'Buster' Crabb," my friend Peter said, with a slow nod.

Peter is an officer attached to the 'stone frigate' H.M.S. *Vernon*—a Royal Naval Diving centre at Portsmouth. He is what is called in Fleet Street—but never in the Royal Navy— a frogman. And I wanted to pick his brains about that remarkable character who met an unknown end—Lieut.-Commander Lionel Kenneth Philip Crabb, O.B.E., G.M., R.N.V.R.

"Crabbie had lots of pals," Peter said reminiscently, "and they'll all talk their heads off about what he did during the war. He got the George Medal, you know, which they don't give away with a packet of detergent."

"And what do his pals say about his disappearance?" I asked.

"Not a damn word! As soon as you mention it they all close

up like startled clams. It seems clear to me, Colonel, that the
Faceless Men traced and interviewed each of Crabbie's friends
and told them to keep their mouths shut, or else——"

"Including you, Peter?"

"No, they missed me. Or they thought I was too dumb to
matter, and of course they could have been right. Actually I
wasn't here in 1955. But a pal wrote and told me he'd had a
drink with Crabbie in Pompey."

"1955? But surely Crabb disappeared in 1956."

"That was his second visit to Pompey. And his last. On
both occasions Russian warships happened to be paying official
visits. Which could have been a remarkable coincidence, of
course."

"Did you see him during his last visit?"

"In this very bar, Colonel. I must have been one of the last
men to buy Crabbie a drink. It was the 18th of April in 1956—
I'll never forget the date—and he was flying all his recognition
signals."

"Such as?"

"Such as the old pork-pie hat, the monocle in his top left-
hand waistcoat pocket, a horrible ten-and-sixpenny red-
checked shirt, and the ebony sword-stick some Spanish pal
had given him, with a gold crab on the handle."

"Did he mention why he was in Portsmouth?"

"I asked him. It seemed a fair question. He said, 'Just looked
in for a quick haircut and shave, Peter.' Then I knew."

"Knew what?"

"Knew he was back at the old cloak-and-dagger racket
again. That was his stock reply. Meaning, ask a silly question
and you get a bloody silly answer."

"So you think that Crabb came here twice to have a look
at the visiting Russian ships—presumably below the water-
line?"

"Why else? But don't you go and quote me on that. I'm not
what the reporters call 'an Admiralty spokesman.'"

"Well, there's no harm in a little guessing game, Peter.

What do you think he could have been looking for? Some secret
underwater gadget sticking out of the hull?"

"I can see I must start from the beginning, and proceed in
words of one syllable. In the first place, *nothing* sticks out of a
ship's hull, as you express it. No, you don't find great bumps
and things sticking out of a warship's hull under water. They
would reduce speed in a ship whose fighting value depends on
its manœuvrability. See what I mean?"

"Yes, I do."

"Furthermore," he continued, "it would be a physical
impossibility for any diver to make an adequate underwater
survey of the hull of a 12,000-ton cruiser, which is the tonnage of
the Russian ships. A diver's goggles are hooded, so he can only
see straight ahead. And visibility down there varies from about
six feet to as little as six inches. You'd need weeks to go round
the ship, practically feeling your way most of the time."

"But surely Crabb knew what he was doing? If he could not
have been surveying the hull, that seems to leave the rudder and
the propellers."

"It leaves just that. But you can't have a new type of rudder.
It has to be a plane surface which can be set at an angle to the
course of the ship. And it can't be anything else."

"So Crabb was probably inspecting the propellers?"

"We call 'em screws. It seems that these Russian cruisers
had a shade more speed than comparable British ships. And
there is a mathematical limit to the amount of power you can
cram into a 12,000-ton cruiser. Some new design of screw
could be the answer. Which would have given Crabbie a
definite point at the stern to aim at when he was swimming out
under water."

"But if Crabb was doing two similar jobs, in 1955 and
again in 1956, why should one apparently succeed and the
other fail?"

"Simply because the jobs weren't similar at all. One was dead
easy. The second was sheer suicide, as poor old Crabbie must
have realised. You see, in 1955 the Russian cruiser *Sverdlov*

was berthed in the dockyard—moored to shore bollards in a protected position a few feet from the quay. In April, 1956, the *Ordzhonikidze* was anchored in Stokes Bay—two or three hundred yards from the shore probably. So, in addition to whatever job he was doing, Crabbie would have had to swim under water for a quarter-mile or more."

"And that would have been difficult?"

"It would be damned near impossible. I've dived in Stokes Bay scores of times, and conditions are so dodgy that we always work in pairs roped together. Like climbing the Alps in reverse. I've often had to swim with my face literally no more than six inches from the sea-bed. That wouldn't be easy in still water, but Stokes Bay is tidal, and a one-knot current could take you miles from your objective. Even with a wrist-compass you can only check your theoretical course—not your actual course. You can't allow for drift. And if you're on a hush-hush job you can't keep on surfacing to check your bearings. Add to all that the fact that you can only work for an hour at a time——"

"Why is that?"

"Well, you must dive at the period of minimum drift, else strong underwater currents might wash you out into the Solent, to drown when your air gives out. So you work only for a half-hour before and half an hour after the turn of the tide."

"But surely the Admiralty must have weighed up all these dangers before asking Crabb to do whatever it was?"

"The Admiralty would have done, certainly, Colonel. But are you suggesting we should be so inhospitable as to have been spying on our official guests? Not quite cricket, eh?"

"I'm afraid there are no moral standards in what you vulgarly call the cloak-and-dagger racket, Peter."

"You're telling me! But at a lower and more practical level, there isn't much the director of Naval Intelligence doesn't know about foreign warships. Certain other naval Powers aren't quite so well informed. Three guesses?"

"I'd put my money on the Americans. Russian warships have never visited United States ports as far as I know. So the most convenient spot where their Intelligence agents could have inspected any Soviet ships would be here."

"I see that you have studied the implications of what we may call the Mysterious Affair of Mr Smith."

"I haven't. Who was he?"

"Well, on the 17th of April, 1956, Crabbie and a friend arrive from the Smoke and book in that evening at the Sallyport Hotel in Pompey High Street. The friend signs in as Smith. And I needn't remind you, of all people, that in British Intelligence, even if your name really is Smith, you are not allowed to use it. It creates an unfortunate atmosphere of suspicion. Even a couple slipping off for an illicit week-end at Brighton have more sense than to use the name Smith. It shouts aloud."

"Agreed. Well?"

"So Crabbie arrives accompanied by some foreign Intelligence type who is going to brief him. This type can pass as an Englishman, but is inadequately acquainted with what we laughingly call the British way of life. He is unaware that by calling himself 'Smith' he is shouting, 'I'm a phoney' from the house-tops. Or am I wrong?"

"I think you're right. I think you've picked on one of those tiny significant details which even the lynx-eyed men of Fleet Street missed."

"Not all of 'em, Colonel. The journalist that even the Royal Navy respects is Chapman Pincher of the *Daily Express*. And a few weeks after Crabbie disappeared Pincher wrote that he had definitely been doing a job for United States Intelligence. Which fitted all the facts, including the acute embarrassment of the Prime Minister—Sir Anthony Eden as was—when he was heckled about Crabbie in Parliament. Do you remember what he said?"

"No," I replied.

"Well, I happen to recall his exact words, because they just don't add up. The P.M. said, 'What was done was done without the knowledge or the authority of Her Majesty's Ministers.' Frank and honest, eh, Colonel? But then he added: 'Appropriate disciplinary steps are being taken.' Who against? No British officer would risk a job like that without authority from the high-ups. So if Crabbie wasn't doing a job for our Government, against whom were the disciplinary steps to be taken?"

"Yes, as you say, it doesn't add up. What do you make of it?"

"Crabbie had obviously been in touch with British Intelligence previously. He was approached in 1955—either independently or through our people—to do a diving job for a friendly foreign Power. And you can take it that he would never have worked for a potential enemy. He was broke and needed the money, so he agreed. He tipped off his British Intelligence contacts, and they said, 'Okay, "Buster," and the best of luck; and let's know how you get on.' You may agree, Colonel, that no sensible Intelligence bloke refuses a bit of useful guff that the other fellow is paying for."

"These things happen, Peter."

"Yes, but Crabbie's contacts didn't realise what a resounding clanger would drop if the job went wrong. Especially on the second occasion, when the Russian ships had brought Bulganin and Khrushchev on an official visit to Britain. So nobody in authority was told in time to warn Crabbie that the set-up was too dodgy at such a time. And the P.M. was telling an embarrassing but true story when he said that Crabbie was acting without approval at Ministerial level, but that somebody lower down was booked for the high jump."

"You could be right. But what you say doesn't explain the removal of a page from the hotel register. Crabb's disappearance was headlined in all the newspapers by then, and someone using the name of Smith wouldn't have been much help to Fleet Street."

"Not just one page, Colonel—*four* pages were torn out by a member of Pompey C.I.D. And two signatures would occupy two lines—not four pages."

"Go on!"

"Well, my guess is that for the first job—concerning the

Sverdlov in 1955—a couple of high level Yankee Naval Intelligence officers come here in advance, pretending to have nothing
to do with Crabbie but staying in the same hotel, ready to see
him in his room at night, to brief him and take his report. Then
he arrives a day or two later, gets into the dockyard and has a
look at the Russian ship."

"Is it all that easy to get into the dockyard?"

"The crushers would recognise Crabbie as a two-and-a-half-
ringer and would give him free gangway. Then he'd pass a
packet of blue-liners round to some of the dockyard mateys and
they'd give him the guff as to where the ships were berthed."

"Despite the liberties the Queen's Navy takes with the
Queen's English, I gather that the naval police would know
Crabb was an ex-lieut.-commander and admit him. Then he
would hand round some Navy-issue cigarettes to a group of
civilian dockyard workers and ask his way to the Russian
ships."

"Yes, but when Crabbie is taking a good long butcher's at
the *Sverdlov* from the quayside he is spotted by a Russian agent,
who is on the look-out for just such a situation. He assumes that
Crabbie is Intelligence—British or otherwise—and follows him
out of the dockyard to try to identify him. He tails him to
the Sallyport but doesn't go in, in case he should be recognised.
It's not until the next day that the agent books a room at the
same hotel, just so that he can take a look at the register and
make a mental note of recent bookings, which include Crabbie's
name. So after that first job, the hotel register includes three
pages on which there are significant entries."

"Yes, but—well, this Russian agent——"

"I'm coming back to him. Let's move on a few months now
to job number two. The high-level Yanks don't bother this
time. They think the job will be dead easy again. So they send
Crabbie here with just the Smith character. They arrive during
the evening of the 17th of April and you can safely bet that
Crabbie looks up the Admiralty tide-tables and finds that high
tide is about seven-thirty next morning.'

"Have you checked that from the tables?"

"No, but Crabbie knew his job. Who better! So early in the morning of the 18th he goes to Stokes Bay to size up the situation. And he is appalled at the risks."

"Why didn't he go back to Smith, then, and report that the job was impossible?"

"Because he was broke, that's why. A damned shame after all he'd done for the country. He wasn't bankrupt in a big respectable way—not owing thousands like some City so-and-so. Just little irritating debts of a few quid. So he decides to take a chance. And when I spoke just now of the risks of diving in Stokes Bay, Colonel, I was speaking as a young, fit man with regular recent diving experience. And Crabbie was out of practice. Also he was a heavy drinker, aged forty-six. With the Russkies waiting for him, too."

"What makes you say that?"

"They're not fools. If they spotted him snooping round the *Sverdlov*, they'd be waiting for a second attempt during their next visit."

"Agreed. But short of making an official protest—which in fact the Kremlin did make later—what action could they have taken at the time?"

"Well, we can scrap the wild theory that Russian divers went down and fought Crabbie with shark-knives. But a very simple anti-diver dodge is what we used to do in the Eoka days when we were patrolling the coast of Cyprus. We'd just heave a Mills grenade over the side now and then, timed to explode at a couple of fathoms. It doesn't make much noise, but as water is incompressible the shock can disable a diver at a considerable distance."

"Yes, I see. But your reconstruction has taken the story only up to the morning before Crabb disappeared. What happened during the remainder of that day?"

"That was the 18th of April. And I can just imagine his feelings as he stood on the shelving shore of Stokes Bay at the turn of the tide. Facing him was the sea—and possible death.

Behind him was dry land—and his creditors. My guess is that Crabbie spent much of that day having a quiet pub-crawl, while he weighed up the few pros and the enormous number of cons. In the course of which his round includes this very bar, and we have our last drink together. Late that night he goes back to the Sallyport Hotel, tells Smith there is a one-in-ten chance of success, and says he will tackle the job early next morning. Which he does, and you can check the times from the newspaper reports. He probably dived from the shore at about seven o'clock, and at about seven-thirty Russian watchers saw a diver surface between two Russian destroyers. He was afloat for several minutes, then dived again alongside the destroyer *Smotriaschin* and wasn't seen any more. That's what Moscow said in the official Note, and there is no reason to disbelieve it."

"Why should he have surfaced?"

"Well, the obvious theory is that he might have come up for a second or two to get his bearings, hoping that he would be back under before he was spotted. But if he was afloat for a matter of minutes—that suggests bad trouble."

"Breathing trouble?"

"Probably. I don't know what type of gear he was using——"

"Wasn't he wearing an Italian Pirelli diving suit?"

"Yes, he preferred it to Navy Issue. But he might have used either oxygen or compressed-air breathing gear. Probably oxygen, because compressed air causes a trail of bubbles which could have been spotted by Russian watchers. The trouble about oxygen gear, though, is that it isn't safe to use at depths of over thirty feet. I estimate the depths of Stokes Bay at from thirty-five to forty-five feet—a dangerous depth if Crabbie was swimming near the sea-bed as I've had to do at that spot. Only an experienced diver can realise the awful feeling of helplessness when you're fighting for breath six fathoms down. I've had it happen to me and I said all the prayers I knew, which wasn't many at that. And when you fight your way up to the surface, you don't recover in seconds. You're gasping for minutes— which fits what the Russian Note said."

"Assuming that is what happened, then, Crabb recovers and dives again——"

"And one little grenade tossed over the side finished him off, with no wounds to suggest death was other than by drowning. He never returns to the Sallyport, and later in the day Smith settles the hotel bill and clears out, taking Crabbie's suitcase as well as his own. He knew by then that a calculated risk had failed.

"When the story broke," Peter said after a thoughtful pause, "it must have seemed expedient to our Intelligence high-ups to conceal the evidence that Crabbie's recent visits to Pompey coincided with the presence of Russian ships. So Superintendent Jack Lamport of the C.I.D. goes along to the hotel to remove certain pages of the register before Fleet Street can photograph them. He takes the page showing Crabbie's 1955 visit, and another showing his visit in 1956 with Smith. He has also been told the names of Crabbie's other possible contacts in American Intelligence, so their bookings in 1955 makes a third page to be removed. And whilst looking for their entries he happens to spot the booking of the Russian agent I mentioned, and recognises the name as that of a local espionage suspect. So out comes page number four. I don't see any other possible explanation."

"Nor do I, Peter," I agreed. "And so we come to the finding of the body, fourteen months later."

"Pardon me, Colonel. Not *the* body—just *a* body. This body was certainly wearing a two-piece Pirelli diving suit of the type that Crabbie liked to use. And it wore underclothes similar to those he had been wearing. But the features which could have provided evidence of identification—that is, the face, and the hands whose fingerprints could have been developed— were missing. The feet had been preserved, but the pathologist who performed the autopsy did not make any comment as to whether he noticed hammer-toes, which Crabbie definitely had."

"The body was found near Chichester Harbour, Peter," I said. "Is that far from Stokes Bay?"

"About twelve miles. A long journey along a tricky piece of coast for a weighted corpse."

"Weighted?"

"When I dive, my gear weighs up to about eighty pounds. So a dead diver would probably stay down on the sea-bed. If his breathing gear came adrift for some reason, I wouldn't have thought it would have taken over a year for him to turn up near Chichester. But just before this body was found, it was known that Russian submarines had passed down the Channel. Could this be another 'Man Who Never Was'? After all, we did just such a job off the Spanish coast during the war."

"A book has been published about Crabb," I said, "in which it is suggested that he was kidnapped, taken aboard the *Ordzhonikidze*, and after interrogation in Moscow agreed to serve in the Soviet Navy. Any comments?"

Peter's comment took the form of a five-letter expletive in the plural, implying disbelief. "Not on your life," he said vehemently. "I knew 'Buster' Crabb!"

Which was where I came in.

SIX

The Murder of Countess Lubienska

LATER WE SHALL ENCOUNTER the Russian organisation OS2, whose operatives were professional thugs. To them murder meant no more than squashing a wasp. But they had no monopoly of violence. The Russian Secret Service has for long been so complicated an organisation that one section knows nothing of what another is doing.

The headquarters of all the Russian Intelligence Services is in Moscow. But they have a very strong outpost in East Berlin— Mr Khrushchev forgot to mention this in his fulmination about Western spies operating from West Berlin.

In the Karlshorst district of East Berlin is a straggle of buildings which used to be the old St Antonius' Hospital. Here the K.B.G. has its advance headquarters. They are very well equipped and staffed. The K.B.G. in its military espionage often overlaps the G.R.U., which comes under the Ministry of Defence, but it has an important political side. At home, it watches potential opponents of the régime. Abroad, it infiltrates local parties and societies: it has spy networks everywhere, including other Communist states: and it has a special section to watch Russian and other Iron Curtain *émigrés* abroad.

The Deputy Director of this organisation sat one day in his office: with him was one of his active agents.

"I don't like it," the latter protested.

"In our job we have to do a lot of things we don't like. There are far too many Poles abroad, and some of them are dangerous. The Poles are good haters."

"I know that. I don't like murder, that's all. An odd kidnapping, or a spot of torture—that's all part of the game."

"You won't have to do it yourself. You only have to arrange it. The whole affair is quite simple."

"The actual execution, maybe. But I don't like working in England. The police are active—and cannot be bribed——"

"That is not true. *Anybody* can be bribed, if you offer enough money."

"And English comrades don't like this kind of work. In fact, they refuse to do it."

"Listen, Volkov, this is an order. You understand? I never thought that I should have to argue with you about liquidating an old woman," the Deputy Director jibed. "Push her under an Underground train, or run her down by car. You have only to study her habits—let your plan depend upon it. Keep well in the background yourself, of course."

"Very well."

Volkov had no option. He knew quite well that if he refused to accept the assignment his own life would be brief.

"Now, listen. This woman knows too much. She was too well informed about the kidnapping of the Polish Underground leaders near the end of the war. She was in the Underground herself, and knew too much about our own activities. Some of our people made a mistake, and betrayed her to the Germans. The Gestapo put her in a concentration camp."

"Why has the case taken so long?"

"She has only just been traced. She lives in the West End of London—I don't know the address, but she has been seen on the Gloucester Road Station in Kensington. You know our London man—he will help you find her. Here are her details, and a photograph—but that is nearly thirty years old. It's quite a simple job. See that you don't fumble it."

Volkov's London contact was not at all happy when he heard of the assignment.

"You and I must keep well clear of this," he said. "The English police are active—I only narrowly escaped capture in the Coventry sabotage business."

"I'm sure I don't want to appear!" Volkov agreed. "But the Deputy Director told me that you would find me a local man to do the job."

"That's not easy. These English are squeamish—even our alleged comrades are frightened of the sight of blood."

"Couldn't we hire someone for the job?"

"This is England, not Italy. No, I don't know anybody—hell, I do. A youth."

"A youth! I don't like kids in our affairs."

"This one should serve. He's a fanatic—crazy. A touch of hermaphroditism, by my guess. Burning to aid the cause, and all that gush."

"I don't like it. These English——"

"Who said he was English? He isn't. But he lives and works in Walthamstow. Look! First we must identify our quarry—she's probably changed her name, but we've got several good leads. Then we'll prime this youth——"

"How?"

"Oh, any old yarn—he's crazy, I tell you. We'll let him know—as a secret, of course—that this old woman is planning to kill Nikita Khrushchev. Or some yarn like that."

"And he'll swallow that?"

"A fanatic will swallow anything. Look at the yarns which circulate in Russia—and people believe them. Yes, I can see the way. We'll keep in the background—and then lie low for a bit."

On the evening of May the 24th, 1957, an old lady of seventy-two went to a social gathering in Ealing. She travelled back to Gloucester Road late at night—a friend saw her alight from the Underground train. The platform was almost deserted.

A minute later the old lady staggered towards the lift, bleeding from a stab wound. The liftman had just heard the sounds of hurried footsteps, as of someone running up the emergency stairs. Now he found the old lady, bleeding profusely from a stomach wound. As he carried her to the lift she muttered, "It was a bandit, a bandit." The police and an ambulance were called. But her life could not be saved.

Scotland Yard went into action. In all, more than 18,000 people were interviewed. Some of the information secured was very interesting.

The old lady was a Polish aristocrat, Countess Teresa Lubienska. Before the first World War, when the greater part of Poland was incorporated in Tsarist Russia, she was the gay and beautiful wife of a wealthy Polish nobleman and diplomat. He was killed during the Russian Revolution and his estates were confiscated. Destitute, and with a small son and daughter to keep, the Countess worked as a clerk in a Warsaw bank.

On the outbreak of the second World War her son was killed in a hopeless cavalry charge against German tanks. The Countess then joined the Polish Home Army of Underground Resistance fighters. She organised both sabotage and the nursing of wounded patriots. But at last she was trapped by the Gestapo.

She was sent to the women's concentration camp at Ravensbrück. There she was tortured, her captors being determined to make her betray her comrades. They failed. The S.S. interrogators decided that she would never talk, so she might as well be liquidated. She was almost on her way to the gas chamber when the camp guards were disturbed by an R.A.F. raid. In the confusion the Countess escaped—not from the camp, but from the group of prisoners about to be murdered. She attached herself to another party—this consisted of those about to be transferred to Auschwitz. There she was branded with her number, 44747, and this she bore for the rest of her life. Her courage constantly inspired her fellow-prisoners.

Communist Poland had no attraction for her, so at the end of the war she escaped to the West and succeeded in reaching London. She was too old and broken by her torture to work, and lived on the meagre National Assistance allowance. She had a tiny bed-sitting room in Cornwall Gardens, Kensington, where she lived in near-poverty. Her brain was still active, however, and she organised social functions among the exiled Polish Catholics.

An old lady of seventy-two could scarcely have been the victim of a sex murder! The police are suspicious of theories about political murders—it is well known that such things do not happen in England! Yet all the evidence favoured such a theory. Countess Lubienska had not been robbed: and the knife which stabbed her was no Teddy-boy weapon—it was a large penknife, its blade two and a half inches long. Naturally, the Countess was not a Communist—she had every reason to hate the Russians as much as the Germans. But her activities in London had been social—she had taken little part in the politics of the exiled groups.

Surely the bloody hand of the Russian Secret Service had not been stretched out against a poor old lady living in a tiny bed-sitter? She was scarcely a menace to the mighty Russian Empire! It was all very confusing.

The police obtained no information to support an arrest. They could scarcely be expected to be interested in a crazy foreign youth from Walthamstow who was raving in a mental hospital.

Volkov was light of heart as he approached St Antonius's Hospital. He had satisfactorily completed a very awkward and unsavoury assignment. Doubtless his skill and zeal would be duly appreciated.

But when he reached the Deputy Director's room he was

appalled. The chief was glaring at him in fury. "You bloody fool!" he shouted. "You bloody fool!"

"What do you——"

"You bloody fool—*you killed the wrong woman!*"

SEVEN

The Disappearance of Father Borynski

THE MEAGRE EVIDENCE in the case suggested that the priest had been kidnapped and hurried behind the Iron Curtain. But I discussed the mysterious affair with a Polish general who had no cause to love the Communists.

"I don't believe it," he said. "The Polish equivalents of the Russian strong-arm squads have never been active in Britain. Even the Polish Communist leaders are anxious to keep on friendly terms with Britain. Although they may be perverted by the Communist creed, they belong to a Western people. They just don't do such things. We have noticed more than once that the Poles may start something—but they hand it over to the Russians if it affects Britain."

This was confirmed a few years later, in the Portland spy case. The miserable Harry Houghton got into trouble in Warsaw, was 'developed,' and again approached when he returned to England. From this point the Russians took over.

After the defeat of Poland in 1939, many thousands of Poles managed to escape into neighbouring countries and made their way to the West to fight again. Later they were joined by tens of thousands of others released from Russian prisoner-of-war camps. They fought gallantly in North Africa, Italy, France and Germany: they were men with much to avenge.

But their joy at the moment of victory was not as exuberant as ours. They had not fought Hitler to suffer the tyranny of Stalin. The conduct of the Russians towards their country had been as savage as that of the Nazis. The Poles are intensely patriotic, but tens of thousands of them decided that they could not return to a Poland which knew no freedom. Some emigrated to the U.S.A. or the Dominions, but thousands remained in Britain. They had fought beside the British forces, and many had British wives. Little Polish communities were scattered over our islands, and most of them consisted of good workers and good citizens.

A number of priests had escaped from Hitler or Stalin, and had never ceased their labours. One of them, serving the Polish community at Bradford, Yorkshire, was Father Borynski, a very popular and tireless cleric. He was anti-Communist, as any sincere Christian must be: and he was greatly disturbed at the miseries inflicted on his country during and after the war.

During 1952, the Polish Government made an effort to persuade the exiles to return home. Professional and skilled men were especially needed, and effusive promises were made to them. Few responded: Father Borynski was not half-hearted in his opposition to Communism, and warned his crowded congregations against such incitements.

"You haven't made yourself popular with these visitors," an English friend commented. "Watch out that they don't come for you!"

"Oh, I can look after myself," the priest laughed. He was indeed a powerful man—a six-footer of forty-two years, weighing fourteen stone: a tough proposition indeed for kidnappers.

He lived in a cottage in Little Norton Lane, Bradford. He was content with simple fare, and saved out of his modest stipend enough to send food parcels to his mother, seventy-two-year-old Mrs Anna Borynska, in her humble home in a village near Cracow, the Polish university city.

On the warm, dry evening of July the 13th, 1953, Father Borynski was called to the telephone by his housekeeper, Mrs Elizabeth Beck. He spoke very briefly in Polish. Later she gave a Polish investigator an impression of the word-sounds she had heard: they were translated as "All right—I go."

Two minutes later he put on his raincoat and went out. He was seen to walk up the hill, turning right past St Luke's Hospital—but he was never seen again. Two days later the Russian ship *Gribojedov* sailed from the Port of London for Leningrad.

At first sight it appeared to be an abduction of a type all too familiar in many Continental countries—there have been hundreds in Western Germany alone. But such a thing was very rare in England. The police took the case very seriously, but could find no vestige of a clue.

One or two details demanded explanation. Why did Father Borynski wear his raincoat on a fine summer evening? Did he expect to be absent for hours, when the night would grow cold? Or did he for any reason wish to conceal his clerical collar?

A peculiar coincidence followed. The priest's mother had been writing regularly to him from Poland. Her letters suddenly ceased. His abduction was not mentioned in any of the Iron Curtain newspapers—but the Polish Underground grapevine has no difficulty in evading Communist censors. Its investigators dismissed the idea that Father Borynski had voluntarily returned to Poland: he would be seen and recognised by someone —and then the news would certainly get to England.

The mysterious disappearance of Father Borynski naturally alarmed other Poles: especially the priests, whose links with Poland, via Rome, had never been completely broken, to the chagrin of the Communists. Father Borsowski, padre of the Wheaton Aston hostel for Polish refugees, determined to take no chances. He lived in a small flat adjoining his little chapel. "If I ring the chapel bell except to summon to service, that will be an emergency," he said.

Three months after Father Borynski's disappearance a small

black saloon car pulled up outside Father Borsowski's flat—in the early hours of Sunday morning. Soon afterwards he heard unmistakable sounds of intruders on the roof.

He ran through to the chapel, rang the bell, and hid behind the altar. Some of the Poles who lived near by telephoned the police, and others ran towards the chapel. They witnessed the rapid departure of the car and its occupants. The episode revived the many conjectures which had been made about the abduction of Father Borynski, but the police could discover no actual links.

I admit that at the time I regarded the Borynski affair as a typical exploit of the Russian Branch for Special Tasks, so closely did it adhere to the usual type. My conversation with the Polish general, however, induced me to make further enquiries. I admit that I was not very successful. Nevertheless, by abandoning the political angle I did elicit certain suggestions and fragments of information. I do not pretend that my reconstruction is accurate in all its details—but it does explain the points at issue. The names, other than Borynski, are fictitious.

In the Polish community at Bradford was a man named Stanislas Orava. He had fought gallantly as a fighter pilot in the Polish Air Force, but the course of events had seared his soul. He felt it a monstrous crime that Poland, the first country to stand up to Hitler, should be handed over to Stalin. There was no justice in the world, he decided. Nothing mattered: in effect, he declared war on society. He could have done well as a skilled mechanic, but he lacked interest in any job. Then he met a local prostitute—who liked him so much that she was content to work for him.

Now he lazed his time away, brooding over the evil world into which he had been unlucky enough to be born. But then his girl caught the disease almost inseparable from her trade, and money grew scarce.

It was then that he took to crime—at first casual house-breaking and the like. He was lucky, and this made him over-confident. His fence introduced him to a small gang of house-breakers with the suggestion of a partnership.

The leader of the gang was a husky brute called, for some inverted reason, Dolly. There were few of the tricks of the trade which he lacked. He was exceedingly skilful at breaking into premises—the gang progressed from private houses to factories and shops—my Bradford readers will recall the spate of burglaries which afflicted their city in 1952 and early 1953.

The organisation of the gang was simple. There was the man who drove the van, a girl who acted as the look-out. Dolly effected the entry, and Stanislas did the actual robbery—Dolly joining him inside if heavy goods were involved.

The man and the girl were not entirely reliable, it seemed: the man drank too much in between jobs, and his mouth opened too easily. Dolly and Stanislas at last decided that they could work with more confidence by themselves.

They did very well, not limiting themselves to Bradford. But one evening the defences of a factory in Leeds defeated them. In their anger, they decided to rob a near-by shop: this was foolish, for they had not studied their objective—usually they spent a considerable time over preliminary investigations. So they could not know that the owner and his wife lived above the shop. It was the woman who disturbed them. And Dolly panicked, striking her with his jemmy. She fell dead, the blood staining her grey hair.

Stanislas's horror rendered him helpless. He had no qualms about theft: that was part of his revenge on an unjust world. But the murder of a woman who had done him no harm was quite another matter.

The pair separated and lay low. Stanislas was miserably unhappy, constantly brooding and utterly restless. They seemed to have escaped suspicion, but that was no comfort.

One day he happened to pass the church which served the Polish community. On an impulse he went inside: he had been brought up as a Catholic, but since the war he had completely

lapsed. The calm quiet of the church could not give peace to
his tortured mind. He was sobbing when Father Borynski found
him kneeling before the altar.

Stanislas recovered and ran away, but returned. Father
Borynski recognised the symptoms: the man was sick in his
soul. He treated him gently, and with great patience.

Stanislas drew from the priest's faith and moral strength.
The time came when he asked Father Borynski to hear him in
confession. Naturally, I know nothing about what happened,
but could deduce it from subsequent events. He confessed
everything—describing the murder in agonised detail.

The priest sought to comfort him and urged him to gain the
repose he needed by surrendering himself to justice. But
Stanislas was not quite ready for so drastic an action—which
would betray his companion as well as himself. He must consult
him, he decided.

He met Dolly one night in a public house at Cleckheaton.
After a drink they drove in the small van to a quiet lane to talk.
Then Stanislas unburdened himself: he had confessed to a
Catholic priest.

It was unfortunate that they sat in the dark, or he would have
seen the fury in Dolly's eyes. But the man was cunning. At first
he was merely doubtful. Was Stanislas certain that the priest
would not talk? The seal of the confessional meant nothing to
Dolly—he had often vulgarly boasted that his only visit to
church was inside his mother when she was married. Stanislas
tried to reassure him: in his eagerness he had no suspicion of
the workings of Dolly's mind.

"I've got to see this priest of yours before I'll feel safe," Dolly
declared.

Stanislas was delighted. Dolly was bound to succumb to
the personality of Father Borynski.

They arranged to meet the following evening at a spot
nearer to Bradford. It was Stanislas who telephoned the priest
from a call-box. Father Borynski was quite willing to come to
meet him: here was a further chance to rescue a man whose

conscience had fallen by the wayside. A bus journey was involved: he might be late—a searching of the soul cannot be hurried—so he took his raincoat.

He had no difficulty in finding the rendezvous. There stood the van, behind a haystack—and Dolly was beside it.

"Your friend's inside," Dolly beckoned.

Father Borynski climbed over the tailboard, then gasped in horror. His friend was inside—dead.

Now Dolly was beside him. An iron pipe swung savagely, and the priest collapsed with scarcely a moan. Dolly, satisfied, drove to a rural area near Dewsbury. Here was an abandoned quarry which he had often used for the disposal of anything dangerous. There he disposed of the most dangerous possession he had ever handled. The two bodies fell hundreds of feet, to splash into the deep pool which flooded the bottom of the pit. Lead piping—stolen!—had been inserted into the clothing to keep the bodies submerged. Then Dolly drove the van back to Bradford, to clean it out thoroughly before using it again.

Post Scriptum. In October, 1962, a self-confessed Russian assassin captured in Germany is reported to have confessed to the murder of Father Borynski. M.I.5. sought confirmation, but so far none has been forthcoming.

EIGHT

Dr Graves—the Spy who won a War

ONE EVENING in the early spring of 1912 a tall, dark-complexioned man arrived in Edinburgh from England. He left the Waverley Station, strolled along busy Princes Street to the Bedford Hotel and booked a room.

He said his name was A. K. Graves, which was true. He also said he was an Australian doctor, which was a lie. He was a man of mystery whose parentage was unknown and whose nationality was never established. He was a highly trained professional spy, sent by Captain Tappken of the German Naval Intelligence Department to report on the new British naval base at Rosyth in the Firth of Forth.

In those days spies had not yet begun to use radio. So elaborate arrangements had been made to prevent any suspicion that this friendly Australian doctor was communicating with the German Admiralty. His innocuous-reading instructions were written on letter paper forged in Berlin. The paper and envelopes bore the printed address of Messrs Burroughs, Wellcome and Co. of London. It would not seem unusual for a doctor to correspond with a firm of wholesale chemists.

Orders from Berlin for Graves and other spies in Britain were sent in bulk to Karl Gustav Ernst, a barber in Caledonian Road,

London. He re-posted them to obtain London postmarks. Reports by Graves were sent in code to three different individuals on the Continent. One was a businessman in the rue de Venise, Brussels; another was the proprietor of the Hotel Stadt in Copenhagen; another was a lady who kept a small lingerie shop in the rue de Rivoli, Paris.

Britain had recently tightened up the Official Secrets Act. And only a few months before Graves arrived in Edinburgh, that brilliant spy-catcher, Sir Vernon Kell, had organised the new counter-espionage department, M.I.5. Already M.I.5 knew all about Karl Ernst and his contacts in Britain. M.I.5 also knew the German Secret Service pillar-boxes abroad. All mail to these addresses was intercepted and photographed. From the very start of his mission Graves did not stand a chance.

But before he could be prosecuted he had to be allowed to do a little spying to provide the evidence. So while he loitered near the Forth Bridge he was carefully watched. And during his absences his luggage was searched and his secret code was copied.

After a week or two Graves moved to Glasgow, where he hoped to obtain details of the new 14-inch naval guns being made by Messrs William Beardmore. And there on the 14th of April, just after he had dressed for dinner at the Central Station Hotel, he was arrested.

His trial opened on the 23rd of July in the Edinburgh High Court. No reference was made by the prosecution, of course, to M.I.5's knowledge of the German pillar-boxes. We wanted to continue watching them, and did so, in fact, until the very day when the first World War began. Then we staggered the Germans by mopping up every spy in Britain.

But sufficient proof of guilt was found in Graves's luggage. The forged Burroughs, Wellcome letter paper could not be explained. And the secret code, which related to naval-base defences and movements of warships, was deadly evidence. Sentences for spying were lighter in those days. Graves was found guilty and sent to prison for eighteen months.

So one of Germany's dangerous spies was taken away to the grim prison of Barlinnie. He did not know that there were certain shrewd men in Whitehall who had begun to plan his future for him.

The British Government knew that war with Imperial Germany was practically inevitable. And nobody thought that in the early days the small British professional army might be a vital factor. War on land was visualised as a struggle between the huge conscript armies of Germany against those of France and Russia. Britain's main task would be to keep control of the seas.

So it became important for Britain to be able to find the German fleet when the clash came. This could best be done by intercepting German Admiralty orders sent out by cable or by the comparatively new invention of radio. These would be in code; hence Britain must know that code.

Getting a copy of the German code was clearly a task for a spy. Indeed, it was a task for a super-spy—a man of high intelligence and wide experience, trained in the technicalities of naval espionage. And as British Intelligence authorities rightly tend to distrust the mercenary spy, the man they now required should be actuated by either love of Britain or hatred of Germany —it scarcely mattered which. The far-seeing men in Whitehall soon perceived that just such a man was sewing Post Office mailbags in Barlinnie Prison.

Actually Graves did not at that time hate Germany. But the theory of brain-washing was not invented by the Chinese Communists. Britain had mastered the technique of 'turning' a spy fifty years ago. Graves had been in prison only a few weeks when he had a visitor. He called himself "Captain Johnson." And during a friendly conversation he happened to mention that the British could not take any credit for catching such a brilliant spy as Graves. British methods were too old-fashioned and inefficient. What had happened, according to "Captain Johnson," was that the Germans had become afraid of Graves because he knew too much, and had deliberately betrayed him.

The proofs offered by "Captain Johnson" were not really very convincing; the German motives seemed inadequate; and their methods appeared clumsy. It would have seemed simpler and safer to recall Graves to Berlin and put him out of the way.

But Graves's account of that momentous interview is on record. He was convinced of the German duplicity. His vanity was hurt, and he wanted revenge. After a period of the self-induced mental process known at Scotland Yard as 'cooking,' he was offered a chance to get his own back on his betrayers—by working as a spy—for Britain. He accepted.

Next morning Graves reported sick. He was transferred from Barlinnie, ostensibly to a prison with better hospital accommodation. A prison official took him by train to London. There he was met at Euston by the mysterious "Captain Johnson"—and disappeared.

Looking ahead a little, let us refer to the Hansard report of Parliamentary proceedings on the 12th of June, 1913. Mr King, a Liberal Member, asked the Secretary of State for Scotland to say whether a German spy named Graves was still serving his sentence for espionage; if not, when and why had he been released. The Secretary for Scotland replied that Graves had in fact been released, believed to have been in bad health at the time. Shortly afterwards the Speaker intervened, and the matter was abruptly dropped.

All the foregoing facts are on record. It appears that Graves was sufficiently loyal to his new paymasters to keep silent about his mission for "Captain Johnson." What was that mission?

It is now suggested for the first time that Graves was sent to Berlin. His pockets were full of money—his heart was full of hatred for the nation which he believed had betrayed him. He had a new identity and a new mission—but he remained the keen-brained spy, trained in the technique of naval espionage and with inside knowledge of the most secret sections of the Admiralty building in Berlin, Königergratzerstrasse 70.

He did not burgle the safe and steal the codes. Indeed, his method was devoid of drama—but effective. He knew personally some of the men who had access to the naval code which would come into operation the moment Germany was at war.

He spent some time in studying their circumstances. One was a heavy drinker, and always short of money. Another was hopelessly in debt as a result of maintaining two 'wives' instead of the conventional one. A third was in serious distress —a sick wife, with a large family needing attention.

This was the man Graves chose. He pretended that he was a secret agent of the German Naval Intelligence staff, and needed a sight of the code books. Maybe his victim persuaded himself that this was true—though the fact that he accepted a heavy bribe suggests otherwise. Graves must have had possession of the code book for many hours in order to photograph its pages. Then it was returned to its place of security, with no one in authority any the wiser.

It is a *fact* that a deal was made with some official. It is a *fact* that an advance copy of the code reached Whitehall not long before the first World War broke out. It is a *fact* that from somewhere in Europe Graves fled across the Atlantic and turned up in the United States. American reporters traced him, and there was no longer any need for him to deny his identity. He had served the purpose of the delighted British spy-masters and was of no further use to them.

In Intelligence jargon, Graves had 'worked his passage.'

On the 4th of August, 1914, the great radio aerials high above the Admiralty building in Whitehall broadcast a grim message to His Majesty's ships in all the seas of the world: "Commence hostilities, midnight."

And waiting cable-ships sped to play their rôle in reverse. From the bed of the ocean they fished up thick, slimy, barnacled coils—the deep-sea cables between Germany and the rest of the

world—and cut them. There was just one cable they left uncut
—that between Germany and Britain. The Germans apparently
thought this omission accidental.

Radio in war then had—and still has—limitations. Broadcast
messages can be heard by enemies as well as friends. But deep-
sea cables can only be tapped on shore. So almost throughout
the war Germany's most secret messages were sent abroad by
cable—the cable that the inefficient British had omitted to cut,
and which they were even foolish enough to let Germany use
for secret orders and reports to her embassies in neutral
countries.

And if sceptical German officers suggested that it was
rather dangerous to send this top-secret material through the
enemy capital, they were assured that the wonderful German
code was unbreakable.

British cryptanalysts in the Admiralty's Room 40.O.B.
could not have cared less. Had not a friendly hand passed to
them a copy of the German naval code? From time to time the
Germans changed this code, following standard Intelligence
practice. But the replacement was always a code of the same
type—and presented no serious difficulty to a brilliant staff of
British code-breakers.

There came the day when they deciphered a message from
Berlin to the German Embassy in Washington that was almost
too appalling to be credible. It was the notorious *Spurlos
Versenkt* order to all German U-boats—the order to sink all
ships at sight, even neutrals. The Zimmermann telegram went
further than this. In the event of war between Germany and
U.S.A. resulting, it proposed alliance with Mexico—which
would receive New Mexico, Texas and Arizona after a German
victory.

Obviously such a barefaced proposal would arouse wide
indignation in U.S.A. But there was a strong anti-British
faction—mainly of German or Irish origin—which would
certainly decry the Zimmermann telegram as a forgery, a trick
by the ruthless and cunning British to inveigle America into the

war. Further, Britain could not afford to let the Germans suspect that all their secrets passing through London were being deciphered. Hence Washington was asked to take the credit for a great Intelligence coup! It was arranged that the Americans should announce that they had obtained a copy of the German despatch from South America. By official request a leading article was printed in the London *Daily Mail*. It congratulated the Americans on the success of their Intelligence Department. It strongly criticised British Intelligence for being so inefficient! And it deceived the Germans into thinking that their messages passing through London could not be deciphered.

The Zimmermann telegram was an incident which helped to bring the United States into the war. The result was vital. America had at first only a small regular army, and was able to take only a minor share in the actual fighting. But her enormous industrial and financial potential was now at the disposal of Britain and France, whose resources were more than severely strained. Further, the vast American armies which could be raised would ensure victory by 1919 at latest.

If America had not declared war on Germany, it is probable that the allies would have lost—for Russia was already beaten to her knees and near to revolution. If British cryptanalysts had not deciphered the Zimmermann telegram, American participation in the conflict might have been too late, or might never have occurred at all.

Hence is it not obvious that the vital American decision derived in part ultimately from the acquisition of the German naval code by a disgruntled German agent?

NINE

Karl Lody — the Spy who lost a War

NO INCIDENT of the first World War has been so much disputed as the Battle of the Marne. Even the course of the battle was utterly confused. A woman questioned General Joffre, the French Commander-in-Chief.

"Tell me, General Joffre, who *did* win the Battle of the Marne?"

"I do not know, madame. But if it had been lost I know who would have lost it!"

The battle was the decisive clash of the war. The Germans had driven the French and British out of Belgium into the heart of France. They were poised for a final victory when suddenly they halted, and the hard-pressed Allies recovered.

The Battle of the Marne decided the course of the war. The allies won it—but still needed four years to defeat the powerful German forces. But if the Germans had triumphed in the Battle of the Marne it seems more than likely that they would have overrun the whole of France and won the war.

Who lost the Battle of the Marne? Why and how? The answer lies in one of the most grotesque and ridiculous combinations of circumstances in all history.

The troop train from Scotland made an unscheduled halt at

a village station in the South of England. As the halt was prolonged, the men got out to stretch their legs. The air resounded to strange accents as the platform was crowded with soldiers.

The village porter stared at the unexpected invaders in amazement. He was not bright—indeed, was barely literate. He could scarcely understand a word the soldiers uttered—to him broad Scots was as incomprehensible as a foreign language.

"Where be you from?" he asked of a sergeant.

"Ross-shire."

The porter knew no geography, and the sergeant's accent was heavy. Just then the engine hooted, and the soldiers rushed to join the train.

"Aye, there was thousands of 'em," said the porter that night in the village inn. "Great big chaps, talking like rubbish."

"But what was they, Henery?"

"I aksed them that. They was Rooshians."

"What? You be sure?"

"I tell you, I aksed 'em. 'Where be you from?' I says, and this chap, he says, 'Rooshia.' "

So the legend of the Russians was born. It swept the country like wildfire, gathering definiteness as it scurried from town to town. The single battalion of Scots became an army of Russians, with whiskers on their faces and with snow on their boots.

Thousands of people actually *saw* them, as they passed through every station in England—in railway carriages with drawn blinds. There were no Russians, of course, but Mr Asquith—a lawyer as well as the Prime Minister—declared that no incident in history was so capable of being proved in a court of law as the passage of the Russians through England in September, 1914.

Karl Lody was a German spy. He had been a naval officer, then a travel courier: he spoke English with an American accent. He had ample courage—but was untrained and incompetent as a spy.

He was a replacement for Dr A. K. Graves, whose peculiar spy career is chronicled in the previous chapter. His task was to watch the British fleet—whose war-time bases were in Scotland. He passed as an American tourist. It was not difficult to pick up oddments of information, for the British are talkative and unsuspicious.

But Lody attracted attention to himself in a peculiar fashion. He sent business cables—or so they appeared to be—to Adolf Burchard, apparently a businessman in Stockholm. And after each he appended a patriotic message: "Hope we beat the damned Germans soon." He was pleased with his own cleverness. This touch would stamp him as a loyal Britisher, he thought.

Now it is unusual to cable such phrases at eightpence a word —especially from Scotland. The telegraph clerk decided that the police ought to know. They passed on the trivial piece of information to M.I.5—to whom it was not news, for the address in Stockholm was known to be a cover for a German espionage centre: Burchard's name was on the Censorship Stop List.

Now Lody was watched. His letters and cables to his contact Burchard were held up—all save one.

The amazing rumour about the Russian troops was afoot. A Member of Parliament had even asked a question about it in the House of Commons. He received the conventional reply: "It is not in the national interest to give out information as to troop movements."

Yet Lody could scarcely make a report on the basis of a rumour. He chanced to meet an old acquaintance, a Canadian journalist, who was attempting to run the report to earth. Together they journeyed to Edinburgh. There, on Waverley Station, they saw trains moving south—with all blinds drawn! This so exactly confirmed the current story that the two men never thought of the obvious alternative—that the trains were full of British troops who wanted to sleep undisturbed.

In the following days Lody met solid citizens in Edinburgh and Dundee who had *seen* the Russians passing south. Another had seen a trainload of furs—evidently part of Russian uniforms. Then Lody himself saw a trainload of men in blue uniforms and round peakless caps. These could not be British, he decided. He never thought of Marines, but jumped to the conclusion that they must be Russians. There could be no further doubt.

He was so excited that he neglected his codes and wrote openly to Adolf Burchard in Stockholm: "Will you please communicate with Berlin at once by wire (code or whatever system you have available) that on September 5th great masses of Russian soldiers passed through Edinburgh on the way to London and France. Estimated about 60,000 men. I went to the station and noticed trains passing at high speed, blinds drawn. Landing in Scotland took place at Aberdeen." This was the letter which the censors allowed to go through.

Lody never knew that he had inadvertently helped to lose the war for Germany. Long before its end he had been arrested, tried, condemned, and shot in the rifle-range in the Tower of London.

General von Moltke lived in the shadow of the great reputation of his uncle, who had so significantly defeated the French in 1870. The younger Moltke was no genius, but he was a competent soldier with a staff as good as Germany had ever known. He had every reason to be pleased with himself. The French and British armies were in full retreat before his powerful and well-organised forces. Soon they would be bound to halt. Then there would be a final battle and the war would be won—for Germany.

Sir George Aston has described the orders given to him. He was to land at Ostend with a brigade of Marines—not to fight, for there were no Germans near, but to advertise his presence. His men were to dash about the countryside, showing themselves everywhere, making a brigade look like a division. Soon the news would get to the Germans, who would doubtless detach a force to counter this threat to their flank. Then Aston's task would have been accomplished. At the first sign of attack he could bring his men home.

General von Moltke listened to his Intelligence officer with some anxiety. "You are sure of this?"

"Quite sure, sir. I ordered special patrols when I heard that enemy forces had landed at Ostend. They captured two English soldiers—on bicycles. These two men have been interrogated. They were not very intelligent or well informed, but from such information as they could give it is quite obvious that the English are establishing a bridgehead around Ostend."

"A bridgehead!" snapped von Moltke. "But what for? They have no major forces left to deploy—you reported yourself a week ago that all their active divisions were already engaged."

"So they are, sir. My information suggests that the English are not preparing the bridgehead for their own use."

"What? Then why are they wasting their time?"

"I have a report from Sweden, sir—we have an Intelligence centre there. It has received a disquieting message from a highly reliable agent in Scotland. Russian troops have landed there, and are moving southwards. There are even reports that they have already landed at Ostend—men in blue uniforms have been seen."

"Russians! Are you sure?"

"Yes. We have checked on the message. Agents report the presence of the Russians from many places in England—so many, in fact, that the Russians must be present in considerable force."

"How considerable?"

"I could only estimate, sir. But, based on the reports on Russians seen, I should say at least an army corps."

"An army corps! If it landed at Ostend it could be dangerous. Right. I'll discuss it with Colonel Hentsch."

Hentsch was von Moltke's Deputy Chief of Staff. The two men adjourned to the map room of their headquarters. There a giant wall map gave the war situation at a glance—the German battle divisions advancing farther into France, now in the region of Soissons; and the long lines of communication across Belgium.

It was to this section that Hentsch pointed. "This is our weakest point. The railway is overcrowded with supply trains moving to France. Even a temporary interruption would be serious. A prolonged interrupton would be disastrous—we have been unable to maintain more than two days' ammunition in the forward zone."

"Suppose an enemy army corps debouched from Ostend——"

"That would be more than dangerous. If they were firmly led they could cut our main supply lines at Namur or Maubeuge. We could detach forces to drive them off—but, as I said, the interruption could be disastrous."

"Precisely my idea. It must not happen. We must contain them at Ostend. On no account must they be allowed to break out. Have we enough effective troops in Belgium?"

"No. Only second-line units. And one estimate gives 40,000 British and 80,000 Russians at Ostend. These figures are probably exaggerated. But we shall certainly have to withdraw forces from the Army in France."

"Very well. Withdraw two divisions."

"Two divisions!" Colonel Hentsch sounded dubious. "That will seriously weaken our striking force."

"That can't be helped. At all costs we must contain Ostend, and prevent the cutting of our lines of communication."

"You are right. I will issue the orders."

"No. Go and see General von Kluck yourself."

So Hentsch hurried to von Kluck's headquarters with von Moltke's orders.

"But I can't spare two divisions," von Kluck protested. "I have suffered the wastage of a long advance—most units are below strength—the loss of two divisions would seriously weaken my army."

"You could not afford to let the enemy cut your lines of communication, could you?"

"Of course not."

"Well, the English are continually disembarking fresh troops on the Belgian coast. There are reports of a Russian Expeditionary Force in the same parts. A withdrawal is becoming inevitable."

Hence two divisions were withdrawn from the pursuit of the retreating French and British forces and despatched northwards. There they took up their positions around Ostend, awaiting the Russian attack—which never materialised.

General von Moltke now regarded the war map with satisfaction. His vital lines of communication were secure. Now he could prepare his final annihilating blow in France.

But the Battle of the Marne was not developing according to plan. There was a bare minimum of actual fighting. Two gaps had appeared in the German line. French and British halted their retreat and marched northwards into the gaps. Commanders of adjacent German divisions were apprehensive of being outflanked, and hurriedly withdrew. It is much easier to start a retreat than to halt it.

So the Germans lost the Battle of the Marne, and with it their chance of winning the war. In 1937 I attended German manœuvres. At a subsequent party German officers began to question me about the background to the battle. At long last they had got to the bedrock truth, and were full of queries about the Russian rumours of 1914. (I did not know it then, but the Germans were preparing to use the rumour weapon themselves in the second World War.)

One senior officer was highly critical of the unfortunate spy, Karl Lody, whose message to Stockholm had started off a trail of events so tragic to Germany. Yet this was not the beginning of the episode: Captain B. H. Liddell Hart, the famous British military historian, has suggested that we ought to erect a monument to the unknown village porter who first started off the rumour!

TEN

Spy Round-up

IN COUNTLESS BOOKS OF FICTION and alleged fact, the
German Secret Service has been presented as a huge, sinister
and highly efficient organisation. Before and during the two
world wars there were reports of spies everywhere: before the
first World War they prepared tennis courts as howitzer sites,
and in the second they had radio aerials up their chimneys.
Actually the German spy organisation in Britain was almost
completely ineffective and remarkably feeble.

This is the story of two German Secret Service 'pillar-box'
systems, which operated in Britain before the first and second
world wars respectively. The story of the first 'broke'—
officially if not publicly—on the day the first World War began.
The German espionage system in Britain was smashed over-
night. It was at that time the greatest such triumph in Secret
Service history.

German authorities later tried to belittle the achievement.
The otherwise fairly reliable Colonel Nicolai, former chief of
German Military Intelligence and Counter-espionage, wrote in
1924 of the pre-war activities of his service: "Time and means
had not sufficed to extend this organisation to England." This
was true as far as military matters went, because the German

General Staff had never been interested in Britain's meagre military resources.

But the German Admiralty had long been very interested indeed in the powerful British Navy, and had built up a Naval Intelligence network in Britain about which they simply had not troubled to inform the German Staff. In such matters the clockwork German efficiency at low levels contrasted with fierce inter-departmental jealousy at the top.

The side of the picture never revealed to Colonel Nicolai was described in 1930 by the smug, blundering, comic-opera German self-styled spy-master Gustav Steinhauer. He wrote: "Spies and agents were recruited in practically all the important seafaring [sic] ports of the United Kingdom." He gave their number as at least forty, but he was such a liar that everything he says should be divided by half. The actual number was twenty-two, all of whom came under the close observation of M.I.5 for years.

The fact is that Nicolai's organisation was not very successful. German visitors who abused our hospitality sometimes suffered baffling setbacks. Poor Steinhauer's maddening experiences among the incompetent British have been described by Detective-Inspector Fitch, who was then an officer of Scotland Yard's Special Branch. "On the whole," he writes, "that must have been a very trying trip to the visitor's temper. Every time he tried to meet an acquaintance something went wrong. His letters were delayed and mis-delivered; telephones broke down at his touch, or else gave innumerable wrong numbers; public clocks in buildings where their correctness was usually almost sacred were either fast or slow. His own watch, which disappeared on the first morning of his stay at the hotel, was miraculously discovered behind a dressing-table on the day he departed, and was returned with profuse apologies. The joy of the thing was that the man, who was no fool, came in the end almost to suspect his own shadow but he could not prove a single thing, and with his doubtful identity" (he was calling himself "Max Westhaus") "he was not really in a position to make much of a fuss." Kipling was not far wrong in calling British Secret Service work "the Great Game."

Even Steinhauer had to admit that "most of the so-called German spies captured in England immediately prior to the outbreak of war . . . owed their fate to the carelessness of an officer who was visiting London."

Kaiser Wilhelm II of Germany attended the funeral of his uncle, King Edward VII, in 1910. Among his suite was a German naval officer, a baron, who had once been naval attaché to a South American state—where his 'official' spying had been rather too blatant. Naturally, therefore, he was closely watched when he visited England.

After the funeral, he took a cab to a shabby barber's shop in the Caledonian Road—scarcely the place where a German baron would go for a haircut! The barber, Karl Gustav Ernst, was a naturalised British subject of German origin. The detectives soon discovered that Ernst was a spy post-box. His employers sent his instructions as wrappings for shaving-soap, and he distributed them to German agents in Britain. Hence, by watching his outgoing post—Ernst used the nearest pillar-box—we had the names and addresses of all German spies in the country.

We did not arrest them at once—the Germans would have promptly established another spy ring. But we were *very* interested in the instructions the German spies received.

The now well-known climax was that when the first World War broke out twenty spies were arrested, one committed suicide, and one escaped in a neutral ship from Hull. Germany was left without a single source of naval information in Britain, and the trickle of replacements—mostly half-trained mercenary neutrals—who crept into Britain during the war were scooped up without much difficulty and sent to penal servitude, the gallows, or an old kitchen chair in the Tower of London rifle-range.

When planning the second World War, the German spy-masters decided to organise *two* spy rings. One was to advertise itself, so that the British would break into it. Then they would rest content. But the British broke into *both* spy rings, and another general round-up followed in September, 1939.

It might be thought that their disastrous experience with Ernst would have given German Intelligence a 'thing' about hairdressers. But apparently not, for in 1937 they were using another hairdressing shop in Britain as an espionage 'pillar-box.' This time it was the establishment of Mrs Jessie Jordan in Kinloch Street, Dundee.

It was an intelligent Scottish postman who noticed that Mrs Jordan was receiving suspicious quantities of mail from Germany and the United States, among other places. It did not seem to make sense that eager clients should write from Berlin and Brooklyn to make hair-do appointments in the city of jam, jute and journalism—distant Dundee.

In this case, as in many others, the German spy-masters showed a complete lack of ordinary common sense. Some of the German agents of the first World War, for example, had posed as cigar salesmen, and their reports to Berlin were in the form of a clumsy code indicating sales by the hundred thousand in such places as Chatham and Portsmouth. But sailors seldom smoke cigars in wholesale quantities: in those days they could not afford them; they preferred Woodbines. Mrs Jordan might have escaped attention for a little longer if her cover occupation had been some mail-order business with likely connections abroad—as a dealer in foreign stamps, for instance. But the Germans will never learn.

Mrs Jordan's correspondence was not, in fact, about hair-do appointments. It revealed that she was, in the words of American G-man Leon Turrou, "a mail relay station for a vast international Nazi spy-ring. Nazi spies over half the world, writing for instructions from Nazi headquarters, sent their mail to that address."

Among the hair-raising schemes dealt with in some of the hairdresser's mail was a plot to steal U.S. Army Air Corps secret codes; a plot to kidnap the Commandant of Fort Totten,

New York, when he had in his possession the plans for U.S. Eastern seaboard defences; and a scheme to copy President Roosevelt's signature on forged White House notepaper in order to obtain blueprints of the latest U.S. aircraft carriers. All of this information was quietly passed by M.I.5 to a startled American Ambassador in London, through whom it eventually reached Edgar Hoover's F.B.I. All that the British public knew at the time was that Mrs Jordan was arrested for espionage and sentenced to four years' imprisonment.

The American people were not spy-conscious in those days, and indeed there was no particular reason why they should have been. They did not want to attack anybody, and they could not imagine why—or even how—any other country should attack them. But when Washington received from M.I.5 packets of sensational photostats of Mrs Jordan's mail, the G-men swung, rather belatedly, into action. That was in January, 1938, and although counter-espionage is a game of patience that should never be rushed, eighteen persons were indicted on June the 20th of that year before a Federal Grand Jury. America woke up at last and learned about the sinister schemes of Hitler's Germany.

The trials had a frankly propagandist angle, and U.S. Attorney Lamar Hardy said, "The important point is that the American public must be made aware of the existence of this spy plot and impressed with the dangers." Of the eighteen accused, G-man Turrou said, "Indictment of most of them was, of course, purely a gesture to show how indignant the United States was over the plot."

It is amazing how the German spy-masters adhered to well-worn devices from one war to another. In view of Germany's attachment to methods that had been tried and found disastrous, it might be an idea to arrange that on the next outbreak of hostilities every hairdresser in Britain should be interned!

We have seen how on the outbreak of both world wars, an

Intelligence Iron Curtain dropped round Britain compared with which the post-war Russian effort was a mere flimsy draping of light muslin.

So in August, 1914, and again in September, 1939, the Germans were faced with the considerable task of building up new Intelligence networks in Britain. With their customary lack of imagination they adopted similar methods. With their customary shocking bad luck in such work, they achieved similar lack of success.

The method they adopted twice in that eventful half-century was to send to Britain a trickle of mercenary agents—not the competent but unimaginative officers of the Abwehr, not even trained and experienced agents of Colonel Nicolai and Admiral Canaris, but mostly drunken and frightened barrel-scrapings of the European underworld. I shall tell the story of one group in a later chapter.

ELEVEN

The Trial of Mata Hari

MATA HARI was shot as a spy in the moat of Vincennes, near Paris, soon after dawn on the morning of October the 15th, 1917. She was innocent: of that particular offence, that is—she could legitimately have been charged as a prostitute. But this does not carry the death penalty!

Two legends have been built up about her. The first concerned her career as a dancer. Her stage name Mata Hari was the Malay for "Eye of the Morning." She claimed to be Indonesian—or, if it suited her, Indian. Actually she was Dutch.

She married a Dutch officer on leave from the East Indies. One of his friends, for a joke, inserted a matrimonial advertisement in his name, and Margaretha Gertruida Zelle, aged eighteen, answered it. She was already pregnant when she married the officer. In the East Indies she was lazy and unfaithful. The marriage broke up, and eventually she was divorced. Returning to Europe, she began to make a living by presenting exotic dances. She had no great talent, but was a novelty—she danced in the nude. Save for a jewelled brassière, that is to say, for she had pendulous breasts.

During the first World War she came to live in Paris, where

she at last attracted the attention of the French counter-espionage, and was arrested as a spy, tried, condemned and shot. Then the second legend began to form. Mata Hari was the greatest woman spy in all history—the prototype of the beautiful woman spy of modern fiction. She was responsible for the death of thousands of French soldiers. She had betrayed important Allied secrets to the Germans—secrets obtained in bed from her lovers. When condemned, her highly placed lovers strove to save her—kings, princes, prime ministers, and the like.

The legend was built up by journalists and retired spies who published their 'memoirs.' All of the latter claimed to have worked with Mata Hari in various countries: most of them had slept with her. There were no bounds to her exploits. Even today most people accept the story that she was a dangerous German agent, for in espionage few are qualified to separate fiction from fact. *All* the fantastic stories of Mata Hari as a spy are sheer fiction—all!

The legend of Mata Hari was substantiated by the evidence of the perfect witness. Sir Basil Thomson was chief of the C.I.D. at Scotland Yard. The son of an archbishop, he was a barrister, and had been successively a colonial administrator and Governor of Dartmoor Prison. He interrogated Mata Hari when she was taken off a ship voyaging from Spain to Holland. Naturally, his account of the woman was adopted by subsequent writers as the basis of their fantasies. Yet Thomson's account was largely based on hearsay, and in it he made one peculiar error—his dates are a year too early! This made all the difference to her story.

No French lawyer is proud of the Mata Hari trial. Were she being tried today, she would certainly have been acquitted—indeed, it is very doubtful if she would ever have been brought to trial. Let us consider some of the 'evidence' which sent her to her doom.

1. On the day war broke out, she was seen in a car with von Jagow, chief of the Berlin police. It was alleged that this proved

that she was a German spy. But police chiefs have nothing to do with espionage—save, in some countries, to arrest spies unmasked by the official counter-Intelligence agents. They certainly do not employ spies. The fact is that von Jagow was one of Mata Hari's lovers.

2. She had been a German spy long before the war. This was proved by her code number, H.21. The prefix H was only used by pre-war agents. In intercepted telegrams a German spy-master referred to her as H.21, and also mentioned money payments to her.

Mata Hari admitted both of these charges—that she was H.21, and that she had received money from a German spy-master. But she claimed that he was her lover, and that the money was her fee. She was expensive, she admitted, and charged as much as £1500 for a course of love-making. This particular lover could not afford so much, so had hit upon the happy idea of putting her nominally on his spy roll, and paying her out of official funds. Indeed, this was no new idea—the history of espionage provides many examples.

For that matter, one was in being at the very moment of Mata Hari's trial.

One of the first French women aviators was Marthe Richer. Her husband was killed early in the war. Burning to avenge his death, she offered her services to the Deuxième Bureau, the French Military Intelligence service. Captain Ladoux, one of its officers, saw possibilities.

Marthe was a very beautiful woman. She went to Madrid, became the mistress of a German naval attaché, and was able to gather fragments of information which meant a great deal when considered by expert brains. She rendered great service to her country.

She was deliberately extravagant, and her lover was hard pressed to maintain her on his official pay. So he, too, put his mistress on his spy list, and paid her out of Secret Service funds —which no accountant ever questions.

Captain Ladoux was an honest man. When Mata Hari

claimed that her lover had paid her out of Secret Service funds,
her judges jeered at her "fantastic" explanation. Captain
Ladoux did not explain to them that at least one of his agents
was involved in the same process. This is so different from his
normal standards of conduct that only one explanation is
possible—that he had been *ordered* to say nothing.

3. Mata Hari herself was at one time the lover of a German
naval attaché at Madrid. From this it was deduced that she had
passed on information to him. No details were forthcoming
as to the nature of the information or how and whence she
obtained it.

4. When the French began to suspect Mata Hari, it was
alleged that she sought to placate them by revealing secrets
told her by her lover. One piece of information was especially
useful to the French. She informed them that two German
submarines were to land cargoes of arms at the port of Mehadiya,
in Morocco. The arms were to be handed over to Moroccan
rebels, who would then be able to harass the French. Fore-
warned, the submarines were sunk by French destroyers.

Not the slightest tittle of evidence was produced to support
this theory. The French officers involved were not called to
give evidence. Reference to a map and war records would have
shown the yarn to be the most fantastic of fiction—there is
no Moroccan port named Mehadiya; and *no* German submarines were at any time sunk off the Moroccan coast.

No attempt was made to prove that Mata Hari had ever been
to the places reputed to be the scenes of her exploits. Yet her
press-cutting albums were available, and would have proved
that she could *not* have been in some of them. Not even a spy
could extract information from over-sexed officers at a French
spa and dance in Italy on the same night.

5. Because of her spy activities, Mata Hari was responsible for the deaths of at least 50,000 French soldiers and
sailors.

No proof was forthcoming that she was responsible for the
death of even one man. But one of her judges later admitted

that he accepted the statement as a fact, and was influenced by it.

6. It was alleged—again without a fragment of proof—that she had reported the French mutinies of 1917 to the Germans.

But German records show that this was one of the war secrets which the Germans did *not* learn. If they had, they would have attacked the French—and might well have won the war. Moreover, at the time of the mutinies Mata Hari was already under arrest!

So the amazing trial continued. It seems incredible that any court could accept such palpable hearsay and rumour. But Mata Hari was duly condemned.

What of the kings, princes and prime ministers who had been her lovers and fought to save her? This, too, is complete fiction. Not one highly placed lover moved to aid her—for the simple reason that they had never even heard of her.

The air of utter unreality persisted. One of her lovers, the Marquis de Montessac, attempted to rescue her. This story was widely published. But no such person existed!

Even her execution was enveloped in fantasies. By one yarn, de Montessac bribed the execution squad to load their rifles with blank ammunition. Mata Hari duly fell 'dead,' and her lover carried her off. The credulous who believed this fantastic story forgot that after the execution squad has fired, an officer gives the *coup de grâce* with a bullet from a pistol.

An alternative version is more intriguing. As the soldiers were about to fire, she opened her fur coat—to reveal her naked body! The soldiers were so affected by the sight that they, one and all, missed!

Unfortunately for such an ingenious yarn, a photographic record of Mata Hari's execution is available. As usual, she was tied to a post before being shot, so could scarcely have opened her fur coat! She was not wearing a fur coat, anyway.

The whole story, then, was a tissue of fanciful fairy-tales devoid of proof. There was evidence that Mata Hari was willing to sleep with any man of any nationality if he had enough money to pay her fee, but none that she had ever spied against France. Yet she was executed. Why?

The French army had borne the brunt of the early part of the war, badly equipped and stupidly led. Regiments were flung into one blood-bath after another, incurring shocking casualties. By the spring of 1917 they had had enough, and there was a widespread series of revolts. These were not German-inspired—as we have seen, the Germans knew nothing about them. They were a protest against the senseless offensives which gained yards of ground at an enormous price in blood. "We will defend the trenches, but we will not attack," cried the disgusted poilus.

Neither politicians nor generals are accustomed to accept blame: they are always right. Yet someone had to be blamed, to divert suspicion from men in high places. And the victim must be well known.

Mata Hari was the obvious choice. She was vaguely under suspicion of espionage—and was *very* well known. If the case were suitably handled, the blame for the mutinies could be diverted from the political and military leaders to the spy. Treachery is a potent thing, always liable to exaggeration. The French Press would doubtless make the most of the unique news value of the trial: it did!

Since then the legend has refused to die. A book, *Inquest on Mata Hari*, published in 1956 proved conclusively that Mata Hari had been judicially murdered. But innocent journalists and authors still continue to peddle and garnish the old story. If a woman spy ever gets into the news, she is always dubbed "a second Mata Hari." But at least she is likely to get a fairer trial than did Margaretha Gertruida Macleod, *née* Zelle.

TWELVE

The Case of Napoleon Reilly

"A CORSICAN LIEUTENANT OF ARTILLERY trod out the embers of the French Revolution. Surely a British Intelligence agent could make himself master of Moscow!" So wrote Captain Sidney Reilly, the British spy who decided to fight the Russian Bolsheviks single-handed.

Sidney George Reilly was Russian by birth, having been born in Odessa in 1874, but the nationality of his parents was never ascertained. According to his own statement he was a mixture of Irish and Jewish. As a young man in his twenties he dropped his original name of Rosenblum and adopted the name of Reilly.

As Reilly he was a partner in a firm of timber merchants at Port Arthur, scene of the famous siege during the Russo-Japanese War of 1904-5. He later became an agent for shipping and armaments firms, and while working for the next ten years in China, Japan and the United States he made a fortune.

In 1916 he was in Canada, where he joined the Royal Flying Corps and whence he was later sent to England. It was then that talent-spotters of British Intelligence picked him out as a man of great ability and a brilliant linquist, fluent in seven languages. He was often sent into Germany as a spy, and his

disguise as an officer of the German Imperial Navy was never
penetrated.

After the Russian Revolution in October, 1917, Britain
became alarmed about Bolshevik foreign policy, not so much
on political grounds as because we wanted to keep Germany
fighting on two fronts, whereas Lenin favoured a peace treaty
between Red Russia and Kaiser Wilhelm's Germany. So early in
1918 Reilly was brought back to England for re-briefing, and a
few weeks later he turned up in Petrograd (now Leningrad) as
M. Massino, an agent for Turkish and Oriental wares.

Reilly had an intelligent face, with sensuous lips and a restless
glance, was always expensively dressed, and was as irresistible to
women as he was persuasive with men.

But he was too late to influence Soviet plans, and the Treaty
of Brest-Litovsk was signed on the 3rd of March, 1918.

An example of Reilly's consummate nerve is the fact that soon
after arriving in Russia he went to Moscow, called at the
Kremlin and demanded to see Lenin, saying that he was a
special emissary from the British Prime Minister, Lloyd
George! Most Intelligence officers would be appalled at such
tactics on the part of one of their agents, but I can say from
experience that a spy of exceptional brilliance—as was Reilly—
sometimes succeeds with a bulldozer approach to some high-
level source of information. Reilly did not see Lenin, but he did
get as far as an interview with the latter's close friend Bonch-
Bruevich. It was this sort of exploit which tended to support
Reilly's claim to Irish blood.

Soon, however, he had reverted to more common methods.
The most fantastic cloak-and-dagger story would have seemed
easily credible in the Russia of 1918, when everybody was
plotting against everybody else. In such an atmosphere he
revelled. He obtained false identity papers describing himself
as a Commissar—in those days the key to almost every door.

It was not difficult to find well-placed sub-agents, and soon
Reilly was sending useful information to London. But he was
after bigger game. Lenin and his friends—who could not trust

the Russians—had to depend on mercenary bodyguards of Letts. Reilly proposed to suborn the Letts with an offer of higher pay and to use them to overthrow the Bolsheviks! His plan was by no means impossible: at that time Russia was in utter confusion, and Lenin's hold was tenuous indeed. But the British Embassy strictly forbade this proposal: to them the enemy was Germany, not Russia. It was at this moment that Reilly proclaimed himself as the Napoleon of the Russian Revolution. If Britain refused to support him, he would go it alone.

His first plan was sensational: he expounded it to a group of friends, including a French journalist. The Letts would seize the Communist Central Committee, including Lenin, while they were in conference. (Reilly proposed to kill their influence by ridicule—by parading them naked through the streets of Moscow!) At the same moment thousands of anti-Communists would rise in revolt.

Again, in the confusions of the day, this fantastic plan was by no means impracticable. But there was something Reilly had overlooked. The Communists, too, were masters of intrigue and infiltration. The French journalist to whom he had outlined his plot proved to be a Communist spy!

Now Reilly was on the run, with the whole force of the Cheka (as the Soviet Secret Police were then called) after him. Hundreds of hostages were shot, but he escaped into German-held territory—though here too he was wanted as a spy. But he was a master of illicit movement, and in September, 1918, he made his way to Finland and thence to England. He had not wasted his time. While in German territory he had acquired much useful information about German naval forces in the Baltic.

Winston Churchill—who thought highly of him—sent him back to Russia, via the Black Sea. He could only play a minor part in the confusion of Red and White armies, but his reports at least helped to clarify the situation.

The story of his life at this period reads like chapters from a sensational thriller. Intrigue, ambushes, captures, escapes, treachery, achievements, failures, fights, and danger were intermingled. His intelligence and subtle brain got him out of endless difficulties. And unlike most of his opponents he knew where he stood and what he wanted.

One week he would be advising a White commander, the next picking up information behind the Red lines. He had available a whole variety of rubber stamps, and made out convincing passes for all purposes—especially as most of the people who challenged him were unable to read. He depended not so much on physical disguise as on the utter confusion of the time and region.

He was to discover nevertheless that war is impossible where men no longer have the will to fight.

By this time he had decided that it would be best to work with the Russian anti-Communists in exile. By this time, too, the British Government had wearied of its efforts and the Bolshevik power seemed by now to have become unshakeable. But Reilly was not yet beaten. In September, 1925, in the company of three Russians he 'invaded' Russia from Finland. On the following day *Pravda* announced an affray on the Finnish frontier: four smugglers had been encountered and shot dead.

This was the apparent end of Sidney Reilly, *né* Rosenblum. But in view of his past history, exaggerated as it spread from mouth to mouth, it was almost automatic for rumours to circulate that Reilly was not dead. For once rumour was no lying jade, for two years later the Russians admitted that the four smugglers had not after all been killed. One had been wounded, and had admitted under interrogation that he was Captain Sidney Reilly, the "notorious British spy." The Russians claimed that he had made a full confession, which they published. Thereafter all was silence.

Thereafter, too, writers on espionage gave full play to their imagination. Reilly had often been reputed dead, but had turned up again alive and confident. History would repeat itself.

Newspapers and books published details of his extraordinary adventures. They were probably no more fantastic than the events in which Reilly had actually figured, but to make them comprehensible a full account of the situation in Russia would be necessary. For this, space was not available—and few people could have written it with accuracy, anyway. Moreover, few readers would have bothered to wade through it.

Reilly had nothing to do with the Army Intelligence organisation—he was supposed to be attached to the political branch. But I had friends who knew as much about him and his contacts as anybody, and I am quite confident that my account of the last phase of his career is accurate.

He was *not* wounded in the affray between the Russian frontier guards and the four 'smugglers'—who in fact did not exist. On the contrary, Reilly reached Leningrad safely, and re-established contact with Yakuslev, leader of a widespread anti-Communist organisation inside Russia. The two men had often worked together: but Reilly, for all his experience and shrewdness, had never suspected that Yakuslev was an OGPU agent deliberately infiltrated into the dissident ranks.

But at last Reilly had cause for suspicion. The OGPU (the new name for the old Cheka) were unusually active: a villa in which the conspirators were to meet was surrounded by a medley of unhealthy-looking characters who might easily have been OGPU agents: they were.

Reliable sources suggest that Yakuslev strove to avoid the proposed arrest of Reilly—it would arouse suspicion if the man were captured while Yakuslev went free. Surely it was better to maintain the latter's unique position as a traitor ensconced in the dissident faction than to jeopardise it by arresting one spy. But someone high in the OGPU ranks decided otherwise.

Reilly was riding unsuspectingly in a car when handcuffs were suddenly snapped on his wrists. To satisfy Yakuslev, the fiction about the smugglers on the frontier was concocted. For some time longer Yakuslev was able to betray the groups plotting against the Communists.

Reilly was well treated. His prison was carefully guarded—but was very comfortable. His food was good and his drinks unlimited. He was taken for motor drives in the country—under guard!—and encouraged to begin work on a book relating his adventures: this would be at least as interesting to the captors as to their prisoner!

Reilly hoped to talk his way out of prison, as he had done more than once before, but this time the Russians were determined. Their interrogations grew sharper and sterner. To break his nerve, he was taken to see executions in the cellars of the Lubianka prison. The victims were brutally knocked about before a bullet through the back of the neck—still the Russian method of execution—ended their agonies. He was himself tortured: at last he was persuaded to talk—but even *in extremis* he deceived the Russians by mingling fiction with fact.

When they decided that he had no more of interest to tell them, his doom was sealed. One morning in November, 1925, he was taken for his usual walk in the countryside south of Moscow. He was given no hint, and of course there was no trial: he was simply shot in the back.

This was not known at the time: the legends continued, their imagination never flagging. By some Reilly had escaped, and was a spy again: by others—on the authority of fellow prisoners—he had been driven mad by torture. Or he had been 'turned round,' and was now working for the Communists. There was no evidence to support these stories, but they will doubtless persist. His remarkable career gave more rewarding opportunities for imaginative fiction even than the romances of Mata Hari.

THIRTEEN

The Assassination of Trotsky

IN SEPTEMBER, 1950, Dr Alfonso Quiroz Cuaron, the famous Mexican criminologist, was in Paris after an international conference on crime. Before returning home he paid a flying visit to Madrid. He wanted to test a theory that an unidentified murderer held in Mexico might be a Spaniard.

Dr Cuaron called at Police Headquarters and introduced himself to the officer in charge of the Fingerprint Department. He handed over a photograph of a criminal record sheet.

"I wonder, señor, whether by any chance you happen to have a record of this fellow," he said.

The Spanish officer glanced at the ten rolled prints. "Who is he?" he asked.

"When we arrested him," Dr Cuaron said, "he carried the passport of Frank Jacson, a Canadian journalist. But Jacson has been dead for years. This man has also said he is Jacques Mornard, or Vandendreschd, the son of a Belgian diplomat. But the Belgian Foreign Office tell us that no officials of such names have ever appeared in their diplomatic list. Briefly, señor, we have no idea who is this man whom we have held in prison for the past ten years. It is a little embarrassing."

"I will do my best to assist you, Doctor," said the Spanish

officer. "But your police are very efficient. What they have failed to do in ten years I can hardly hope to do in ten days. Could you call back at the end of next week?"

"I must return to Mexico at the earliest possible moment," Dr Cuaron said. "I apologise for troubling you, but may I wait while you make a quick preliminary search?"

"Of course," said the Spanish officer. "But it may be a rather long wait. There are newspapers and magazines on that table. I will set my clerks to work at once. If they have not succeeded by the end of the morning, perhaps you will have lunch with me."

"You are very kind, señor," said Dr Cuaron.

Left alone in the waiting-room, Dr Cuaron looked at his watch. Then he glanced idly at the magazines on the table. He picked one up, prepared for a long and boring wait. But before he had had time to sit down, the Spanish officer rushed back into the room. "We have found him!" he exclaimed.

Dr Cuaron was amazed. He again looked at his watch. The successful search had taken exactly one minute and forty seconds.

"My sincerest congratulations, señor!" said Dr Cuaron. "Do your records show the man's real name?"

"Yes, Doctor. He is Jaime Ramon Mercader del Rio Hernandez, member of a well-known Spanish family. It seems that he was arrested on the 12th of June, 1935, as a secret member of the Barcelona Communist Party."

"I am most grateful, señor," said Dr Cuaron. "This is a historic moment."

"Why should it be historic?" asked the Spaniard. "What did this misguided young man do in Mexico?"

"He murdered Leon Trotsky," said Dr Cuaron.

During the years that immediately followed the Russian Revolution in 1917, Stalin had been jealous of Trotsky. The ambitious but plodding Georgian worked in the background under Lenin, whilst all the limelight shone on Trotsky, who was not only a fiery orator but was the organiser and leader of the rabble that he drilled into the successful Red Army.

After Lenin's death, their mutual dislike flared up. Trotsky claimed that Communist Russia would not long be allowed to exist in a capitalist world. Imminent attack by Western capitalist powers must be forestalled. In self-defence, Red Russia must organise world revolution—now. But Stalin maintained that it would be years before any such attack would be made. In the meantime the Soviet Government would be better employed in first setting its own house in order.

Political differences were aggravated by personal antipathies; they were completely opposite personalities. And the outspoken Trotsky's tactless habit of referring to the beetle-browed Georgian as "that Caucasian cockroach" did not endear him to the vain and revengeful Stalin.

Trotsky was skilfully ousted from power and sent to live in a remote district of Russia. The only reason that he survived was that he had followers all over the world, including many in Russia, who appreciated the vital part he had played in the success of the Revolution. His murder might have triggered off a dangerous anti-Stalin movement.

So Trotsky must be killed, but—not in Russia. Once he was on foreign soil, his murder could be blamed on hot-headed non-Russian Communists. And Soviet censors could prevent the news from reaching the people of Russia.

When Stalin felt that the latter had had time to forget Trotsky, the fallen leader was hustled over the frontier and took refuge in Norway. And at the same time Stalin summoned the grim-faced chief of Section OS2 of the N.K.V.D. The official title of this deadly branch of the Russian Secret Police was the Department for Special Tasks. But to those of us in the British Service who were actively engaged in the death-struggle of the international underworld, OS2 operatives were known as the "Travelling Executioners."

Under Kremlin pressure, Trotsky was expelled from Norway in 1936. The order was made by the then Minister of Justice, Trygve Lie, later first Secretary-General of UNO. Trotsky found refuge in Turkey.

But there was little rest for him there, and OS2 squads chased him out of the country and into France. He had plenty of friends and followers in that tolerant country, whence the Trotskyist movement in Europe was directed by his son, Leon Sedov.

Stalin was determined to exterminate his old enemy and all his followers. During the nineteen-thirties there were numerous OS2 killings in France. And during the chaotic conditions of the Spanish Civil War, N.K.V.D. men sent from Russia, ostensibly to help the Republicans, actually spent most of their time secretly kidnapping and killing Trotskyists, including some British subjects fighting in the International Brigade.

There was one intriguing sideline to the Spanish Civil War. Before the volunteers of the International Brigade went into action, their passports were collected by one of their officers— a Russian agent. The volunteers were persuaded that since their passports would reveal their nationality in the event of their capture, it would be safer to leave them behind.

None of the volunteers ever saw his passport again. Since 1936 they have been turning up in all parts of the world—all of them used by Russian agents.

Trotsky had to flee from France and across the Atlantic to America, where he finally settled into a large house on the outskirts of Mexico City. He was worried about the safety of the extensive records of his world-wide movement, so before leaving he deposited them with the Paris Institute of Political Science.

OS2 had been ordered to get those records. And what OS2 wants it usually gets. One night in 1937 the Institute was burgled, and no less than half a ton of Trotskyist documents were stolen. This brilliantly planned operation must have required the use of a number of agents and a lorry. But no trace of the burglars or the papers has ever been found.

Later in the same year another deadly blow was struck. The intelligent, studious and completely healthy young man known as Leon Sedov was admitted to a Paris hospital. He was suffering from a mysterious internal complaint, of which the symptoms were consistent with poisoning.

Under skilled hospital treatment, Sedov, with nurses at his bedside day and night, made a good recovery. And one evening orders were given by telephone that, since the patient was so much better, the nurse on night duty should be withdrawn. Subsequent exhaustive enquiries failed to trace the source of the telephone call.

But at 4 A.M. Sedov was found, naked and incoherent, staggering along a hospital corridor. He was muttering, "They've poisoned me!" He died shortly afterwards.

There was reason to suspect that one of the hospital staff might have been involved. But the inquest jury returned an open verdict. This was the end of Trotsky's much-loved son, the leader of European Trotskyism, as well as of the records of the movement. The old man himself was next on the death-list. After he was 'liquidated' there would not be much left of the once dangerous Trotskyist movement.

During 1938 two incidents occurred which were to have repercussions two years later. Trotsky, in Mexico, engaged as his secretary and guard a young New Yorker named Robert Sheldon Harte. And in Paris Sylvia Ageloff, courier and trusted friend of the Trotsky family, was introduced to a young man who called himself Jacques Mornard. He was handsome, cultured, quiet and considerate in his manner, and Sylvia fell in love with him.

Several books could be filled with the story of the years during which OS2 harrassed Trotskyists with spies, kidnappers and assassins. The operation is estimated to have cost the Kremlin half a million pounds. But we must move ahead to 1940.

Trotsky's house near Mexico City was virtually a fortress. The gate in the outer wall was guarded by Mexican Secret Service men, provided by the Government for a refugee from the murderous dictatorship of Stalin. Inside the walls armed Trotskyists patrolled the grounds. At night seachlights swept the lawns. On the roof were machine-gun nests. It was quite a problem for OS2.

A well-planned attack took place during the early morning of the 24th of May, 1940. An Army officer and several policemen approached the gate, showed their credentials and were admitted. Once inside, they held up guards at pistol-point, and admitted a number of others. They were all, in fact, OS2 agents wearing stolen police and military uniforms.

A pitched battle ensued, the attackers using pistols, machine-guns and incendiary bombs. Machine-gun bullets poured into Trostky's bedroom: incendiary bombs set his study on fire. Yet almost miraculously Trotsky and his wife escaped. They had flung themselves to the ground when the firing began, and the hail of bullets missed them. In the meantime the defenders were stout-hearted and resolute, and the OS2 men had to retreat. They took with them Robert Sheldon Harte, now revealed as an OS2 agent, on whose information the attack had been planned.

One of the attackers was later captured by the Mexican Secret Service, and under interrogation he revealed the location of a local OS2 hide-out. A search of the premises brought to light Harte's body buried under the kitchen floor. In OS2 there is only one penalty for failure!

Two of the gang escaped to Russia—a significant place of refuge! The local leader of the plot, under OS2 orders, was David Alfaro Sequeiros, a Mexican Communist. He claimed that murder was a legitimate punishment for "one of the greatest renegades of the cause of world revolution."

Communists take the trouble to cultivate friends in high places. Sequeiros was arrested, charged with murder—and released on bail! Naturally, he got away. Later he was re-arrested in Chile—and the Mexican Ambassador secured his release! He has never been tried.

Nevertheless, the attack had been a complete failure, and a serious loss of face for Stalin. He demanded a further operation—and this had better be successful!

The next and final scene of the Trotsky tragedy took place three months later, on the 20th of August. By then Sylvia Ageloff, close friend of Mme Trotsky, was back in Mexico. Closely following her was the young man who called himself Jacques Mornard. He explained that he had managed to get hold of a false passport as Frank Jacson, a Canadian journalist. He did not mention—perhaps he did not even know—that the owner of the passport had been killed fighting in Spain, and his passport had reached Mornard via Moscow.

For Mornard also was an OS2 agent and his successful courtship of Sylvia had been planned and ordered by the Kremlin. He may have inherited his talents, as his mother was another OS2 agent—an accomplished knife-thrower who boasted that she had killed twenty enemies of Soviet Russia.

Sylvia explained to Trotsky that her lover was eager to write articles about the Trotskyist movement. And the old man—quite a kindly person in private life—welcomed Mornard into his house, discussed Communism and world affairs with him, and advised him on his writing.

Soon after five on a hot August afternoon the young man was shown into Trotsky's study. He had a packet of manuscript in one hand and a raincoat in the other, both of which he laid on the table.

As soon as Trotsky had begun to read the manuscript, the young man snatched from his raincoat pocket an ice-pick. He shut his eyes—then drove the pick with all his force into Trotsky's head.

The old man gave a long and dreadful scream. Under interrogation later, Mornard said, "It still seems as if that scream is piercing my brain." The tough old fighter sprang at his attacker and bit his hand. He was knocked to the ground. But somehow he struggled up, and with blood spurting from his head staggered out of the room to where guards were about to rush in. "See what they have done to me!" he muttered.

Three guards, Robins, Hansen and Cornell, dashed into the study with drawn pistols. Speaking slowly and painfully,

Trotsky told them from the open doorway, "Not to kill. He must be made to talk."

Reluctantly the guards obeyed their revered leader. Mornard was standing aside, desperate and frightened. "They made me do it!" he cried. "They have something on me! They are holding my mother in prison!"

He did not escape unhurt. Holding the pistols by the barrels the guards bashed his head until the butts broke off the weapons. Meanwhile they fired questions at him. Several times he became unconscious, but they revived him, then went on with the questions and the beatings.

An ambulance arrived to take Trotsky to hospital. Then Sylvia arrived in a taxi. The revelation that the man she had loved was an OS2 agent had almost unhinged her mind. "Kill him! Kill him!" she screamed. Police took her away to a prison hospital, where she suffered a severe nervous breakdown.

Trotsky was tough. At the time of the attack he was sixty-two years old. The ice-pick had penetrated his brain to a depth of three inches. Yet he retained enough strength to fight back, and the killer's hand long showed the scar of his victim's teeth. The old man died twenty-four hours after the attack.

During and after the trial, the killer insisted that he was Jacques Mornard. There was never any doubt of his guilt, and as there is no capital punishment in Mexico he was sentenced to twenty years' imprisonment.

It is interesting to note that shortly after the sentence, an OS2 agent named Ramon Mercader was awarded in his absence the Order of Hero of the Soviet Union for "a valorous act." And an old lady named Caridad Mercader was taken to the Kremlin by a delighted Lavrenti Beria to be presented by Stalin with the Order of Lenin.

It was, as we have seen, not until ten years later that Jacson, alias Mornard, was identified by Dr Cuaron as Ramon Mercader.

And ten years after that, the man who still maintained that his name was Mornard was released from a Mexican prison.

He received no remission for good conduct, on the grounds that by continuing to deny his identity he had refused to co-operate with the authorities.

A few days after his release, a Soviet ship sailed from a South American port for Russia. It was assumed that Ramon Mercader was on the ship. But he has never been heard of since. If he ever lived long enough to claim the medal of his Order, it is improbable that he wore it for very long. He knew too much.

FOURTEEN

Mother of a Murderer

I QUOTE ONE INTRIGUING SENTENCE from my last chapter:
"And an old lady named Caridad Mercader was taken to the
Kremlin by a delighted Lavrenti Beria to be presented by
Stalin with the Order of Lenin." At the same time she received
the Order of Hero of the Soviet Union on behalf of her son, who
was unable to attend the ceremony in person.

Many prominent psychologists have studied the effects of
heredity in criminal records. There is no definite natural law,
but crime does seem to run in certain families—criminal
surroundings do, of course, increase any hereditary tendency.
"Like father, like son," is an old saying, but in extremist
political circles it could be more accurately amended to "Like
mother, like son."

A baby girl was christened on the 31st of March, 1892, in a
Catholic church at Santiago de Cuba. She was given the name
of Eustacia Maria Caridad del Rio Hernandez. Her parents were
prosperous minor Spanish aristocrats.

Caridad was sent to Europe to be educated, just as British
children born in India were sent to school in England to avoid
their acquiring the chi-chi accent. At a convent in France, and

later at another in Barcelona, Caridad received a good education, especially in languages, and soon learned to speak almost perfect English and French as well as her native Spanish. She also picked up the distinctive Catalonian tongue.

In 1910, soon after she had completed her education, her parents returned from Cuba to live in Barcelona, and she served as a novice in the barefooted order of nuns of the Carmelite Descalzas. She was then a beautiful girl of eighteen, nervy, eccentric and of uncertain temper.

But Caridad was not destined to live in permanent religious seclusion. Her parents noticed that she could not conceal her interest in men, so they found her a husband, as is the Continental way, and in January, 1911, she was married to shy, conventional twenty-six-year-old Don Pablo Mercader Marina, of an impoverished aristocratic Catalonian family.

Caridad bore four sons and a daughter. And her second son, Ramon, was destined to live in the history books long after his aristocratic forbears had been forgotten. He was to help unify the Communist world by murdering Stalin's most influential opponent, Leon Trotsky.

It was hardly to be expected that such a young woman as Caridad would settle quietly down to the rigidly conventional life of a Spanish society matron of those days. She began to brighten the dull days of domesticity by taking up the study of painting. This brought her into touch with artists of highly unconventional views, of whom there were plenty in revolutionary Catalonia, where even Marxists were regarded as rather 'pink,' and political strikes were organised by the Anarchists and Syndicalists. Already the most powerful working-class organisation was the Iberian Anarchist Federation, which was to distinguish itself later in the Spanish Civil War as the F.A.I. by fighting Franco's forces with sticks of dynamite brought from the Basque mines.

By 1925 the increasingly unstable Mercader marriage finally broke up. Thirty-three-year-old Caridad left her husband and took her children to live with her, first in Toulouse and

later in Bordeaux. Her husband followed her, got a job with
Air France and tried, but failed, to persuade his wife to return
to him.

Caridad did not want her husband, but she did want love.
She went to live with a Frenchman and shared not only his bed
but his political views. This had its indirect effect on the course
of history, for he was a fervent Communist.

Don Pablo returned at last in despair to Spain. Caridad moved
to Paris. And their children lived an unsettled life, shuttling
back and forth between their parents' homes.

In the political hothouse atmosphere of the Left Bank in
Paris, Caridad became more and more enthusiastic for love and
revolution, and highly successful in both.

It is not quite clear which was cause and which was effect,
but she was soon the mistress in turn of most of the French
Communist leaders, and also of a trusted Communist courier
between the capitals of Europe, for which her command of
languages made her eminently qualified. Whether or not her
lovers considered her equally qualified as a mistress is less
certain. Her idea of a joke at a cocktail party was to describe a
former lover as he appeared when haranguing the Paris mob,
and then to compare his appearance as he stood naked in her
bedroom a little later.

When the Spanish Civil War broke out, Caridad was in
Barcelona on a Communist assignment. She joined the Republican Army, was wounded, and after she had recovered was sent
on an official mission to Mexico.

It is a measure of her abilities that she successfully carried out
several tasks simultaneously. Her legal status, as far as the
Mexican Government was concerned, was that of a political
refugee, which implied that she should take no part in local
politics. Her overt task, as set by the Spanish Republican
Government, was to finance the resettlement of hundreds of
orphans of the Civil War. Her secret task was to organise
support by Mexican workers for Republican Spain. And above—
or, more accurately, underneath—all she was an active

representative of OS2, the dreaded Soviet Department for Special Tasks.

Caridad was then forty-four years old, tall and still beautiful, with a mass of black hair beginning to turn slightly grey. She was a powerful and passionate speaker, and at her public appearances, which included a speech to the Mexican Chamber of Deputies, she wore the blue fighting denims of the Spanish Republican Militia.

After she had addressed scores of great public meetings and had her photograph published in the Mexican newspapers, the Government could hardly agree that she was living the life of a non-active political refugee from Fascist tyranny. But before her deportation could be ordered she had seen the red light and had escaped into Spain, with an extensive and intimate knowledge of the Mexican scene which increased her value to the plotters of OS2.

In Spain, Caridad now met a sinister figure with whom she began to plunge still more deeply into love and conspiracy. He was then known as General Kotov and commanded the Spanish Section of OS2, in which capacity he had recently organised the murder of Trotsky's secretary, Erwin Wolf. His real name was Leonid Eitingon and he had a long list of OS2 crimes to his discredit, including the kidnapping in Paris of General Kutyepov in 1930. To Spaniards who knew nothing of such an organisation as OS2, Eitingon was known as Comrade Pablo—a name which the wife of Don Pablo Mercader must have found conveniently easy to remember. Under that name he had organised a number of sabotage schools—not mere back-room study-groups, but each with hundreds of 'students.'

It would not seem that Caridad and Eitingon, each living several active secret and semi-secret existences, would have had much spare time for romance. But the passionate Spanish aristocrat and the burly, bearded Russian fell genuinely in love with each other. He even suggested that they should get married. This was the height of Caridad's ambition, but the proposal was quietly dropped when she found out through sources of her own that he had a wife and family back in Russia! But she stayed with him, enjoying his brilliant conversation, his passionate love-making, his easy charm at conspiratorial cocktail parties, and his gourmet's talent for ordering the most delicious dishes and the most delicately flavoured wines. Except for the fact that he was a highly skilled professional murderer, Eitingon was every woman's dream of the perfect lover. He was a tribute to the OS2 talent-spotters.

Early in 1939, Franco's forces achieved victory. Republican leaders fled to Mexico to form a Government-in-exile. Vast numbers of Republican supporters escaped to France, to be herded into camps in miserable conditions. But the Kremlin sometimes looks after its own, and a number of high-level refugee Communists were brought to Moscow, including the famous woman agitator known as La Pasionaria, and such valuable OS2 operatives as Caridad Mercader: and among them was Eitingon.

Vast quantities of documents disappeared towards the end of the Civil War. Many were burnt during bombing raids; many more were deliberately destroyed; and some which might have future use, such as all the impounded passports of the Republican International Brigade, safely reached Moscow.

Hence I found it impossible to refer in detail to documentary evidence of Caridad's activities during the Civil War. But some of the people with whom she became friendly in Moscow have revealed that she boasted of having personally 'executed' about a couple of dozen Trotskyists. Other sources state that it was well known at that time that she was a crack shot with an automatic pistol, and could kill at a dozen yards with a throwing-knife!

Caridad spent a few delightfully romantic months in Moscow with Eitingon, and the records are discreetly silent as to what had happened to his wife and family. Then early in 1940 Stalin sent his trusted murder-planner to Mexico. The brilliant anti-Stalinist Trotsky had been at large far too long. He must die, and Eitingon was the man to arrange his death. For this tricky operation the OS2 leader called himself Leonov. And back to Mexico with him went, of course, Caridad Mercader.

The story of Trotsky's murder (told briefly in the previous chapter) is a matter of history. A detail not generally known is that three powerful OS2 cars were parked near Trotsky's house at the time. One was a getaway car for Ramon Mercader if he should manage to escape after the killing. In another was Stalin's personal representative, Eitingon, alias Leonov. In the third was the murderer's mother, Caridad Mercader.

But, as already described, Ramon did not get away. People rushed down the road shouting, prematurely, that Trotsky had been murdered. In the distance were heard the wailing sirens of ambulances.

Two cars revved up their powerful engines and shot off in opposite directions. The third car was no longer required. Before nightfall Caridad and Eitingon had separately crossed the Mexican frontier. By escape routes carefully organised in advance by OS2, they made their ways separately back to Moscow. There the lovers were reunited in the bright sunshine of Stalin's approval.

It was Lavrenti Beria himself, head of the N.K.V.D., who took Caridad to a Kremlin reception. Ramon Mercader had proved himself the worthy son of a worthy mother, and she was formally invested with the Order of Lenin for her part in the Trotsky murder. She was also given custody of her son's Order of Hero of the Soviet Union, pending his release in twenty years' time. She was tremendously proud of these medals, for a short time, and showed them to all her friends.

So Caridad, officially provided with what passed in the Soviet Union as luxury, lived happily—but not for ever after. She became, in fact, progressively disillusioned with the régime which she had so ardently and so violently supported in the days before she had had any first-hand knowledge of how it actually worked in practice. She was distressed at the hard labouring work and meagre rations given to Spanish Communist refugees in Russia. She was horrified when Spanish teenage orphans who, bereft of their parents, had become minor delinquents were shot on the ridiculous charge of being secret Falangist supporters of General Franco.

The American historian of the Trotsky murder, Isaac Don Levine, published an interesting letter in his valuable study of Ramon Mercader entitled *The Mind of an Assassin*. This letter is from a former leading Spanish Communist, Enrique Castro Delgado, who was a close friend of Caridad Mercader in Moscow during 1943. Señor Delgado wrote to Mr Levine: "She was tall, slender, with white hair, her face angular with thin lips. She was incredibly attractive, spoke rapidly with a slight Catalan accent . . . She smoked uninterruptedly, lighting one cigarette from the stub of the previous one. She gave the impression of being a great lady."

To Señor Delgado, who had also been disillusioned about Russian Communism, Caridad opened her heart. "We have been deceived," she told him. "This is not Paradise—it is the most terrible of hells known to man." One day she said: "Here I am doing nothing . . . I merely die, bit by bit." And again, "Still another night I have not slept. If I don't get out of here soon I shall go mad . . . But even if we do get out, we shall still be under sentence of death."

Caridad openly confessed to Señor Delgado that she had travelled back and forth across Europe tracing Soviet spies and diplomats who had defected, "so as to assassinate them pitilessly," she said.

Then she took from a drawer the Orders awarded to her son and herself. "Many people do not know the high price of these *merdes*," she said. "For the assassin of Trotsky is my son Ramon, whom I, in the name of the sacred interests of the Revolution and of Socialism, drove to this crime, and I am a thing to inspire horror!"

But Caridad had to conceal her real feelings from the Soviet authorities, because she could think of nothing but of getting her son out of his Mexican prison. She suggested diplomatic representations, and if these should fail, she asked to be allowed to go to Mexico herself to organise his escape.

At that stage of the war, Stalin would not consider any overt approach which might jeopardise his delicate relations with any Government in America, North or South. But he was not entirely ungrateful, it appeared, and he authorised Lavrenti Beria to finance Caridad's escape plans by handing her a bag of jewels. Their value in English money was about £20,000. So she crossed the Atlantic once more, and took an apartment in Hamburgo Street in Mexico City.

But when she resumed contact with some old friends in the Communist Underground of Mexico, she began to wonder how genuine, after all, had been Stalin's appearance of gratitude. She was disconcerted to find that the OS2 were already in action—and that she had no part in their proceedings. She began to pick up horrifying hints of Stalin's real plans for her son's future. Ramon knew too much, and even after twenty years' imprisonment he might possibly let slip some indiscreet remark which could inconvenience the dictator of the Kremlin. Caridad began to perceive that Ramon's escape from prison, which was being planned by OS2 groups unconnected with herself, was in order that he might be permanently silenced at the earliest possible moment.

It is very significant that Ramon Mercader consistently refused to take part in any plans for his own escape. It is known that his mother, living so near to the prison, never once attempted to visit him. I have reason to believe, however, that through her own underground contacts she managed to warn him that outside the safety of the prison walls he would find waiting not a getaway car but an OS2 bullet. And he served, as we have seen, his full term of twenty years.

Caridad stayed in Mexico City for about twelve months, uneasily conscious that she was surrounded and watched by OS2 agents whose plans for her son's future were very different from her own. Even the honoured holder of the Order of Lenin was not safe from the OS2 murder squads. She narrowly escaped death by being run down by fast cars. And at last in despair she went to the French Embassy and told a convincing story which secured her a visa for France. She determined that in the safety of the French capital she would wait until, as an old lady of sixty-eight, she would at last be reunited with the son whom she loved and had deceived.

She took an apartment in Paris near to her married daughter, Montserrat Dudouyt, whose husband ran a Left Bank antique shop. Her son Jorge was also in France. Another son, Luis, was somewhere in Soviet Russia. And her lover Eitingon . . . ?

News that reaches the outside world about ordinary Soviet citizens is scanty. News about leaders of OS2 murder squads seldom leaks beyond Soviet frontiers. All that Caridad ever learned about the man she had loved so well was that Eitingon was arrested for treason at the time of the downfall of Lavrenti Beria, and was never heard of again.

In 1960 there emerged from a Mexican prison the murderer of Trotsky—Jacson alias Mornard alias Ramon Mercader. Reporters from the whole world's newspapers rushed to interview him. But his mother knew that he would come first to her, and in her little Paris apartment she prepared to welcome him and cherish him and keep him on what was left of the proceeds of Beria's jewels.

But a couple of days later a Soviet ship left a South American port, and Ramon Mercader was never seen again.

FIFTEEN

The Lucky Star of Franz von Papen

AT PRECISELY TEN O'CLOCK in the morning of the 24th of February, 1942, a British Intelligence officer put down the field-glasses through which he had been looking out of the window of a house in Ankara.

"I've seen him off again," he said to a colleague. "Punctual old so-and-so, isn't he!"

The lady and gentleman he had been watching had emerged from a large house and had now passed out of sight into the Boulevard Ataturk. They were the German Ambassador, Franz von Papen, and his wife, who every morning enjoyed the short walk from their home to the Embassy.

The morning was sunny but cold. It is not generally known that parts of Turkey suffer almost a Siberian winter, and at that time starving wolves were nightly prowling about the suburbs of the Turkish capital. So at a time when most men had gone to work and women had not yet come out to do their shopping, the Boulevard, in its icy sunshine, was almost deserted. Von Papen and his wife thought that they were alone on the wide Boulevard, and did not notice a man lounging inconspicuously in a doorway.

Suddenly there was a violent explosion, and the couple were

flung to the ground. Windows were broken for hundreds of yards in every direction. Von Papen scrambled up almost unhurt and looked wildly around. There was nobody in sight.

As he helped his wife to her feet a taxi came racing across the Boulevard. He hailed it and told the driver to go for the police. Then he and his wife continued their walk to the Embassy. He had cut his knee slightly in falling, but otherwise he and his wife had not suffered a scratch. But his wife's dress was drenched in blood.

The efficient Turkish police were soon on the scene; they cordoned off the area and searched for clues. There was blood on the ground and a few scraps of mangled flesh. From the branches of a tree hung a bloodstained shoe. That was all— except for a dead man's blood on Frau von Papen's dress.

The plot to murder the German Ambassador had been hatched in the office of the Russian Consul-General in Istanbul. It was directed by a high official of Department OS2 of the Soviet Secret Service—the Travelling Executioners—who had been sent specially from Moscow, with a very ingenious device in the diplomatic bag.

The plan was that von Papen should be shot as he took his invariable morning stroll to his office, and two Macedonian agents of OS2 had spent weeks at target practice with automatic pistols inside the Consulate-General. There was nothing very original in such a plan, but what sets this crime apart from similar outrages is the method devised to prevent the murderer revealing the identity of his employers. He was issued with a small appliance which he was told was a smoke-bomb. Immediately he had shot his victim he was instructed to pull out a firing-pin and to evade capture by running through the dense cloud of smoke it would emit.

It is quite clear that the agent decided to improve on this procedure by pulling the pin first and shooting afterwards, on the assumption that it would take a sufficiently dense smoke-cloud several seconds to form. But the device was not a smoke-bomb. It contained high explosive. It certainly caused the killer to disappear. It blew him into unrecognisable shreds before he had time to fire his pistol.

In distant Berlin certain high officials of the Gestapo smiled contemptuously when they heard of the Russian failure. They were planning to murder their own Ambassador themselves—not for the first time—and were determined to make a better job of it.

Much has been written about Franz von Papen's fifty-year career as soldier, diplomat and politician. He has been pictured variously as a super-plotter who organised vast rings of spies and saboteurs in the United States during the first World War, and as an almost comic bungler who habitually mislaid incriminating secret documents which were patiently collected and published by British Intelligence. He could hardly have been both. The truth is—as usual—somewhere between the extremes.

He certainly did some foolish things, but though he often found himself in situations of appalling complexity, sometimes of deadly danger, he always emerged safely. To my mind the outstanding—and hitherto overlooked—feature of his career is his consistent good luck, of which the episode of the Ankara bomb is a fair sample.

Von Papen must be the only diplomat who ever represented four European powers at the same time, by whom he was accredited simultaneously to two other Powers who were mutually at war! He must be the only war-time Ambassador who was the target of assassination plots organised both by the enemy and by his own Government.

The table talk of Adolf Hitler—surprisingly often shrewd, original and entertaining, in contrast to his public rantings—was for some years recorded in shorthand for the edification of posterity. On January the 24th, 1942, when he was dining with his Gestapo chief, Heinrich Himmler, he gave a fairly accurate snap judgment of the man who was to be his Ambassador in Vienna and Ankara. "Personally von Papen was an inoffensive man," said Hitler, "but by a sort of fatality he surrounded

himself with people who all had something on their conscience."
Hitler was not far out.

Von Papen was born in 1879 of an old Westphalian family
whose records can be traced back to the thirteenth century. His
father had been a cavalry officer and young Franz began to
train for the German Army as an eleven-year-old cadet. He did
well, learned English and French, and often stayed with friends in
England, where he conceived such an admiration for the British
way of life—as seen from country mansions and shooting-
lodges—that fellow-officers used jokingly to say they were
surprised he did not wear British uniform. By the comparatively
early age of thirty-three he was an officer of the German General
Staff.

Later in the same year, 1913, Kaiser Wilhelm II appointed
him Military Attaché to the German Embassy in Washington,
and accredited him also to Mexico. At that time there was no
military diplomatic representation in the United States or
Mexico for Austria-Hungary, Bulgaria or Turkey, so he acted
for those countries as well as his own. When the U.S.A. went
to war with Mexico, and later when the four European Powers
took part in the first World War, the complications of von
Papen's duties are almost unimaginable.

As the charming and cultured member of an aristocratic old
family, he was popular in Washington, and became friendly
with two young men who were to be heard of later—one a
soldier, Captain Douglas MacArthur, and the other a civilian,
Franklin Delano Roosevelt. He also met and began a lifelong
friendship with a young lieutenant in the German Navy,
Wilhelm Canaris, destined to have some influence on European
history as chief of the German Secret Service.

One of the lucky von Papen's early escapes from death
occurred during an official visit to Mexico. That country then
had so many enthusiastic rebel leaders that the calendar became
overcrowded, and revolutions sometimes had to take place two
at a time. During von Papen's visit the Government was
fighting both Pancho Villa and Zapata, and the German

Military Attaché went near the firing line for first-hand impressions. He was strolling away after a friendly chat with a sentry when the young conscript seems to have had second thoughts as to the purity of his visitor's motives. So he gave chase, firing his rifle, and a very undignified episode ensued as the smartly uniformed attaché ran for his life pursued by the shouting and shooting Mexican, who fortunately missed with every shot.

Back in Washington, the outbreak of the first World War in 1914 plunged von Papen into an underworld of spies and saboteurs of which he had no experience and for which, it would seem, little talent. Nor had he the advantage of advice and assistance from his Government. Transatlantic radio was very unreliable in those days, and the great German wireless station of Nauen was frequently made inaudible by atmospherics. The British Navy had, of course, cut the undersea cables.

"The German Embassy became completely ineffective," von Papen writes. "It was some months before Bernstorff" (the Ambassador) "was again able to send reports to Berlin, via Sweden." Also, for reasons involving the complexities of American politics, "Bernstorff had practically no contact with President Wilson." It is surprising that the harassed Military Attaché accomplished as much as he did.

I need not dwell on the activities for which von Papen was most often criticised during the first World War. Some of his anti-British schemes were perfectly legal, such as his efforts to persuade skilled German-born mechanics to leave American factories working for Britain, or his placing of large German orders with armaments firms which would otherwise have accepted British orders. It was his duty to do such things.

More dubious enterprises were the interruptions to troop movements which his agents caused by blowing up key points on the Canadian Pacific Railway. It was legitimate to do this on the soil of Canada—a country at war with Germany—but not to organise such sabotage under the protection of diplomatic immunity in a neutral capital, and even von Papen admits this gross breach of protocol.

He seems to have had some success at planting bombs in British ships in American ports, but there are discrepancies between the accounts of such exploits written by himself and those by Captain von Rintelen, with whom he had little in common. It is possible, indeed, to draw interesting parallels between these two and the situation in Moscow three years later, when the official Bruce Lockhart and the free-lance Sidney Reilly similarly agreed to differ as to their means of combating Bolshevism.

The beginning of the end of von Papen's service in Washington came when British Intelligence heard from an agent in New York that an American journalist was on his way to Berlin in a Dutch liner with incriminating documents. The ship was searched at Falmouth and the papers were impounded and published as a White Paper. They included a private letter from von Papen to his wife in which he referred to the "idiotic Yankees," which infuriated his American friends. He was declared *persona non grata* and sent home.

When his ship called at Falmouth, British Intelligence ignored his protests of diplomatic immunity and seized all his papers, which included cheque-book stubs showing payments to secret agents, some of their payments falsely noted as for laundry bills. And in a very bad temper he arrived home in Germany during the first week of January, 1916.

He seems to have done his best to persuade the German authorities, correctly, that the programme of unrestricted U-boat warfare was a psychological blunder likely to bring America into the war against Germany. But most of his contacts seemed afraid to disagree with the Kaiser, who brusquely told von Papen that he preferred to believe his friend Ballin, chief of the Hamburg-Amerika Line. And one cannot blame Herr Ballin if he had felt that the more Allied and neutral liners that were sunk, the more business there would be for his own ships after the war.

A Press conference was arranged for Von Papen to explain his views, but a few hours before it was due to take place he was ordered to go immediately to the Western Front as battalion commander of an infantry regiment. His exploits in Flanders, and later in Turkey and Palestine, were credible but not sensational. After the Armistice, he fell out with General Liman von Sanders and, faced with arrest and court-martial, escaped in disguise to Germany—then suffering chaotic post-war revolutionary conditions—and resigned his commission.

He now decided that he could best serve his country as a politician, and was elected to the Reichstag as a Conservative member of the Catholic Centre Party, considerably assisted by the fact that he was something of a favourite with the popular old Field-Marshal von Hindenburg, who became President of the German Republic. He viewed with alarm the rise of the upstart Austrian Adolf Hitler, and in 1932, urged by von Hindenburg, accepted the unenviable post of Chancellor after an election in which Hitler had polled over thirteen million votes.

With either much courage or little tact, von Papen offered Hitler the post of Vice-Chancellor. But Hitler—who could never imagine himself as anybody's deputy—stiffly declined. A few months later positions were reversed. Hitler became Chancellor and von Papen Vice-Chancellor as well as Reich Commissioner for Prussia.

It is to von Papen's credit that he did not conceal his misgivings at the extreme policies of the Nazis, and in what came to be known as the "Marburg speech," made at Marburg University in Mid-June, 1934, he said that "he who threatens to employ a guillotine may be its first victim." This was a brave thing to say less than a fortnight before the "Night of the Long Knives," when Hitler in a few hours smashed all trace of opposition in his own ranks, particularly among the leaders of the Brownshirts who had raised him to power. It will never be known how many hundreds were shot or hacked to pieces that night. Among them were two anti-Nazi members of von

Papen's staff. Von Papen himself was arrested, but after a few days under 'house arrest' he was set free—another piece of remarkable luck in a situation which for so many was fatal.

Three weeks later a squad of black-uniformed S.S. men came to von Papen's house at two o'clock in the morning. He prepared for quick death from a bullet or for re-arrest and slower death in a concentration camp. His son seized a loaded revolver and opened the door. But the S.S. officer who entered was smiling and apologetic. It was important that Herr von Papen should immediately telephone the Führer at Bayreuth. Von Papen did so, and was astounded when Hitler asked him to go at once as German Ambassador to Austria. He was not merely to be allowed to live—he was to be promoted! His lucky star was still shining brightly.

Dr Dollfuss, the Austrian Chancellor, had just been murdered by the Nazis. The German Ambassador in Vienna would have to be—to use Hitler's expression, unusual in diplomacy—court-martialled. Mussolini was behaving in an unfriendly manner by massing troops on the Brenner Pass. "We are faced with a second Sarajevo," Hitler shouted hysterically. Von Papen accepted the offer.

For over three years he adequately filled a difficult post in a country moving steadily towards the Anschluss. It was not moving quickly enough for Hitler, however, and Gestapo leaders thought of a simple and easy means of expediting matters. They arranged for Nazi secret agents to murder von Papen, which would officially shock and horrify Berlin and justify the occupation of Austria by German troops "to restore order."

But von Papen's lucky star must have guided the Viennese police. On the 25th of January, 1938, they raided the offices of a Nazi underground organisation called the Committee of Seven and seized a mass of documents which have become known to historians as the Tavs Papers. One of these revealed the proposal to assassinate the Ambassador. As he took the necessary—and successful—precautions, he must have reflected that diplomacy had become a much more dangerous profession than when he had first entered it a quarter-century previously.

Then the light of the lucky star waned a little, and exactly ten days after the murder plot was uncovered von Papen was sacked. The telephone rang late in the evening of February the 4th, and in the brisk Nazi way—so different from the leisurely correctness of the Kaiser's Foreign Office—he was told: "The Führer wishes me to inform you that your mission in Vienna has ended." Five weeks later German troops marched into Austria, and close behind them came the Gestapo, who found von Papen's anti-Nazi friend and colleague, Ketteler, and brutally murdered him. On the following day von Papen, prepared for the worst, was baffled to learn that he had been awarded the Nazi Party Gold Medal!

And on the day after that he was rushed by air back to Vienna with the rank of Federal Governor of Austria, to join Hitler at a saluting base before which paraded vast crowds "in a state of ecstasy," as von Papen puts it.

Loyal to his friends, von Papen at once started enquiries as to the disappearance of Ketteler. He consulted Goering, who produced a file on Ketteler's "treasonable activities," including a plot to assassinate Hitler, which Ketteler had in fact discussed with a now very nervous von Papen. "I was speechless," he writes, and one can well believe it. Ketteler's body was found in the Danube a few weeks later.

A year afterwards, von Papen was offered the post of Ambassador to Turkey, a country which then feared an attack by Fascist Italy on the Dardanelles. And after two refusals he accepted on Good Friday, 1939—the day on which Mussolini invaded Albania, as a fairly obvious preliminary move to advancing on Turkey via the Balkans. Once again von Papen was heading for a trouble-spot.

Now more than ever he needed the help of his lucky star. President Inönu of Turkey received him and explained how worried he was by the Italian moves, and said he was considering a proposed pact with Britain and France. It was von Papen's duty to oppose such a pact, as in the event of war Germany would not want the Allies to control the Dardanelles. So he wrote a strong appeal to Hitler to restrain Mussolini, and rushed back to Berlin, where, he says, "I found myself caught up in the festivities that marked the signing of the German-Italian alliance."

There could not have been a more hopeless occasion for von Papen to introduce a discordant note between the two dictators. He tried to explain his views to Count Ciano, the Italian Foreign Minister. Ciano protested to Ribbentrop, who went red with rage and was very rude to his Ambassador. The only result of von Papen's well-meant efforts on behalf of his country was that the Italian Ambassador in Ankara was warned to watch his German colleague very closely.

Soon after the second World War broke out—during the stalemate in the West that became known as the 'phoney war'—certain countries such as Holland, which was still neutral, wanted to act as intermediaries in peace discussions, of which von Papen approved as he did not think Germany could win the war. But when he went to Berlin to put these suggestions to Hitler, Ribbentrop went so far as to forbid any Foreign Office official even to speak to their Ambassador to Turkey—an amazing example of how the Nazi amateurs conducted their foreign affairs. But although officially sent to Coventry, von Papen remained Ambassador.

When Germany invaded Russia, the Red Army had an unusual ally in its battle against the Wehrmacht. The Travelling Executioners struck against enemy diplomats. One result was the attempt to assassinate von Papen which has already been described.

But it was not only his enemies whom he had to fear. Two or three months after the Russian attempt, the head of the Nazi Party in Ankara held a private meeting of the Embassy staff, and told them it was high time that the Ambassador was either murdered or sent to a concentration camp, a fact which duly came to his knowledge. Von Papen must have felt that the only people who knew his every movement but courteously refrained from trying to murder him were the British Intelligence officers who—as he was well aware—seldom let him out of range of their field-glasses.

It is understandable that he would have welcomed the collapse of the murderous Nazi tyranny, and he was indiscreet enough to discuss a *coup d'état* with Bismarck and Helldorf in the Union Club during one of his visits to Berlin. He agreed to foster secret approaches to President Roosevelt on his return to Ankara, but these were fruitless.

I describe elsewhere the sensational exploits of the German agent in Ankara known as "Cicero," whose reports passed through the German Embassy. One of von Papen's more dangerous indiscretions was to mention to the Turkish Foreign Minister a piece of information which he could only have obtained from a British Embassy source, and this did not pass unnoticed in Berlin.

Then occurred an incident which must have thrown a great strain on von Papen's lucky star. Dr Vermehren, chief agent in Istanbul of the Abwehr—the German Secret Service—defected to the British. As an indication that German interests in Turkey were not being very well supervised by the Ambassador this was bad enough. Worse still was that the defector took with him his wife, who might otherwise have been held in Berlin as a hostage, but who had been permitted to join her husband through von Papen's efforts. Still worse again was the fact that the lady, the Countess Plettenberg, was a relation of von Papen and had influenced her husband against the Nazis by converting him to Catholicism. And von Papen, too, was a Catholic!

Britain now knew all about the Abwehr organisation in Turkey, and there was panic in Berlin. Admiral Canaris was removed from control of the Abwehr, which was combined with Himmler's Gestapo. And high Nazi Party officials accused von Papen of having organised the defection and demanded that he be brought to Berlin and put on trial.

It was very tactless of von Papen to choose that stage for

trying to persuade Hitler to reverse his decision to combine the
Abwehr and Gestapo, an amalgamation which it had long been
Himmler's ambition to achieve. So the jealous Himmler began
to make plans for a squad of Gestapo agents to be flown to
Ankara to kidnap von Papen. This scheme had the approval of
Ribbentrop, which seems a peculiar attitude to be adopted by a
Foreign Minister who could more easily have issued a formal
notice of recall 'for consultations,' to use the diplomatic phrase
for what is, under a dictatorship, an invitation to death.

Von Papen learned of Himmler's plans—and was not
kidnapped. Then on the 2nd of August, 1944, Turkey severed
diplomatic relations with Germany, and he was ordered to
return to Berlin within twenty-four hours.

Von Papen had seldom been in such deadly danger. Less than
a fortnight previously a group of officers had attempted to kill
Hitler with a bomb and seize power. They had failed, and a
'purge' of officers and aristocrats—whose massacre was being
demanded by Nazi leaders—was in progress. Many of von
Papen's anti-Nazi friends were either dead or under arrest,
including Bismarck and Helldorff and his lifelong friend
Canaris. And he could not have derived much comfort from a
speech that day by Mr Churchill, who said, with reference to
the break between Turkey and Germany: "Herr von Papen
may be sent back to Germany to meet the blood-bath he so
narrowly escaped at Hitler's hands in 1934."

He could have been excused for following Dr Vermehren to
seek asylum with Britain. He would not have been betraying his
country but quite sensibly escaping from a blood-thirsty
tyranny. But he did what he conceived—rightly or wrongly—
to be his duty. He travelled by train to Berlin and thence to
Berchtesgaden. He was received by a white-faced and trembling
Hitler, a nervous wreck with his arm in a sling as a result of the
bombing attempt. It seems likely that von Papen trembled too.

In the course of an hysterical tirade about the bomb plot
"Hitler narrowed his glaucous eyes as he looked at me, then
forced out the words, 'This bunch of aristocrats—they don't

deserve anything better!' " writes von Papen, to whom it must have seemed that the axe was about to fall.

What happened next was the very last thing he could possibly have anticipated. Hitler calmed down, made a complimentary little speech, and presented to him the Knight's Cross of the Order of Military Merit! Then they parted for the last time.

Von Papen retired to his home at Wallerfangen, and after a few months of well-earned peace he was arrested by American troops on the 10th of April, 1945.

After some time in labour camps and prisons, and being beaten almost to death by a lunatic S.S. man who was a fellow-prisoner, he was tried as a war criminal at Nuremberg. He was one of the only three of the accused who were acquitted.

During the past forty-five years von Papen has often been abused or laughed at. It seems time to re-assess his character. Without being snobbish, one may say that his virtues were those of a soldier and his faults those of a gentleman. He was loyal to his country and loyal to his friends. Like many of us, he was not always tactful. It is not greatly to his discredit that he did not descend easily or successfully into the underworld of espionage and sabotage. And it may be agreed that the outstanding feature of his varied career is his really colossal luck!

SIXTEEN

The Hooded Men

FRANCE IN 1961 was racked with division.

The Algerian war had reached a stalemate—but still counted its weekly toll of dead in hundreds. President de Gaulle was determined to end the strife. He was to find that it was easier to placate the Algerians than some of his own people.

Algeria then had a population of nine million Moslems and a million Europeans. Only a small minority of the latter were rich farmers: most were small traders and craftsmen. Algeria was their homeland—most had never seen France in their lives: they were fifth- or sixth-generation Algerians. Why should they give up all they had worked for to these ignorant Moslems? Whatever arrangements were made, it was quite obvious that there would be no future for Europeans in a Moslem Algeria. They were sturdy folk, prepared to fight for their 'rights,' and they were increasingly incensed at the succession of murders which were a feature of a very dirty war.

They were supported by a section of the Army, where officers and men alike had a feeling of frustration. One after another the French colonies had been lost. But Algeria was legally a part of Metropolitan France. There the French had exercised their 'civilising mission,' conferring innumerable benefits on a backward country. If Algeria were not to stay French, why trouble to fight?

Frustration and fear are alike disquieting, and doubly so when they appear together. They lead to acts of desperation: they breed extremism and a narrow outlook. Here they were the progenitors of the O.A.S.—*Organisation d'armée secrète*. Now France found herself involved in a three-cornered war, with the O.A.S. against the Moslems and the French Government alike.

Every day there were bloody outrages on both sides. Bombs of the *plastiqueurs* brought the conflict into Paris. There was one moment when the capital awaited an attack from the skies by her own paratroops. The project appeared fantastic—but not to the older Frenchmen. To them it was no more desperate than the project, twenty-five years before, to capture Paris not from the air but from the sewers. Heavily armed, and with their heads shrouded, many thousands of what were called the Hooded Men were to assemble in the maze of sewers beneath Paris. At a given moment they were to stream up through manholes in the streets and take over the city.

The plot was fantastic—but it was feasible. It had behind it vast sums of money, huge stores of arms, and an estimated force of over 100,000 conspirators. And it came to light through one of those trivial incidents which have so often influenced the course of history.

Jean-Baptiste Duchamp was a minor businessman of Lille. He was a person of fixed opinions, despising the Government of the day and all men of the Left. He was an obvious recruit for an underground organisation of Fascist tendencies. France had had enough of puerile democracy, and needed a long spell of discipline and firm government. The organisation was engaged in the customary bid for power, and its methods included the murder of opponents and other dramatic outrages meant both to call attention to the cause it represented and to remove or intimidate opponents.

Jean-Baptiste had been sent on a mission to Belgium to arrange for the purchase of weapons ostensibly for Spain but actually for the organisation. His suitcase was heavy with papers, and on his return he deposited it in the cloakroom at Lille Station. Then he went off to meet his friends. He expected a warm reception, for his mission had been successful.

Instead, he found himself under 'arrest.' Half a dozen grim-faced men were facing him in an empty house.

"Traitor!" one of them snarled.

"What?"

"You cannot deny it. We *know* that you betrayed Grimopont to the police."

"What rubbish! Here I return with good news about supplies from Belgium——"

"And you have doubtless lined your own pocket well in the transaction."

"What do you mean?"

"You know! And we know. We know what you made out of that purchase of grenades in Czechoslovakia—and where you have banked the money in Switzerland. There is no more to be said. There is only one punishment for traitors!"

Much later a police informer described the scene. Two men held the miserable Jean-Baptiste while a third plunged a dagger into his neck. It was a peculiar dagger, made from a sawn-off army bayonet. It made an easily recognisable triangular wound, the trademark of the Hooded Men.

This was long after dark. The 'trial' had occupied only a couple of minutes. The body was buried on the spot.

In the meantime, two other men had gone to search Jean-Baptiste's home. They found one or two incriminating items, but nothing of serious importance. They did not know of the suitcase in the cloakroom—and the ticket which might have led them to it was lying in the victim's crude grave.

Some weeks later a railway official was making a routine

check of the cloakroom. All the items long deposited were produced for his inspection. He had a rare collection of keys and pick-locks, and opened one case after another in the hope of tracing their owners.

One contained large envelopes full of papers. Doubtless these would give him the clue he needed. Instead, three minutes later he closed the suitcase, took it to his office, and called the police.

The same evening the Chief of the Police was in urgent communication with the Paris Sûreté. He reported that he had chanced across astounding details of the secret society later known as the Hooded Men.

The society which became known as the Hooded Men was called by its members C.S.A.R. These are the initials of French words meaning the Secret Committee for Revolutionary Action. And its secrets were well kept. Most members did not know each other even by sight. At secret meetings they borrowed a trick from the Spanish Inquisition and the American Ku Klux Klan and wore hoods over their heads.

The French word for a hood is *cagoule*, and when the sinister story began partly—but never completely—to leak out, a well-meaning journalist tried to ridicule the organisation by calling its members *Cagoulards*, or Hooded Men.

That was a bad psychological blunder. It is always a mistake to popularise an opponent. The journalist who christened William Joyce as "Lord Haw-Haw," and thereby ensured him first-class publicity, inadvertently did his country a grave disservice.

The name Cagoulards attracted instant attention. Something called C.S.A.R. might have seemed just one more of those strings of initials which confuse the uninitiated. But the picture formed in the public imagination of a vast organisation of Hooded Men caused terror among the peace-loving many, and excitement among the adventurous few. Large numbers of young Fascist-minded Frenchmen with a taste for mystery and secret back-stabbing swelled the ranks of Cagoulard killers.

The founder and leader of the Cagoulards was a man of dominating personality named Eugène Deloncle. He was a wealthy shipowner who possessed a gift for leadership, a lust for power, and the money, transport and foreign contacts which enabled him to smuggle into France huge quantities of arms and equipment for his devotees and dupes.

A meeting is recorded between Deloncle and two of his highly placed sympathisers—that doddering old anti-democrat Marshal Pétain and that notorious Anglophobe Pierre Laval. At that meeting Deloncle told them that he had 120,000 armed members ready to turn France into a totalitarian state by force. The meeting was in November, 1936, and the story of it has been told by so reliable a source as Commissioner Jean Belin of the French Sûreté, whose task it became to investigate the Cagoulards.

Neither Pétain nor Laval seems to have lifted a finger to save their tottering country from a movement which was already organising murders to assist the Italian Fascists, and which later collaborated eagerly with the German Nazis. Indeed, it was not until months after the meeting that a railway clerk examined that suitcase, and the Sûreté began thirty months of secret war against the terrorists upon whose trail the police had thus accidentally stumbled.

The Sûreté detectives discovered that the Cagoulards were elaborately organised on a basis which combined military and Communist principles—with brigades subdivided into regiments, battalions, units and cells. When they drilled in secret on the country estates of landowner Cagoulards, they wore steel helmets, leather tunics and cavalry breeches. They had great stores of arms, ammunition and explosives, and private shooting-ranges in the main French cities. They would have welcomed plastic bombs had those deadly devices then been invented.

The first rule of the organisation was impenetrable secrecy.

The only penalty for revealing its secrets was death. 'Executions' were carried out by stabbing victims in the neck with savage daggers made from Army bayonets.

A few examples will show the deadly efficiency with which the Cagoulards organised murder. A highly placed member had a beautiful mistress named Letitia Tourneaux, who was suspected of having repeated indiscreet remarks he had made to her in bed. On Whit Monday, 1937, she was seen in the afternoon at Charenton boarding a train on the Paris Métro. Exactly thirty seconds later the train stopped at the next station. A passenger entered the coach and found it empty but for Letitia. She was dying in her seat, with a Cagoulard dagger left sticking in her neck. No clue to the killers was ever found. That must have been one of the most brilliantly planned murders of all time.

It was only a week or two later, in June, 1937, when the Cagoulards kidnapped the Italian brothers Carlo and Nello Roselli, and murdered them in a Normandy forest. The Rosellis were political refugees who had offended Mussolini, and their murders are two of many crimes which completely refute any claim by the Cagoulards to be genuine patriots. The organisation wanted wealth, weapons and power at any cost. Its death-squads were available on payment of adequate blood-money as the hired assassins of foreign Fascist paymasters.

In return for the murder of the Rosellis, Mussolini gladly paid his debt to the Cagoulards in arms and cash. These murderous traitors were also presumably paid for their later services to the Germans. During the war hundreds of Arab Cagoulards came from the North African lodges to hunt down and kill heroic Frenchmen of the Resistance movement.

Energetic action against the Cagoulards was ordered later in 1937 by M. Max Dormoy, who was then Minister of the Interior. He was accordingly marked down for assassination. But it was four years before his killers found an opportunity to strike. They killed him at last on the 26th of July, 1941, in circumstances so strange as to be—like so many Cagoulard exploits—almost incredible.

The ruthlessly enforced security system of the Cagoulards ensured that no group should know anything of the activities of the other groups. This is a safe policy in principle, but it has certain operational disadvantages, especially in the matter of overlapping assignments. It is known, for instance, that in the course of years several Cagoulard death-squads were given identical orders and even identical equipment for the murder of M. Dormoy. And it would appear that, when at long last a suitable opportunity occurred, two separate squads acted independently and—by a remarkable coincidence—almost simultaneously.

What can be deduced from police investigations is that the first squad gained access to M. Dormoy's room in a Montelimar hotel, took away a deed-box stored under his bed, and replaced it by a time-bomb in a replica of the box. On the same day the second squad carried out an absolutely identical routine. They took away with them what they imagined to be the genuine deed-box and left in its place a third deed-box of identical appearance.

In the middle of the night an explosion took place and M. Dormoy was killed. And shortly afterwards three Cagoulards who had fled to Nice with the second deed-box were blown to pieces. It was poetic justice.

There were other dangers to the Cagoulard organisation in its virtually impenetrable secrecy. When Sûreté detectives had gathered sufficient information to start mopping-up operations, it was actually of assistance to the police that members remained unaware of how close the detectives were on their trail. A raided unit could not pass on a warning to neighbouring units because Cagoulard security precautions prevented direct contact.

After more than two years of difficult and dangerous investigations, and some official obstruction by high-placed sympathisers, the patient, tenacious Sûreté men swooped at last. Over seventy leaders of the organisation were arrested. It is a pity that the traitor Laval and the dotard Pétain were not among those detained and discredited. They had long known what was going on, but had kept their mouths shut—putting their dubious totalitarian schemes before the safety of the great democracy they claimed to serve.

But luck was still—for a time—with Deloncle. The second World War broke out a few weeks after the first wave of arrests, and France had to face a more immediate peril from without than from within. High-level wire-pulling secured a postponement of the Cagoulard trials, and even the release of some of the prisoners on the excuse that they must be mobilised for military service.

Stabbed in the back by the dagger of Cagoulard treachery, France soon collapsed, and genuine patriots of the Resistance began to be hunted down and knifed by imported Cagoulard assassins. And doubtless Deloncle began to see himself as Hitler's French Gauleiter.

But even Hitler did not trust traitors, as Vidkun Quisling found out to his disappointment. And after being used for a time as a Nazi cat's-paw, the disillusioned Deloncle announced in 1942 that he proposed to retire from political life.

It might seem that he had not sought approval for this step from the masters whose methods he so much admired. Whatever the reason, Gestapo representatives called to see him, and in the course of a mysterious interview, of which we shall never know the truth, Deloncle was shot dead.

The official end of the amazing Cagoulard story came quite quietly in 1948, and there were probably few people in Britain who ever heard of it. In that year took place the trials which had been postponed nine years previously. But during the war many of the accused had died or disappeared. Twenty-three survivors were sent to prison; others were acquitted.

Frenchmen were then much more concerned with repairing the ravages of recent war than with punishing the ten-year-old crimes of the almost forgotten Hooded Men. The once dreaded name of Cagoulard had long ceased to be headline news.

But a study of the names of known leaders of the O.A.S. reveals a remarkable coincidence. They include senior Army officers and Algerian *colons*. They include others who in their youth were leaders or active members of the Hooded Men, and now in their middle age are just as active in the O.A.S. *Plus ça change, plus c'est la même chose.*

SEVENTEEN

Operation Sea Lion

"I DON'T BELIEVE THE LION WILL EVER ROAR," said Admiral Canaris. "It can't swim, to begin with."

Hans Pickenbrock, head of Section I of the Abwehr—the branch directly concerned with espionage—nodded agreement. He was normally a cheerful and fun-loving Rhinelander, and certainly a first-class spy-master, but on the morning of July 4th 1940, he looked careworn and anxious.

"But we've got to do something," he muttered. "This is a direct order from Hitler—the Abwehr is to speed up at once the collection of the necessary intelligence for Operation Sea Lion, the invasion of England."

"Sea Lion!" Canaris repeated, scornfully. "Why, the very code name gives the whole show away. Half of our army and navy know what's in hand. I wouldn't be a bit surprised if the English know all about this impossible animal Sea Lion already."

(Canaris was very nearly right. On July the 16th, 1940, Hitler issued his "Directive 16/40, Directions for a landing operation against England." Within four days full details of its contents were received in London.)

"Well, I suppose we shall have to do something to make a show," the Admiral continued. "But improvisation in war-time

145

is dangerous. If the Nazis had kept out of my pre-war plan, we should have been in England now."

As related in another chapter, in 1910 the Germans had a well-placed spy ring in Britain. But our counter-spies broke into it—aided by almost incredible stupidity by the Germans.

Soon after his appointment as head of the Abwehr in 1935 Canaris had thought out a better plan. It comprised *two* spy rings in Britain. One was deliberately flamboyant, so that the British would soon discover it—which we did. Then, the argument ran, they would feel secure: spy history would repeat itself—and the second ring could operate undisturbed.

Unfortunately for Canaris, the British broke into the second ring—again because of German stupidity, for which Canaris rightly blamed Himmler and his amateur spies of the Gestapo. The round-up in September, 1939, was comprehensive, the German organisation was wrecked, and Canaris had to begin again.

One German spy, who was dropped by parachute, did manage to remain at liberty for quite a time. But as a menace to the British war effort he was almost as big a joke as the others. And he suffered under several fatal handicaps which made inevitable his farcical adventures and his tragic end.

Why he remained at liberty for as long as eighteen months is because he was not in security-conscious Britain but in neutral Eire. He was dropped on the 5th May, 1940, at the wrong place and miles away from his equipment. This was found by Irish Security officials, and the British Government was notified that a German agent appeared to be at large.

An almost incredible detail of this farce is that the German spy-masters do not seem to have realised that there were no serious restrictions on passengers travelling to neutral Eire. The doomed parachutist could have travelled in much greater safety and comfort and without arousing suspicion by passenger ship.

This experienced spy was an officer of the Luftwaffe Reserve, and one prepares for the thrilling story of a trained, efficient and ruthless mystery man, going secretly about his sinister work in our midst—or at least in Eire's midst. Actually, the poor man hardly dared to show his face, which was well known from newspaper photographs to most private citizens and to all Security officers. For there was not much mystery about him. He was Dr Herman Goertz, who had been sent to prison for some rather ineffectual espionage in Britain four years previously.

It should have seemed, even to German spy-masters, vital that there should be nothing about Goertz to arouse suspicion of his being a German spy, especially as his task was connected with a projected German invasion of Eire. But his appearance did not, in fact, suggest a typical inoffensive Irish citizen. As a spy he was a sort of musical-comedy figure wearing Luftwaffe breeches and jack-boots, a woollen sweater and a very small black beret. In his pockets were his Luftwaffe cap and his first World War medals. And his forgetful masters had omitted to tell him that his ample supply of English currency was legal tender in Eire, so that for a time he wandered wearily about the countryside with a pocketful of English notes which he was afraid to produce, and nearly starved to death.

By a piece of luck which the Berlin spy-masters cannot take credit for having foreseen, Goertz got into touch at last with some of the members of the Irish Republican Army whom he had met in Maidstone Prison. With their help he got hold of a radio transmitting set, and remained in hiding, and after a long silence he got into radio communication with Germany. But such information as he sent did not encourage Germany to invade Eire, and of course his activities did not do Britain the slightest harm. He was a danger only to the Irish, whose neutrality his activities threatened. And the German Minister in Dublin, who was trying hard to keep Eire out of the war, was probably the most nervous man in Eire when he knew of this amateur at large.

Goertz was picked up rather belatedly by the Eire police in November, 1941, detained until 1947, and when about to be released and sent home to Germany he committed suicide.

If we compare the results of German attempts to infiltra
agents into Britain during the first year of each world war, 1
figures are not merely similar—they are identical. This see
to be beyond the bounds of coincidence, and suggests that
Germans were incapable of learning by their mistakes.

During the first two weeks of June, 1915, seven German
spies—six men and a woman—were caught. During four weeks
of September, 1940, seven German spies—six men and a
woman—were caught. Desperate to obtain information from
inside war-time Britain, the unimaginative Germans adopted
the same methods in the same circumstances—the recruitment of
low-grade mercenary spies who were expendable. The loss of
their comparatively worthless lives neither helped the German war
effort nor provided examples of what to avoid in the future.

Canaris hoped to do better by using men of the I.R.A. But
he found it difficult to find recruits—the I.R.A. might be anti-
British, but was not pro-Nazi. If Sea Lion were a success,
Canaris considered, the British might move into Eire to carry on
the war from there. The obvious answer was an I.R.A. rebellion.

The few members of the I.R.A. who could be persuaded had
a small training-school at Chiemsee in Germany. They were
joined by Sean Russell, an Irish exile from U.S.A. He was
well known: he could surely promote a revolt. But the ill-luck
continued. Russell sailed for Ireland in a German U-boat, but
died of a hæmorrhage on the voyage.

The Irish were a real disappointment to the Abwehr, who
were misled by their violent talk about England—and did not
notice that Oliver Cromwell (who had been dead for quite
some time!) was the principal object of their abuse. Canaris's
plans were not aided by the mutual suspicion and even enmity
among the German leaders—Goering obstinately refused to
supply aircraft to drop spies in Ireland, for example.

Eventually Canaris persuaded a yachtsman friend to land
three agents in Ireland—two Germans and an Indian. The
latter was scared and gave himself up as soon as he landed: the
other two soon joined him in prison.

So now Canaris and Pickenbrock were discussing the next step, without much enthusiasm.

"There's this man Waldberg," said Pickenbrock. "He's done very well in France and Belgium, and as a stool-pigeon in a P.O.W. camp. But he can't speak a word of English!"

"Hell! And that's the best you can raise?"

"There's an enthusiastic Nazi named Meier—but he demands a high fee. We have two Dutch smugglers—they were black-mailed into 'volunteering' for service."

"This is utterly ridiculous!"

"There's worse to come. A German merchant named Drueke and a Swiss named Waelti—with a few dozen words of English between them. All of these are willing to go to England—so long as the German Army follows them within forty-eight hours."

"Don't be funny!"

"We have one other, Herr Admiral. A woman."

"A woman! Useless—except for seduction."

"She's brighter than the other six put together. And she speaks English very well."

"Is she German?"

"No. Cosmopolitan. Danish or Norwegian in origin. Her name is Erikson. Quite young—blonde, good-looking, good nerves—she soon made herself unofficial leader of the group. They'll do anything she tells them."

"Six men and a woman against England!" Canaris muttered. "And only the woman speaks English. Hell!"

The Admiral's apprehension was justified. Yet, being responsible for the Abwehr, he cannot escape liability for the folly of sending untrained and unintelligent spies—there must always be the suspicion that he was indeed only interested in making a show: he was a clever man, and knew that their careers as spies could be reckoned in hours. They were actually paraded in Le Touquet as heroes before they set off on their mission! To Canaris, they were expendable.

The first pair of German agents who landed in Britain were put ashore near Hythe, on the Kent coast, at dawn on the 3rd of September, 1940. For them it was a tragic anniversary of the outbreak of war.

The Dutchmen had been brought across the Channel from Le Touquet, apparently dead drunk, in a French fishing-boat. There was reason to believe that they were crooks who had been blackmailed into serving as spies. Their chances of survival were small, but at least slightly better than survival in Dachau or Belsen. They were comparatively untrained, could hardly speak any English, and one was very obviously half-Japanese. Their sketchy equipment included a crude sort of schoolboy code, and among the oddments hung round the half-caste's neck were field-glasses and his best pair of shoes. He was not, at first sight, a typical British South Coast holiday maker! They were both caught within an hour or two, suffering from what seemed remarkably like a hangover.

From the same fishing-boat another pair landed later a few miles away at Lydd. One of these was another Dutch traitor, the only one of the four who spoke a little English. But he was fatally unfamiliar with British licensing laws—which could, admittedly, have been drafted by cunning counter-espionage officers for the purpose of baffling and confusing the enemy—and when he rushed to the nearest public-house and ordered cider for breakfast, the intelligent landlady sent for the police. His companion, a German who was caught twenty-four hours later, suffered from a handicap which even the German spy-masters should have realised would hamper his efforts to ferret out British military secrets—he could not speak a single word of English.

The spies' kit included radio transmitters, money, and a German sausage. This last item was an invariable feature of the equipment of Nazi spies in England, and was used as evidence against them. It was a type of foodstuff not unnaturally excluded from the British rationing scheme!

Drueke and Waelti, the remaining pair, set off with confidence.

Operation Sea Lion had been postponed until October, so they had had some training. And Fräulein Erikson was going with them!

They were taken by seaplane from Norway to Scotland, and landed on the Banffshire coast by rubber dinghy—getting wet on the way. Once ashore, they separated. Drueke and Fräulein Erikson walked to a near-by station. All the signs had been removed, and the spies had to ask where they were! A good beginning, indeed!

Worse was to come. It was a fine morning—but their legs were wet. Instead of leaving the talking to the Fräulein, Drueke joined in—speaking with a very heavy accent. The station-master phoned the police. They searched the couple, and in the man's pockets they found a pistol, ammunition, money—and a German sausage. It was as if the Berlin Gestapo had arrested a suspected British spy, and found his pockets full of fish-and-chips in a bag printed with a London East End address.

In the meantime Waelti had managed to catch a train to Edinburgh. He left his bag in the cloakroom. When he returned to pick it up, the police were there—Fräulein Erikson had given a good description of her second companion. There was a moment of drama; Waelti reached for the loaded German automatic in his pocket, as if about to shoot his way out. But he was quickly overpowered. His suitcase carried a radio set, maps, money—and, need I add, German sausage.

Both men were tried, condemned and executed. Sir William (later Earl) Jowitt, who as Solicitor-General conducted the prosecution of both groups, wrote: "If the cases of which I had experience were a fair sample of German espionage, then that espionage must have been remarkably inefficient."

In Berlin Colonel Pickenbrock commiserated with his chief.

"The British have announced the capture of all six of our men," he said glumly. "Just as you said."

"It was bound to happen. What of the woman?"

"No mention of her. She's our only hope."

"H'm!" Canaris muttered.

"I know. She has no special military knowledge, but she ought to be able to give an idea of British forces along the South Coast."

"Let's hope you're right."

After the war the records of the German staff were captured. They showed that information had indeed been received from England during the autumn of 1940. The estimate was that the British forces totalled 1,640,000 men: the actual figure was just about half. Estimates of guns and other equipment were just as exaggerated. Even if the German air force had won the Battle of Britain, it is doubtful if an invasion would have been launched—the military chiefs would have hesitated to risk an attack in the face of such considerable defences.

What they did not know was that the information on which their estimates were based had kindly been supplied to them by the *British* Intelligence service.

"It only remains to add that it was decided to take no proceedings against Madame Erikson. I have no doubt that she was detained here during the war, and it may be that she was able to be of some use to our authorities," wrote Lord Jowitt, in masterly understatement. Fräulein Erikson *did* stay in England for the rest of the war: she *was* of very considerable use to our authorities—in sending misleading information to Germany.

This was the end rather than the beginning of her service. Much earlier she had been infiltrated into the Abwehr; she was actually a British agent, and her particular task was to spy on Nazi spies. The six men were doomed long before they came to Britain. Operation Sea Lion was equally doomed by the picture of a massive resistance to an amphibious invasion.

Today a lady keeps a pleasant little hotel in a Norwegian village. She has reverted to her own name, which was not Erikson. She is still easy to look at, active, and with a sprightly figure: she has attractive eyes and a very friendly smile.

Even her relatives and friends cannot fill in details of what happened to her during the war years. True, a good many people had strange experiences at that time. There are rumours that she was (*a*) a prominent member of the Resistance, (*b*) in a Nazi concentration camp, (*c*) an interpreter with the American forces, (*d*) the lady friend of a well-known statesman. But when challenged, Fräulein Erikson just smiles. Her Service was Secret.

EIGHTEEN

The Invasion that never happened

ALL THE WORLD KNOWS that in 1940 the Germans were
ready to invade Britain. Warships, aircraft, hordes of troops in
thousands of invasion barges were all waiting for Hitler to
name the day. But he never did so.

Even today, however, more than twenty years afterwards, few
people have any idea why the hitherto irresistible German
forces held back from attacking a small island left almost
defenceless by the loss of practically all its tanks and heavy
guns at Dunkirk.

There were two main reasons why the invasion plan was
repeatedly postponed and finally abandoned: one was that the
incompetent German Intelligence were completely ignorant of
Britain's appalling defence weaknesses; the other was that
Hitler had a psychological dread of the sea.

The origins of Hitler's sea-phobia are interesting. He was,
of course, sexually abnormal. The story of his strange liaison
with Eva Braun is well known. Less familiar is the unpleasant
story of his earlier association with his own niece, Geli Raubal,
twenty-one-year-old daughter of Hitler's half-sister, Angela.

Geli was a brainless but coarsely attractive young woman,

who in 1930 was living with Hitler in his nine-roomed apart-ment at 16 Prinz Regentenplatz, and her circle of lovers included even Hitler's chauffeur. In those early days Hitler always carried a heavy whip, and when he cracked it Geli would shrink into a corner shuddering with horror. "He is a monster," she said to a friend. "You wouldn't believe the things he makes me do."

Hitler fancied himself as an artist, and drew a number of what his friend "Putzi" Hanfstaengl described as "depraved, intimate sketches of Geli." This came to light as early as 1930 when a blackmailer stole the erotic portfolio, and Franz Schwartz, the Nazi Treasurer, had to buy it back with a large sum of Party funds.

Geli's end came on the 18th of September, 1931. We shall never know what refinements of depravity Hitler demanded of her, but, promiscuous as she was, she refused. There was a violent quarrel, in the course of which the girl was severely knocked about and her nose was broken. That night she shot herself in the apartment.

This sordid tragedy may seem to have little connection with the fact that Britain was never invaded. But it has its place in the psychological case-history of the German leader.

Hitler's abnormal sex-life was due to his freakishly under-developed genitals, and he never recovered from the sneers of fellow-soldiers during the first World War. Thereafter he would never allow himself to be seen in a bathing-costume. This meant that he could never bathe in the sea. And in a process of self-justification familiar to psychiatrists, his sea-phobia re-mained after he had forced the cause of it back into his uncon-scious.

The invasion of Britain required that the then unbeatable German Army must cross twenty-odd miles of sea. And Hitler decided—coming to the right conclusion for the wrong reason —that it was on the sea that he might suffer defeat.

In the Abwehr's ignorance of British defences, history was repeating itself. In 1914 the British Expeditionary Force—the

"Old Contemptibles"—was shipped to France in such secrecy that it was weeks before the German General Staff knew of the presence of British troops on French soil. Kaiser Wilhelm II was furious. "Am I surrounded by fools?" he demanded. "Why was I never told that we have no spies in England?"

Similarly in 1940 Hitler said in an angry speech to his General Staff: "We are divided from England by a ditch 37 kilometres wide, but we are not able to get to know what is happening over there."

Count Ciano, Italian Foreign Minister and Mussolini's son-in-law, wrote in his diary: "It is incredible that we" (the Italians) "do not have a single informant in Great Britain."

So Ciano approached his country's German allies, optimistically believing that they might be better informed. But no. In a depressing discussion with the German General Keitel, Ciano was told: "The intelligence available on the military preparedness of the island" (Britain) "and its coastal defences is meagre and unreliable."

It must be borne in mind that any comments on espionage apply equally to counter-espionage, in the same way that a C.I.D. officer must know as much about the technique of crime as the criminal himself. And the German respect for British methods in these fields was so great as to give them a marked inferiority complex. In preparation for the invasion that never happened, the German General Staff printed a book of instructions for German Intelligence officers whose happy task it would have been to prepare a conquered Britain for its Nazi Government. I examined a captured copy of this book, with its long lists of addresses to be raided (including my own) and its many pages of photographs of individuals to be arrested and shot (which included, amusingly enough, some of the leading officials of Sir Oswald Mosley's pro-Hitler Fascist Party).

The book was called *Informationschaft G.B.* It described Intelligence as "a field in which the British, by virtue of their traditions, their experience, and certain facets of their national character—unscrupulousness, self-control, cool deliberateness and ruthless action—have achieved an unquestionable degree of mastery."

But if the German invasion-planners were ignorant of British military preparedness, or lack of it, they were uncomfortably aware of an equally important factor—British civilian morale. Most Germans obey self-appointed leaders with sheep-like docility. Most British people refuse to do anything of the kind. Centuries of increasing political freedom have made even comparatively uneducated British people into sturdy, self-reliant individualists, better able than any other nation to form their own judgment of a given political or even military situation. This means that when they feel that their cause is just and their leaders are competent, civilians as well as soldiers are ready, in an old but apt phrase, to die on their feet rather than to live on their knees.

So, in preparation for the invasion, the German leaders decided that British morale must be 'softened up.' It was the right idea, put into action by quite the wrong methods.

The main German offensive against British morale was by broadcasting. And it may be news to many British readers that early in 1940 a flood of propaganda began to pour from no less than four German radio stations which pretended to be situated in Britain. Within hours, of course, British radio monitors established by direction-finding apparatus that these stations were in Occupied Europe. And this radio offensive was quite unconnected with such broadcasts as those by William Joyce ("Lord Haw-Haw") from Hamburg, which did not pretend to be other than from inside Germany.

The best-known pseudo-British broadcasts were from a station calling itself the "New British Broadcasting Station" which started to operate during the last week of February, 1940. Its programmes opened by playing *The Bonnie Banks o' Loch Lomond* and ended with the National Anthem. It pretended to take it for granted that German invasion was inevitable and imminent, and professed to give British people friendly advice on a *sauve qui peut* basis unlikely to appeal to the tough national character.

It was one of my war-time odd jobs to listen to the N.B.B.S., which emphasised that everybody should hoard every scrap of food they could get hold of (which was designed to disorganise the food-rationing system) and to leave their homes at once, take to the roads and trek to the North—this was designed to hamper the forces rushing South to repel the German invaders.

Another German propaganda station called itself the "Workers' Challenge," and tried to exploit class difference by abusing Jews and capitalists. Another called itself the organ of the "Christian Peace Movement," with a slogan, "Blessed are the Peacemakers." And a fourth pretended to be the voice of Scottish Nationalism, calling itself "Station Caledonia" in a somewhat unconvincing Scots accent and plugging "Auld Lang Syne." It advocated a separate peace between Germany and Scotland!

Enquiries by a sort of official Listener Research Bureau failed to find that any of this nonsense had the slightest effect.

Desperate at their failure to shake British morale by radio, the German propagandists took the risk of using a fleet of bombers to prepare an elaborate but abortive hoax. This was during a night in mid-August, 1940, and I have not the figures before me of how many of the practical jokers were shot down, wasting their planes and giving their lives in vain. What they did was to fly over the North of England and South of Scotland dropping parachutes, radio sets and fake instructions to non-existent spies, complete with maps and lists of addresses of imaginary Fascist collaborators.

The humourless Germans were very proud of their futile exploit. General Greiner of the Oberkommando der Wehrmacht wrote in his diary: "We dropped pack assemblies in order to feign a parachute landing, which caused great excitement in the British Press." Readers who remember those tense days of 1940 will be able to confirm that the "great excitement" in Fleet Street was not merely an exaggeration—it was a fabrication.

During those tense spring days of 1940, the German Army was consistently successful in Europe; but German Intelligence was consistently a failure in Britain. In only one case did M.I.5 feel any concern. And that was a case in which the defeated Abwehr played no part whatsoever. It was an abortive plot—but might have been a serious plot—dreamed up in a Kensington café.

The background of the plot was an organisation of anti-Semites who called themselves the "Right Club." The founder of the Right Club was Captain A. H. Maule Ramsay, then Member of Parliament for Peebles and Midlothian, an Old Etonian with a creditable record of service in the first World War. He had conceived a pathological antipathy to Jews and Freemasons, but his sympathy for those features of Nazi ideology did not make him an active traitor to the country he had served so well.

But whilst Captain Ramsay sat in his big Kensington house, hating Jews and Freemasons, other members of his Right Club sat in the near-by "Russian Restaurant" arguing that anybody who hated Jews must like Hitler—an illogical and dangerous line of thought that the Nazi leader used freely in his propaganda.

The Russian Restaurant was owned by a Russian named Wolkoff, who had been an admiral in the old Tsarist Imperial Navy before the Revolution. He had escaped to political sanctuary in Britain with his wife and daughter Anna, all understandably anti-Communist, incidentally anti-Jewish, illogically anti-democratic. Anna, particularly, snobbishly resented the fact that instead of taking her place in Imperial Russian society as an admiral's daughter, she had been relegated by forces she imperfectly understood to the social status of the daughter of a Kensington café-owner. And instead of showing any gratitude to the country which had given her and her family sanctuary, when in their homeland they would undoubtedly have been executed, she began to work for the defeat of Britain by her anti-Communist and anti-Jewish idol—Adolf Hitler.

So, night after night at a special table in the Russian Restaurant, a little group met to eat the tasty Russian dishes that Admiral Wolkoff had prepared, and to discuss how they might best fight the bogey of Communism by helping its great adversary Hitler.

And Anna Wolkoff was delighted to find that one of the group was in a position to obtain information which, if conveyed to the Germans, might influence the course of the war in their favour.

That knowledgeable member of the Right Club was a thirty-year-old American named Tyler Kent, employed in his country's diplomatic service. Whilst serving as a cipher clerk in the United States Embassy in Moscow, he had taken it upon himself to disagree with the reports of his Ambassador. And with a view to subsequently making a name for himself in political circles in Washington, he had formed the habit of keeping private copies of his Ambassador's secret telegrams. When he was transferred as cipher clerk to the United States Embassy in London, he continued that treacherous practice.

So that early in 1940 the private dossier of telegrams with which Tyler Kent hoped one day to startle and impress Congress, to his own advantage, included decoded copies of the correspondence that was passing between Mr Churchill and President Roosevelt—information which could only be described as 'vital.'

Anna Wolkoff soon perceived the potential value of Tyler Kent's information in her efforts to build up a Nazi Europe to oppose Communist Russia. And it was not long before Kent was persuaded to transform words into deeds—to hand to Anna secret American diplomatic papers of which she had photostat copies made. It was not easy in war-time to transfer such material from London to Berlin, but Anna had a friend who was Assistant Military Attaché at the Italian Embassy in London.

As an example of the perilous possibilities of this conspiracy, President Roosevelt's reply to Winston Churchill about the projected loan of destroyers was received by Mr Churchill on the 18th of May, 1940. It was, of course, decoded by Tyler Kent. And, bearing in mind Anna's friend at the Italian Embassy, it is interesting to note that a few days later an accurate summary of what President Roosevelt had said was telegraphed to Berlin by the German Ambassador in Rome.

It is entirely due to the foresight of M.I.5 in penetrating the Right Club with high-grade agents that all these moves were known to the British Government almost from hour to hour. Action could not be taken immediately. An Old Bailey trial was essential to reveal and destroy the conspiracy—and reports from agents are not proof.

It is not illegal for refugees in Britain to advocate anti-Semitism, even in war-time. But it is highly illegal indeed to give active assistance to the enemy. So the Right Club had to be smashed beyond hope of reorganisation.

Anna Wolkoff continued to receive top-secret information; and she continued to explore new methods of conveying it to Germany. And almost before she had reached home from the Russian Restaurant after these discussions, M.I.5 knew all that had been said.

Anna's last and fatal effort to help Hitler to win the war against the country which had given her sanctuary was when she picked up a piece of news which it seemed urgent to transmit. The best plan she could devise was to try to send it to Hitler's henchman, William Joyce, via the Rumanian Embassy in London. She arranged this through a trusted Rumanian contact, and was very upset to learn later that before the information reached Hamburg via Rumania and Berlin, the message had been vetted by M.I.5 and passed as completely harmless to the British war effort.

In her message Anna wrote to Joyce, "Acknowledge by Carlyle reference on radio." This interested M.I.5 greatly, because, in a British court of law, it was desirable to prove not merely the sending of the message but its receipt by the enemy. A few days later, listening British radio monitors transcribed a talk in English from a German radio station about French culture. "We thank the French for nothing," they said in their broadcast. "Where is their Shakespeare? Who is their Carlyle?" This unanswerable question was fatal for Anna Wolkoff. Her message had got through—she had suggested that the Germans use these phrases as confirmation. And M.I.5 struck.

There were diplomatic complications. Not only was Tyler Kent protected by diplomatic immunity, but a room in Anna Wolkoff's home was let to an official of the Netherlands Embassy, and it was strongly suspected that she might have parked compromising documents under the bed of her un-suspecting extra-territorial lodger.

In hurried but technically impeccable protocol, M.I.5 went first to the American Ambassador, Mr Joseph Kennedy— father of the present President of the United States and a man who misguidedly believed that Britain was going to be defeated. He could not deny the complicity in this espionage plot of his own cipher clerk, and he withdrew diplomatic immunity from Tyler Kent.

So on a day in May, 1940, the way was clear for M.I.5 to supervise a series of arrests and searches carried out by Scot-land Yard's Special Branch. Ex-Admiral Wolkoff was outraged when his home was entered at dawn by Special Branch officers and a representative of M.I.5. "This is ridiculous!" he protested. "I am a respectable person. I used to be an admiral of the Imperial Russian Navy." "Is that so?" snapped the big, tough Special Branch Inspector in an incredulous tone. "Then in that case you will be able to tell me who was the Imperial Minister of Marine at that date." The Inspector did not know, of course; but unfortunately for Admiral Wolkoff, he did not know either. This setback forced him to retire from the verbal conflict and lick his wounds whilst Anna was interrogated and the whole house searched.

Anna Wolkoff and Tyler Kent were arrested that morning and detained pending trial. Captain Ramsay, despite his position as a Member of Parliament, was detained a few days later and sent to internment under Defence Regulation 18(*b*).

Anna was eventually sentenced to ten years' imprisonment, and Tyler Kent was sentenced to seven years and was later deported to the United States.

And what makes this little-known episode one of the big jokes of the war at German expense, is that the Abwehr never knew a thing about it until it was all over. The vaunted German Secret Service spent much time and trouble and huge sums in expenses to establish agents in war-time Britain—all in vain. The only spy ring which might have helped the Germans was that group of Right Club amateurs boasting over their vodka in a Kensington café, blissfully unaware that one of the most trusted members of their circle was reporting everything they said to M.I.5 a few minutes later.

NINETEEN

Dr Sorge—the German who saved Russia

SOME YEARS AGO I was dining with a group of old colleagues. Between us we could claim to know as much about spies and counter-spies as any group in the world.

The conversation over the port got around to an old subject: who was the greatest spy in history? Karl Schulmeister was a possibility—the man who won some of Napoleon's battles before a shot was fired. And Stieber, Bismarck's master-spy—he did really deserve the title often allocated by modern journalists to minor agents. Yet there was fairly general agreement when I suggested Dr Richard Sorge.

We could regard him calmly and professionally, for British contacts with him were slight.

"I didn't know that they existed," was the comment of a retired Director of Naval Intelligence.

"Oh, yes," I said. "He came to England—about 1936, I think it was. He had scarcely been in London a few hours when a man sat beside him in the lounge of his hotel. 'Well, Dr Sorge, and how's Hamburg these days?' Sorge proved his quality by leaving England immediately."

"I haven't got it," said the ex-D.N.I. "The man was one of ours, I take it—but what did 'how's Hamburg' mean? An identification phrase?"

"No. Sorge was born in Russia; of mixed German-Russian parentage—his grandfather was secretary to Karl Marx. He joined the Communist Party at Hamburg, and edited its local newspaper. Yet later he was admitted to membership of the Nazi Party—for all their police state, they did not know that he had been a Communist."

"Ah, I see! And M.I.5 did."

"Yes. Actually, when he came to London he was a Nazi member all right—but he was actually a Communist spy!"

Dr Sorge had a first-class intellect, and was a brilliant linguist—speaking Russian, Japanese, Chinese, French and English as well as his native German.

He worked for German newspapers as a correspondent in war-stricken China, and did the job excellently. All the time he was a Russian spy!

In 1933 he returned to Berlin and won the confidence of the Nazi hierarchy by his accurate and detailed knowledge of the confused situation in China. Dr Goebbels was not too proud to dine with him. When Sorge moved to take up a new post as German newspaper representative in Japan, the Nazis beamed approval. But he was still a Russian spy!

He was astute enough not to be in a hurry—haste has been the downfall of many a spy. He commanded ample funds, and chose the members of his spy ring with great care. It included *no* Russians. A German, Max Klausen, had a cover as good as that of Sorge—he represented a German electrical group in Japan—which explained his experiments with V.H.F. radio. Another, Branko de Voukelić, was a Yugoslav in exile, now acting as correspondent for a French magazine. A Japanese artist, Yotoku Miyagi, had lived for years in the U.S.A., where he had joined the Communist Party. Another Japanese was the most useful of all: Hozumi Ozaki was a journalist who had already worked with Sorge in China. Back home, his knowledge of that country proved to be of great interest and value to the Japanese Government. He soon became the leading adviser on Chinese affairs to Prince Konoye, the Japanese Prime Minister.

Sorge himself enjoyed most useful connections. Thanks to his newspaper reputation and the friendship of Dr Goebbels, he was a regular visitor to the German Embassy in Tokyo. There, indeed, his advice was frequently sought on Chinese problems, and Sorge became a close friend of the military attaché, Colonel von Ott, who later became Ambassador. Thus Sorge was uniquely placed. He was quite happy to put his experience of China at his friend's disposal. At the same time, breakfasting daily at the Embassy, the Ambassador—a military man—freely discussed military as well as political matters with his friend and adviser. He even gave Sorge an office in the Embassy, which was of course immune from search by the Kempēitai—the Japanese counter-espionage.

This was a first-class team—of a quality and opportunity, indeed, almost unparalleled in the history of espionage. No greater contrast can ever be imagined than that between the uniquely equipped and efficient spy ring organised by Sorge in Japan, and the indiscriminate collection of jailbirds and incompetents despatched by the Nazis to Britain. If Sorge had been working for Germany, the course of the war might have run very differently. As it was, he served the Soviet Union magnificently. "Sorge saved us!" cried Stalin, seldom effusive in his praise.

Sorge had no contact with Japanese Communists. The members of his spy cell had their own informants—who thought that they were selling information to journalists!

The discipline of the cell was almost perfect. The radio set was dismantled after each transmission, was never used again from the same place, and the code was 're-scrambled' after each use. All reports were completely destroyed immediately following the despatch of their contents. No member of the cell lived above his apparent means. The spy ring even paid its own way. Klausen set up a business for copying documents and photographs and used the most modern equipment—better than any other in Japan. So good, in fact, that the Japanese Government began to use the Klausen service for copying its own secret documents—in effect, it *paid* the spy ring for receiving the information it thus passed over.

I said that the discipline was 'almost' perfect. The exception was Sorge himself. He was full-blooded and highly sexed, and could not live without the intimate company of women. He was not the first spy to be doomed by this failing.

However, for years he was outstandingly successful. When the Russians were apprehensive of a Japanese attack on Siberia, he was able to reassure them with the news that the Japanese would soon attack China. He was able to obtain full details of the anti-Comintern Pact even before it was signed. Few secrets of Japanese and German diplomacy were beyond the ken of his contacts—and thereby of Sorge himself.

I have often stressed the fact that the spy's hardest task is not to get information but to persuade his employers that it is accurate. Stalin rejected Sorge's reports if they disagreed with his own ideas! He was fully informed of Hitler's plans when he signed his pact with the Nazi dictator. As the war progressed, he was notified well in advance of the German attacks on Norway, Denmark, Holland, Belgium and France. Cynically he did nothing to warn any of them.

When Sorge reported that Germany would shortly attack Russia, Stalin refused to believe it. Britain and America confirmed the warning, but Stalin was obstinate. The information Sorge provided would have convinced anyone except a tyrant over-confident of his power. The Russian people had to suffer bitterly for their leader's incredulity.

When the German attack did develop, Sorge's warnings proved accurate in every detail. From this time onward Stalin accepted his news without hesitation!

Sorge reported that Japan would *not* attack Russia—her present ambitions lay in South-east Asia. Hence the Russians

were able to withdraw their crack troops from Siberia for the
defence of Moscow. The Duke of Wellington would have said
that it was "a damned near thing."

Sorge's lust was so strong that it could never be concealed.
His string of mistresses was indeed the talk of Tokyo: but, as a
leading German correspondent, it was agreed that he could
well afford such luxuries. True, he kept his sex-life quite distinct
from his espionage—none of his women had the slightest
connection with his spy cell.

One of Sorge's friends was Colonel Ozaki, head of the
Japanese counter-spy service—not to be confused with the
journalist Ozaki, Sorge's most reliable assistant. The colonel
was worried. It was quite obvious that Japanese secrets were
escaping abroad. Illicit radio messages had been picked up,
but the Japanese direction-finding equipment was too primitive
to trace their origin.

He began a long and painstaking search. He compiled a list
of all the people who *might* have had advance news of Government policy. It was lengthy, but each person it contained was
thoroughly investigated. After many months of enquiry, three
names remained on the list: Ozaki, Voukelić—and Sorge!

Sorge! It seemed incredible even to suspect him. And Ozaki
was a principal adviser to the Prime Minister! Yet the colonel
had a tenacious sense of duty, and he persisted.

He sent for a young dancer who had just begun her rise to
stardom. Kiyomi came of a good family, and was a virgin. But
Colonel Ozaki persuaded her that it was her duty to yield her
virtue for love of the Divine Mikado.

One day he met Sorge at a Tokyo cabaret where Kiyomi was
dancing. Sorge did not know it, but the meeting had been
deliberately arranged.

"She is really beautiful, isn't she?" said the colonel. "And I'm
told that she's pure—quite unapproachable."

"No woman is unapproachable!" was the verdict of the expert Sorge. He seemed to be justified, for Kiyomi shared his
bed that very night.

Kiyomi was not a trained agent, but she had keen eyes. One evening as she danced—the date was October the 15th, 1941—she saw a man toss a paper pellet away. Casually it fell on Sorge's table. She noticed a flash in his eyes as he read the note it bore: then he stuffed the paper into his pocket.

No wonder Sorge's eyes had sparkled. The note was indeed his greatest war-time coup. "Japanese carrier force attacking United States Navy at Pearl Harbour probably dawn 6 December source reliable. Joe." Joe was the cover-name of Sorge's agent Miyagi.

Sorge had a chalet by the sea. There he proposed to take Kiyomi for the night. She did not resist. On the way he halted to light a cigarette. As he felt in his pocket for his matches, he touched the scrap of paper. He was going to burn it, but failed to find any matches. So he ripped it into tiny fragments and threw them out of the window.

Later, Kiyomi asked him to stop so that she could telephone to tell her mother that she would not be home. But her 'mother' answered the call in a man's voice—Colonel Ozaki.

As she prepared a meal at the chalet, Sorge went for a short walk. Long before this he had bought a large fishing-boat. He used it for drunken parties—frequented by Cabinet Ministers and high ranking officers. They were not to know that below was a secret cabin—unknown even to the Japanese skipper—housing a powerful radio set. And while the noisy parties were afoot, Max Klausen would be tapping off messages to Moscow. Small wonder that the Japanese had failed to track down the apparatus—the fishing-boat ensured that messages were sent from a different place every night. And who would suspect a boat on which were to be found half the Japanese Cabinet and the Emperor's personal staff?

"Get this off quickly," Sorge ordered. "Then you'd better clear out. I have an idea that the Japs are getting warm. Miyagi tells me that one of his informants has been arrested in a round-up. It may be casual, but——"

He ate his supper and went to bed. Kiyomi said later that he had never been so full of love, returning again and again for her embraces.

Early in the morning Colonel Ozaki entered. He said no word: he merely displayed a sheet of paper on which hundreds of tiny fragments had been pasted: the Pearl Harbour warning!

This had been the only spy ring ever to operate successfully in Japan. It had enjoyed amazing success, but now it had crashed because of one of the oldest devices in the history of espionage: a woman decoy.

Now the story of Sorge is well known—the Americans pieced it together during their occupation of Japan after the war, and the C.I.A. published a full account in 1949, *Sorge Spy Ring*. And General Willoughby, MacArthur's Chief of Intelligence, wrote a book on the case. But it soon became obvious that the ex-D.N.I. knew nothing of the amazing sequel.

"Sorge got the punishment he deserved, I presume," he said.

"Well, he and Ozaki were sentenced to death. But——"

"Don't tell me that he got out of a lavatory window and escaped! His real name isn't James Bond, is it?"

"No. But queer things happened. The Russians were active —they owed a lot to Sorge, and he claimed Russian citizenship. He was held in jail until 1944. Then he was allowed to have some teeth extracted and a new plate made and fitted. And a Tokyo tailor supplied a new suit. All for a man about to die."

"You're suggesting that the Russians got him off? An exchange, perhaps?"

"Nothing was ever announced. But you know the Japanese custom? When a man is hanged, his body is handed over to his relatives. If he is a foreigner, his Consul is invited to witness the execution. But that didn't happen with Sorge."

"And he was kept alive for three years?"

"Two and a half, anyway."

"I don't understand it."

"His execution was announced, but——"

"Go on. There's more?"

I turned to a man who had been smiling throughout my recital.

"You tell him, George. You were in China at the time."

"Yes, I was. I knew the two men concerned——"

"Just a minute—*which* two men?"

"An American journalist and a French diplomat. Late in 1947 they were drinking in the Long Bar at Shanghai. Suddenly the Frenchman nudged his companion. 'Look at that man!' He indicated a tall man ten yards away. 'My God, it is! It's Sorge!' "

" 'Sorge!' the journalist echoed. 'You mean the spy Sorge? But he was hanged years ago.' "

" 'I tell you that that's Sorge—I knew him well—I couldn't mistake him.' "

" 'Let's go!' The American scented a story. But the man saw them approaching and disappeared through the crowd to the door."

"So he did get away!"

"Wait. There's a bit more. A few days later Kiyomi was appearing in a Shanghai night-club. She had now added songs to her dance act. One night—it so happened that one of my men was there on another job—she suddenly stopped short right in the middle of a song. She was staring at a tall man who was sitting near the door. He got up to go out—my man got a good sight of him——"

"And he was Sorge?"

"He answered the same description—my man didn't know Sorge personally. But I haven't quite finished. Kiyomi screamed with terror and ran from the stage. She grabbed her coat from her dressing-room and rushed out of the stage door. The door-keeper heard three shots fired—and found Kiyomi dead on the pavement."

"Hell! What a story! You're sure you haven't read it in a magazine?"

"Every word I've said can be corroborated."

"So Sorge got his revenge!"

"Hitherto he had always wanted his women alive. This one was dead. And he should really have taken his revenge on himself, not Kiyomi."

"And where is he now?"

"Your guess is as good as mine. The Russians owed him plenty, didn't they?"

TWENTY

The Escape of the Scharnhorst and Gneisenau

ONE MORNING EARLY IN 1942, two officers were sitting in
a bomb-proof office not far from Whitehall. Far above them the
street was dark and empty after a German air raid. In the
distance was the clangour of fire-bells. It was not yet dawn.

"There's a lot to learn, Colonel," the younger officer said
in a tone almost of despair. He wore the uniform of a captain,
and his green Intelligence Corps tabs looked new.

"You'll pick it up, my boy," the colonel told him in a tired
voice. "Every night brings its own problems, of course. But
they're seldom new problems—usually just fresh twists to old
ones. For instance"—he picked out a paper from a tray on his
desk—"do you remember this report?"

The captain took the document and glanced at it.

"I remember, sir," he agreed. "Received four days ago from
Gall and Philippon, our agents in Brest. They say the German
battle cruisers, *Scharnhorst* and *Gneisenau*, are practically
undamaged after recent heavy R.A.F. raids, and are likely to
put to sea any day."

"Yes," the colonel said with a slow nod. "A rather unlikely
story. Anything else?"

"The radio monitors have endorsed the decoded copy
'Handwriting OK: Security test OK.' "

"Good! And of course you will remember that I explained to you how every secret agent develops an individual style of sending Morse. So that our clever little girls learn to recognise the style as they would recognise handwriting. Is that all?"

"There's the Security test of misspelling a prearranged word, sir. For the Brest agents the test-word is the eighth in each message. And in this report the eighth word is spelt 'reddy' instead of ready."

"Excellent! And the implication?"

"This seems to be a perfectly genuine message from two thoroughly reliable agents, sir."

"Quite! But now have a look at this. It came in an hour ago."

The young captain took the second document and frowned over it. "But—but this is a 'Cat' report which says exactly the opposite, sir. It's almost incredible. It says the German battle cruisers have suffered heavy bomb damage and won't be seaworthy for at least six months."

"Read on, my boy."

"It says Gall and Philippon have been captured by the Abwehr, and under threats of torture are being forced to send false reports. Good God!"

"Well, these things happen in war-time. And this is a good example of what I was telling you yesterday—that an Intelligence assessor's biggest headache is to decide which of two contradictory reports is likely to be true. The most important section of any Intelligence service is its Evaluation Branch."

"I wouldn't have a clue in this case, sir."

"We have to ask ourselves two simple questions. Is the source reliable? And does the information fit the known facts?"

"I've read the personal files of Gall and Philippon. They seem to be clever and completely trustworthy agents, sir. I don't know much about 'the Cat.'"

"Nobody knows much about her. We didn't drop her into France—she appointed herself, and even invented her own code name. But judged by results she's terrific. We made exhaustive checks on information from her Interalliée Resistance group up to three months ago. That was November, 1941. By that time she'd radioed no less than fifteen hundred reports mostly highly important information, and consistently accurate down to the last detail."

"Honours even so far, sir."

"Yes. Which brings us to the second of my questions. I needn't remind you that the existence of two undamaged German battle cruisers in Brest harbour is a powerful threat to our transatlantic convoys. We must either destroy them at their moorings, or fight them if they put to sea."

"If they are really undamaged, sir."

"If, indeed! But it hardly seems likely. Up to this month the R.A.F. have dropped 4000 tons of bombs on Brest. In the course of which we lost 34 bombers and 247 air crew. And we killed an unknown number of unfortunate French people, which Dr Goebbels is emphasising in his propaganda."

"Surely Salmon and Gluckstein[1] must be just scrap iron after all that."

"I quite agree, my boy. Which is why I'm inclined to endorse this 'Cat' report as probably accurate. I think we must work on the assumption that Gall and Philippon have been caught by the Abwehr and 'turned round.' "

"So what action do we take, sir?"

"We tell the R.A.F. they've done a good job at Brest, and they can leave the place alone for a month or two. And we tell the Admiralty they can withdraw the big ships from blockading Brest, as there is unlikely to be a sea-fight in the Channel before next August."

"What about Gall and Philippon?"

"We can only warn M.I.6. and S.O.E. that they appear to be working under enemy control. What happens then is no business of ours. The poor fellows will either be rescued or wiped out, I suppose. They know too much. And I wonder—it might be worth while to take a risk and get 'the Cat' over here."

[1] 'Salmon and Gluckstein' was war-time slang for the *Scharnhorst* and *Gneisenau*.

The date of that conversation is very important. It was the 11th of February, 1942.

The following day the world was amazed at British ineptitude; the British people were in despair; the R.A.F. were incredulous; the Admiralty were apoplectic.

It was the day on which the undamaged German battle cruisers *Scharnhorst* and *Gneisenau* left Brest, steamed up the English Channel and safely reached their home port in Germany.

It can now be revealed that the dramatic escape of the *Scharnhorst* and *Gneisenau* from Brest, which necessitated an immediate revision of British naval strategy, was made possible as the result of a distressing but not unusual domestic situation. A young French woman wanted children, but her husband would not let her have any.

She was Mme Mathilde-Lily Carré, of Toulouse. Shortly after marriage, her husband was shocked to find that there was a trace of hereditary insanity in his family. He came to the reluctant but sensible conclusion that it would be wrong to risk bringing a family of lunatics into the world.

Mme Carré, though passionate to the verge of nymphomania, could have settled down to a normal married life with the love of husband and children. But life without love—which to her meant passionate love—she could not face.

During 1940 she met a Polish officer, fell in love with him, and together they organised one of the earliest French Resistance groups, which they called the "Interalliée." They enrolled a considerable number of members, and later went to Paris, where they lived together in an apartment near the Arc de Triomphe. They extended their organisation, installed a secret radio transmitter, and began to send to London a steady flow of reports from what was by that time a highly efficient circle of loyal French people who were well placed to gather secret information in Occupied France.

As a code name Mme Carré called herself "the Cat," and earned a high reputation in British Intelligence circles for the importance and accuracy of no less than 1500 reports that she had transmitted by the end of 1941.

There then developed a situation which the emotional 'Cat' did not hesitate to exploit. It was instigated by Sergeant Hugo Bleicher of the Abwehr.

The Abwehr—which must not be confused with the Gestapo —was the old professional Secret Service of the German armed forces. Headed by Admiral Canaris, it was not a collection of Nazi thugs but a world-wide organisation under regular officers and N.C.O.'s, who carried on the secret war of espionage and counter-espionage in a manner as decent and honourable as is possible in such dirty work. And Bleicher, a highly efficient Abwehr man, was also a decent fellow with certain standards of fair play.

Towards the end of 1941 Bleicher captured a member of the Interalliée group who, under skilful interrogation, broke down and gave away such secrets as he knew. As a result Bleicher located and seized the secret radio, and arrested over twenty members of the group, including the Pole and "the Cat."

Unknown at the time to British Intelligence, Bleicher's *coup* was virtually the end of the Interalliée group.

The defection of "the Cat" was surprisingly sudden, and is a tribute to Bleicher's powers of persuasion and his personal charm. On the third day after her arrest he obtained her release from prison on parole for an evening. He took her to dinner at the Tour d'Argent and, as was her way with any man who showed her attention, she fell in love with him.

A few days later he obtained her release on indefinite parole, and she went to live with him in his Paris flat. She not only lived with him but worked with him. Within a few weeks she had helped him to trace and arrest no less than 130 more of her comrades of the Interalliée group, including her own mother.

Now it happened that Bleicher had a discarded French mistress—perhaps merely a girl he had seduced in order to make use of her for official purposes. Bleicher was traced by this girl and persuaded to resume their relationship.

"The Cat" had been proving more and more useful to Bleicher, so he continued to live with her. But a jealous and suspicious woman like herself sooner or later senses the facts of such a situation. Realising that she was about to lose her German lover, she decided to have her revenge by changing sides yet again!

The climax came, by another trick of Fate, at Christmas 1941. Anxious to pacify his useful but suspicious helper, Bleicher pulled Abwehr strings to obtain extra rations, and planned a special celebration at his flat for Christmas Day. But urgent last-minute information reached him which demanded that he should make several immediate arrests and searches. These kept him out all night on Christmas Eve.

Convinced that he was spending the night with the other woman, "the Cat" became desperate. In a semi-hysterical state of frustrated eroticism, she told the whole story of her activities to one of the leaders of the Free French in Paris!

If this story were not true, and if such serious issues had not been involved, it would be almost laughable. What happened next has all the elements of French farce.

Bleicher arrived home at his flat early on Christmas morning. He was worn out after a long night of arrests, scuffles with violent prisoners, searches of grubby apartments, repeated interrogations. All he wanted was a long peaceful day and the fine Christmas dinner that "the Cat" would cook for him. Jealous though she was, she could tell that he was speaking the truth when he said how hard he had been working. So she relented, admitted that she had misjudged him, and said how sorry she was that during the night she had betrayed all the secrets of the Paris branch of the Abwehr to a Free French agent!

Poor Bleicher nearly shot out of his chair. All his dreams of a quiet and peaceful Christmas vanished in a flash. He demanded the name and address of the agent, and the now penitent "Cat," back on Bleicher's side again, told him everything. Sternly ordering her to stay indoors and get on with cooking the dinner, he went out.

Next it was the Frenchman's turn to hear a piece of news which nearly brought on a heart-attack. His Christmas, too, was spoiled when a burly visitor announced himself as an officer of the German Abwehr who had heard all about him from Mme Carré and proposed to arrest him as a spy.

Actually, Bleicher was bluffing. If the Frenchman were arrested and interrogated by some Abwehr officer of higher rank, what he might say about the Frenchwoman with whom Bleicher was living was likely to end the promising career of a zealous Abwehr sergeant.

So Bleicher did not want to arrest the man. And he, who knew all about what the Germans did to captured spies, certainly did not want to be arrested. On this basis they arrived at a mutually satisfactory arrangement. Bleicher offered to refrain from arresting the Frenchman if he, in turn, would agree not to report "the Cat's" treachery to London. It is hardly surprising that the other agreed. After this, with slightly lighter hearts, both faced their delayed Christmas dinners.

For about the next six weeks there was not much excitement. Bleicher carried out his difficult duties, living with "the Cat" and making love to his other mistress during the day when he had a few moments to spare. He had taken over "the Cat's" radio, learned her security check, and practised her Morse 'hand-writing.' As a result of this the hitherto accurate "Cat" reports to London began to contain such misleading information as the Abwehr wanted to transmit to the British Government.

This comparatively peaceful situation continued until the 11th of February, 1942. And we have seen what happened on that day.

The escape of the *Scharnhorst* and *Gneisenau* was a major British Intelligence defeat. It had to be investigated. Could it be, after all, British Intelligence demanded, that Gall and Philippon in Brest were still loyal, and that it was the trusted "Cat" who was the traitor? Assessment of all future information from both sources was in the balance. It was worth risking an officer's life to find out. And the officer selected for this tricky assignment was one who was given the code name of "Major Richards."

The first attempt to bring "the Cat" to England failed, the motor-boat sent for her being sunk. But it is a sidelight on the efficiency of British Intelligence that, within forty-eight hours of the escape of the German battle cruisers, the officer called Major Richards, dropped by parachute, was in Paris, grilling "the Cat."

Major Richards soon formed a partially accurate assessment of a difficult situation. "The Cat's" reports during recent months had obviously been a pack of lies. But what was the extent of her guilt? Could she have been an unwitting dupe of the Abwehr?

Major Richards did not mince matters. An account of the interview has been written in German by Count Michael Soltikow. "If I thought you had lied to us purposely," said Major Richards, "I would have you shot like a dog in one of the back streets of Paris." It seems a pity that he did not do so. It would have saved a lot of subsequent trouble!

Faced with this stern interrogation, "the Cat" prevaricated. She said that she had been ill, and during the time she was unable to send her own reports, false reports in her code name must have been transmitted by a colleague, "Monsieur Jean" of the Belgian Resistance. This was at least partly true, as "Monsieur Jean" was one of the names used by Bleicher when he personally contacted Resistance groups.

To check the truth of this story, Major Richards demanded to be taken at once to "Monsieur Jean," and "the Cat" invited him to call at Bleicher's flat. She pretended afterwards to have been surprised and shocked by what Bleicher did. But unless she was a raving lunatic, she must have known that she was inviting a brave British officer to certain capture and, as he was in mufti, probable execution as a spy.

Bleicher, alias "Monsieur Jean," duly welcomed Major Richards to his flat. Then he called in a couple of his men from the next room and the British officer was arrested.

That evening Bleicher went to see his other mistress. And "the Cat"—practically insane with jealousy once more—decided to change sides yet again. So in the middle of the night she paid another visit to the Free French leader, took up her story where she had left off on Christmas Eve, and brought him up to date with the latest news of the activities of the Paris branch of the Abwehr.

Then, having spread panic in the Paris Resistance movement by describing how she had betrayed them all to the Abwehr, she went happily home. And when Bleicher came back next morning, smiling and pleasantly weary after a night with his other mistress, "the Cat" shattered him by telling him all about the latest Abwehr secrets she had spent the night passing on to the Frenchman.

And, as a professional aside, even readers who are not familiar with the work of an Intelligence assessor will sympathise with the difficulty of sorting out, in distant London, the value of reports flooding in every night from people such as "the Cat." It is not surprising that occasional mistakes were made in London.

By this time, Sergeant Bleicher realised that "the Cat" was not merely useless—she was a menace. But the inherent decency of the Abwehr man emerged. He was not a Nazi thug. He had originally promised that if "the Cat" betrayed the Interalliée group, he would ensure that she eventually escaped to England. And, despite all her betrayals of practically everybody she had ever met, Bleicher kept his promise. It was a tribute to the Abwehr tradition created by Admiral Canaris.

So Bleicher got busy with "the Cat's" radio. In her code name he reported to London that she was anxious to get to England in order to clear up any misconceptions that might have arisen concerning her recent reports. At this British Intelligence very readily agreed to make another attempt. More than ever they wanted to have a talk with "the Cat." And once they had got her they were not going to let her go!

"The Cat" was taken to a lonely part of the French coast. A speedboat from Dover crossed in the middle of the night and picked her up. And Bleicher, watching and listening from an isolated farmhouse, heaved a sigh of relief as he heard the waning roar of powerful engines taking "the Cat" out of his life for ever.

In England, "the Cat" was upset when she realised that she was not going to be treated as a heroine of the French Resistance. She was, in fact, flung into prison and persistently interrogated for months. By this time, unromantic British Intelligence officers had elicited all the details of her activities. They recommended that she be kept in custody as a war criminal.

In 1945 the British authorities handed "the Cat" back to France. She was held in Paris on no less than 130 charges of treason. It took French judicial processes—so painfully slow compared with those of Britain—four years to prepare her trial during which "the Cat" remained in prison. Then in January, 1949, she was at long last tried, found guilty, and sentenced to death: but in May of the same year her death sentence was commuted to one of imprisonment for life—and early in 1955 she was pardoned.

Released unconditionally, "the Cat" found consolation for her many-sided past in religion. But historians of Intelligence work began to piece together details of her career, and some of these have been published by authors of various nationalities. And her story was even made the basis of a film.

It is a literary convention that all women spies are brilliant and glamorous. But in the cold-blooded war of spy and counter-spy, women are almost invariably a useless burden. This subject is of some importance, and I deal with it in more detail elsewhere.

For instance, can women spies keep their secrets? The answer is that almost invariably they can not. And "the Cat," whose later exploits were nothing to be very proud of, began to talk as freely to journalists as she had talked to the agents of the

Abwehr, of Free France, and anyone else she came across.

She followed the conventional pattern set by retired spies in our day, and wrote a book. In it she tells part of her story, and a very confusing yarn it is. True, her career was so changeable and complicated that she can scarcely be blamed if she forgot some episodes and got others out of order or perspective. She describes her defection to Bleicher as casually as if it were a description of taking a dog for a walk. She claims that she did it to avoid torture for members of the Interalliée—whose names, but not addresses, were already known to him. The members of the spy cell looked at the episode differently. When "the Cat" arrived at their houses bringing an Abwehr officer with her, they could be pardoned for considering her a traitor.

"Women spies are useless except in bed, for seduction purposes," said Admiral Canaris. Most of them are too emotional and talkative. "The Cat" meant no harm, but simply could not control what the French Prosecutor called her "unbridled erotic impulses." She confirms the theory—to which, after long experience, I subscribe—that women in espionage are a mistake.

TWENTY-ONE

Eight Nazis invade the U.S.A.

DURING THE EVENING of the 14th of June, 1942, the telephone rang in the New York office of the Federal Bureau of Investigation. A bored night-duty officer answered.

"Hello?" he said.

"Is that the F.B.I.?"

"Yep!"

"Well, my name is Dasch—Georg John Dasch. I'm a German secret agent."

"Come again, buddy."

"I'm in charge of a party of German agents who landed on Long Island this morning from a U-boat. Others are landing at different points on the coast."

"Yeah? Listen, bud, you been reading too many spy stories."

"But this is the truth! I want to make a statement."

"Sure, sure! But right now I'm too busy to listen to a story from the pulp magazines. You go home, bud, and have a hot cup of coffee and a nice long sleep. You'll feel better in the morning."

The bored F.B.I. man rang off, and thereby missed his chance of promotion. For the story he refused to hear was true.

During the latter half of 1941, the F.B.I. had scooped in

some thirty German agents. This largely broke the back of the German spy organisation in the United States. One small group of experts remained underground in New York. Their existence was unknown even·to Hitler.

When the latter heard the news of those thirty arrests he became hysterical with rage. He demanded that large-scale sabotage operations be immediately undertaken in America in order to try to restore a little of Germany's lost prestige.

As head of the Abwehr—the German Forces Secret Service, of which Division II was responsible for sabotage—Admiral Canaris did not like the idea at all. In another chapter we have peeped into the twisted mind of this unusual German officer, and have seen that, by his own peculiar standards, he was a man of honour. He disapproved, for instance, of assassination. And he also disapproved of sabotage. He did not regard it as playing the decent Intelligence game.

But Canaris had to obey Hitler's orders. He gave the necessary instructions to his deputy, Major-General Erwin von Lahousen de Vivremont—the tall, bald, monocled Austrian aristocrat who was in charge of Abwehr Division II.

Under Canaris, Lahousen had trained a number of highly skilled professional saboteurs whom the Abwehr called *Vertrauensmänner*, or V-men. But before he could brief any of these experts, further panic directives flooded in from Berchtesgaden. Heinrich Himmler's Gestapo—always madly jealous of the Abwehr professionals—had dug up ten German-American Nazi Party members who had previously lived for years in the United States. It was hoped—rather optimistically—that their familiarity with the American way of life would make up for their complete ignorance of the techniques of espionage and sabotage.

Under Himmler's influence, Hitler gave Canaris no option but to accept these raw recruits. Their transport across the Atlantic in two U-boats had already been arranged.

"The Nazi amateurs have taken over," Canaris commented sadly to Lahousen—his exact words were recorded in

Lahousen's private diary. "It will cost these poor fellows their lives."

But the wily Canaris spoke with his tongue in his cheek. The unfortunate amateur V-men were certainly going to their death. But it was Canaris—not the enemy—who was going to ensure that they did so.

The plan of Canaris to sabotage his own saboteurs might not seem to fit in with what he regarded as his sense of honour. It would appear to outsiders as the rankest treachery. But Canaris had his reasons. And to his delicate but selective conscience, Nazis meant less than the lower animals he loved so much. Nazis were less than human. They were expendable.

And the astute old admiral knew much more than did the Nazi bosses about the personnel of the sabotage group.

The sabotage expedition was given the code name of Operation Pastorius. And the ten Nazi nominees went off for a sabotage course at Lahousen's special training-school at Brandenburg. It is a convenient stage at which to glance at the history of some of them.

The party was to travel in two submarines, five saboteurs with their equipment in each. In charge of one group and in general control of the whole operation was Leutnant Werner Kappe, formerly a reporter on a New York newspaper, when he had been a prominent member of the Nazi Overseas Organisation. It might seem that even the Party bosses in Berlin could have foreseen the dangers of entrusting undercover work to a man known to thousands of Americans as a fanatical Nazi.

In charge, under Kappe, of the group in the other U-boat was Georg John Dasch, who had become equally notorious in America as a Left-wing agitator. In 1941 he had suddenly announced that he was going home to Germany, although his wife was ill at the time. He travelled via Moscow, where he disappeared for several days on mysterious business that was never satisfactorily explained. This was not known to the often staggeringly incompetent Gestapo. But it was known to Admiral Canaris.

Another of the amateur V-men was Ernst Peter Burger, an S.S. colonel who had been imprisoned by the Gestapo for criticising Nazi atrocities, and could hardly have been regarded as completely reliable material.

The training course was completed by May, 1942, during which month the ten V-men arrived in Paris with quantities of explosives and American currency. Whilst awaiting their sailing orders they stayed at an hotel reserved for German officers.

They were very different types from the quiet, shrewd, efficient operators that Canaris usually employed, and they proceeded to have a good time. There were some wild parties, enlivened by the presence of rowdy prostitutes.

One midnight fracas, started by a girl who thought she had been underpaid, was so violent that a number of pyjama-clad Wehrmacht officers rushed out of their bedrooms with loaded revolvers, convinced that British paratroops had seized the hotel. That Paris *poule* must have been tough.

Then one of the V-men developed conscientious objections to the whole operation, and had to be sent back to Germany in disgrace. Another contracted syphilis, which upset the U-boat crew, who did not relish the idea of living for weeks in cramped quarters with the patient. So he, too, was sent back to Germany with a black mark. Other incidents included fights with hotel barmen which brought the eight surviving V-men much publicity and more unpopularity. Lahousen was watching the progress of his pupils, and his reports to Canaris must have made the old admiral smile.

It certainly might have seemed that some hidden hand was busy sabotaging the saboteurs. They decided to make a last-minute check of their funds—the very considerable sum in dollars which had been issued for their expenses in America. It was as well that they did so.

The first few packets of bills they examined were mere waste-paper—ancient dollar notes that had long ago become obsolete and been withdrawn from circulation. Many others were

of fairly recent issue, but bore date-stamps of Japanese banks!
It would have been suicidal to try to pass them in a country still
smarting from the effects of Pearl Harbour.

This deadly stuff had to be dumped, of course, and new
American currency to be rushed from Germany. And the
saboteurs may have prayed that their explosives were not as
faulty as their funds.

It was in the last week of May, 1942, that the German
submarines U-170 and U-202 at last sailed from a French port,
each carrying four saboteurs and their equipment. It could not
have been a very enjoyable trip for the V-men as they huddled
in their cramped quarters, very seasick, and the U-boats, packed
with explosives, plunged and rocked under attack from British
depth-charges.

The first to be put ashore were the U-202 party, under the
leadership of Dasch, at about one o'clock in the morning of
the 14th of June. Dasch had chosen a spot he knew on a lonely
part of the shore of Long Island. But by what might have been
a disastrous error of navigation they actually surfaced miles
away, near a coastguard station.

Fortunately the night was misty, and although they were
spotted and challenged by a coastguard, Dasch managed to
delay action with bluff. So the others were able to bury their
equipment in the sand. They had been instructed to leave no
traces of their landing. They interpreted this order somewhat
loosely, leaving such oddments by the water's edge as empty
German wine-bottles and cigarette cartons, a vest and part of
a German naval uniform.

The party caught an early train to New York and proceeded
to spend some of their expenses in shops—which were better
stocked than those of poverty-stricken Nazi Berlin. And no
suspicion seems to have been aroused when Dasch absent-
mindedly gave the Nazi salute and shouted "Heil Hitler!" as he
entered a drugstore. The Marx brothers could have made
quite a film out of Operation Pastorius.

By this time the operation had cost the Germans months of

high-level planning, long training courses for ten men and an enormous sum of precious dollars in expenses. In addition, two U-boats and their crews had been subjected to grave risk of loss. But the first four saboteurs were now safe on American soil and, back in Berlin, Lahousen began to expect reports of deadly damage to war factories. What Canaris expected was precisely what, in due course, happened.

As leader of the Long Island party, Dasch wasted no time. During their first evening in New York he had a conference with the S.S. Colonel Burger. What was said would have made Canaris give a slow nod and smile, but would have given Hitler one of his most violent fits of frenzy. Briefly, Dasch frankly stated that he was a madly anti-Hitler Socialist, that he hated "those Nazi bastards," and that he intended to go straight to the F.B.I. and betray the whole operation.

Dasch went on to accuse Burger of secretly wanting to retaliate on the Nazis who had imprisoned him for daring to criticise their cruelties, and suggested that Burger had left those highly incriminating oddments on the Long Island shore with the deliberate object of attracting suspicion. Burger hedged. He does not seem to have disagreed, but after one dose of Gestapo treatment he was naturally suspicious that Dasch might be an *agent provocateur*.

As soon as the two double-crossers had parted, Dasch went to a telephone and called the New York office of the F.B.I. We have seen that the reception of his startling news was disappointing. So he took time off to consider his next move, and spent a day or two looking up some old Socialist friends and giving them a good laugh with the inside story of Operation Pastorius.

Meanwhile the Long Island coastguard who challenged Dasch had told his somewhat delayed story. The clues by the shore had been found, and after the New York police had been asked to check a laundry mark on the vest, the news at last reached the F.B.I. Security forces were given a panic warning that German troops were being landed for an invasion of the United States.

Then, with every inch of the Atlantic seaboard being, in theory, closely watched, U-170 safely landed the second Pastorius party unobserved in the middle of the night near Jacksonville on the Florida coast. According to one account, they were interrupted by a patrol whilst busy burying their explosives, but the coastguards did not think the midnight proceedings at all odd and went home to bed. Or perhaps they did not want F.B.I. complaints about their intrusion into a security case.

On the 18th of June, the fourth day after he had been landed, Dasch was in Washington and made another attempt to tell his story to the F.B.I. This time he secured an interview, and, in order to prove that he was not fabricating a story in the hope of a reward, he produced $80,000, which he had in his pocket for expenses. In a land where money talks, that gesture was accepted as clear proof of the purity of his motives.

From details supplied by Dasch, the F.B.I. were able to round up the other seven V-men, and the American radio broadcast to the world a somewhat exaggerated story of the deadly peril of the sabotage offensive, and how Operation Pastorius had been foiled by the unsleeping U.S. Secret Service. The story did not please everybody. Dasch was furious because he was kept in prison and treated not as a hero but as a spy. Hitler was on the verge of apoplexy at what he called "this appalling catastrophe," and demanded explanations and scape-goats.

The Gestapo chiefs—always jealous of the Abwehr—combined public indignation with private glee at what they regarded, rather prematurely, as a major defeat for Canaris. And the old admiral was summoned to Berchtesgaden for what his enemies believed to be dimissal and disgrace.

But Canaris was unperturbed. He readily agreed with Hitler that Operation Pastorius had, indeed, been an appalling catastrophe, and said that it was a great pity that his own Abwehr men had not been employed, although he entirely agreed that the men whom Himmler had insisted should be used had all appeared to be loyal members of the Nazi Party.

Hitler glared with bloodshot eyes at Himmler, who had no answer ready. "You should have used Jews!" Hitler spluttered at last to Canaris.

An interesting sidelight on Operation Pastorius is that as a result Canaris was able to rescue a number of Jews from the clutches of the Gestapo. He smuggled them abroad in groups, saying that he was using them on dangerous missions—by order of the Führer. Himmler blinked his cold blue eyes in frustrated rage, but could not do anything about it.

In August, 1942, the eight V-men of Operation Pastorius were tried and found guilty. All were sentenced to death, but only six were executed. Burger's sentence was commuted to life imprisonment on the grounds that he was not a hired civilian spy, but was under orders as an officer in the armed forces of his country. For his services in betraying the operation, the sentence on Dasch was commuted to thirty years' imprisonment.

In the spring of 1948 Dasch and Burger were released and deported to Germany. And Dasch's subsequent movements are not without interest. He went to the Russian Zone of Berlin and contacted the local Communist Party. But he suffered the fate of most double agents who survive—he found that he was trusted by nobody. His premature release from prison made the East German Communist Party suspect that he had been bribed with the offer of freedom if he would become a spy for the Americans. So with no future in Intelligence work on either side of the Iron Curtain, Dasch opted for a quiet life and became a prosperous businessman.

That is the story of Operation Pastorius as known to most students of Intelligence work—as available from American sources and from the private diaries of Colonel Lahousen.

But is it really possible that the head of the German Secret Service should have deliberately sabotaged his own saboteurs? Why should he have done so? And how? Here is the story behind the headlines.

We are back on the old theme—'the riddle of Canaris,' which is really no riddle at all. The undisputed fact that Canaris was anti-Hitler did not mean that he was pro-British. He was simply pro-German, in the same way that, in 1940, a British officer who was anti-Chamberlain was not necessarily pro-Mosley.

Canaris opposed Hitler not because he wanted Germany to lose the war, but because he wanted her to win it. Canaris believed that the direction of the German war effort would be better in the hands of the old professional-officer class then in the hands of the superstitious Austrian upstart. And he may have been right.

At the time when Hitler insisted on launching Operation Pastorius, Canaris was busy with an operation likely to have more far-reaching effects in the United States than sporadic attacks on war factories by isolated and comparatively useless amateurs. Canaris was involved in nothing less than the projected long-range bombardment of New York.

During the war we had very practical experience of the V.1 and the V.2. At its end we learned that German experiments had been advanced as far as a V.10. Of these types, the V.4 rocket was particularly designed for the bombardment of the United States. It was in effect an early and primitive Polaris—without an atomic warhead, of course. It was to be launched from far out at sea, and to strike the seaboard cities of the East Coast.

It was capable of travelling far greater distances than the V.2. But it suffered from a defect of the earlier model—it was not accurate even within a distance of two or three miles. German technicians, unable to ensure accuracy at the firing-point, began to study the prospects of doing so in the reception areas. At last they devised a method of guiding V.4 rockets to their objectives—and the task of installing the 'home-finders' was handed over to Canaris.

A group of his men were already at work in New York when the war ended. Had it continued for a few months longer,

American cities would have experienced a serious bombardment. Canaris agents were not the absurdly amateurish rabble used in Operation Pastorius: they were experts. Their task was to install tiny short-wave radio transmitters on skyscraper roofs. These would send out beams which would cause the rockets to 'home' on to the skyscrapers.

The question Canaris had had to ask himself was: What effect might Operation Pastorius have on the fantastic but terribly practicable rocket scheme?

There were two possibilities. The fumbling V-men of Operation Pastorius were wretched material, but they might for a time have had some luck. Their especial objective was aluminium plants—damage there would have seriously affected the manufacture of aircraft. One or two successful acts of sabotage would have prompted the F.B.I. to a new pitch of keenness and activity, and so made the task of Canaris's men far more difficult.

The other and more likely possibility was that the Pastorius operators might be caught before they had done any damage and exposed as incompetents. There would be a wave of relief among Americans. Spy-mania would be deflated. And the Canaris radio-men would be able to get on with their work among a populace who thought that they were safe from German agents. So it appeared to the twisted mind of Canaris that the betrayal of Operation Pastorius was a patriotic duty. And if a few Nazis died, the old admiral could scarcely have cared less. He preferred dogs, anyway.

But the betrayal would have to be carefully planned. Canaris could hardly send a friendly warning to President Roosevelt! The ideal plan would be for one of the Pastorius leaders to go voluntarily to the F.B.I. and make a statement. This would have the incidental effect of bringing the Nazi Party into disrepute as a hotbed of potential traitors—and this is what, in effect, happened.

But which leader could Canaris approach? He made a careful study of the histories of the ten original Pastorius recruits.

Werner Kappe, a fanatical Nazi, had to be ruled out. But what about Dasch?

The Abwehr was a much more efficient organisation than the Gestapo, and Canaris knew far more about Dasch than did Himmler. He knew that Dasch had a Left-wing record in America, and he wondered why such a man should have been so ready to return to Nazi Germany, especially when that meant leaving a seriously ill wife. And—above all—he wondered what Dasch had been doing during that lost week-end in Moscow.

The obvious answer was that Dasch was an agent of the Russian Secret Service who had been instructed to penetrate the Abwehr, and sabotage its plans. And nobody was more surprised and delighted than he when he reached Berlin and was secretly contacted by the chief of the Abwehr himself. And when the old Admiral hinted at what he knew about Dasch, and hinted at the painful results to him if Canaris should communicate what he knew to the Gestapo, it became clear to Dasch that if he obeyed the old Admiral's instructions to betray Operation Pastorius, he would get the best of both worlds. He would have a bonus from Moscow for sabotaging an Abwehr operation; he would have a bonus from Canaris; he would be back in America with his ailing wife; and the American nation would, he hoped, treat him as a heroic and public-spirited informer—a hope which was not, in the end, fulfilled.

This is not being wise after the event. These are not theories but facts. It is unfortunate that even now there are many war-time secrets which it might imperil agents' lives to reveal in too much detail.

But it is safe to quote one source of information which has been revealed. That source is M. Jacques Bergier, war-time chief of the famous Marco Polo group of French Resistance, whose agents stole documents that uncovered many German secrets. M. Bergier's Paris agents got on to the muddy trail of the drunken and indiscreet Pastorius men in that Paris hotel, and soon knew all about Dasch. M. Bergier mentions no names, but has given sufficient details to identify this man who, he says in so many words, was "the personal agent of Admiral Canaris."

Intelligence work is essentially dirty work, and its pawns are expendable. In some operations I have been told that they must be carried out "at any cost in money or human life." An Intelligence officer must believe, at least in war-time, that the end justifies the means.

In Operation Pastorius a group of agents were sent deliberately to their death in order that another Abwehr operation might have more chance of success. It is not a nice story—it just happens to be a true one.

TWENTY-TWO

The Murder of Admiral Darlan

ADMIRAL DARLAN'S HEADQUARTERS were in the Palais d'Été, on the outskirts of Algiers. His presence there at the time of the Allied landings in November, 1942, was entirely fortuitous—he had flown over to see his son, stricken abruptly with polio. The subsequent 'adoption' by the Americans of the activist member of the Vichy Government aroused great argument. Eisenhower's outlook was sane, however: Darlan could rally French North Africa to the Allies, and rescue the French fleet from the clutches of the Nazis, and therefore save thousands of American and British lives.

On the morning of December the 24th a youth named Bonnier de la Chapelle walked to the Palais. There he asked to see a friend who was employed there. While inside the building he took the opportunity to have a quick look round.

He returned in the afternoon, and again asked to see his friend. Issued with a pass, he made instead for Admiral Darlan's office. The Admiral's girl secretary explained that her chief was out.

"I'll wait," said the youth.

The girl took a cigarette, but had no matches. He produced a box from his pocket, lit her cigarette, and gave her the box—

an unusually gallant gesture in a town where matches were worth their weight in silver. Then he strolled casually up and down the corridor awaiting Darlan's return.

The Admiral arrived, with his aide-de-camp. The youth touched him gently on the arm and addressed him. As Darlan turned, de la Chapelle fired three shots into his chest. The A.D.C. was the next victim, shot in the legs.

The youth ran to the window and dropped into the court-yard. But the guards had been aroused by the shots and the screams of the girl. De la Chapelle was arrested.

Darlan died on the operating-table an hour later. The senior French officers in Algiers promptly constituted themselves into a court-martial. The youth was condemned to death.

Then followed the most extraordinary feature of the episode. If a man commits murder, he expects to be punished if he is caught, but Bonnier de la Chapelle was exhilarated and confident. "I have liberated France!" he cried. "They will not shoot me!"

But they did, at dawn the following day. Until the very last moment the youth protested his confidence. He went to his fate quite convinced that the firing-squad would use blank cartridges!

Why? And why did he kill Darlan? To answer these questions we must turn back for a few weeks.

German records speak of Hitler's consternation at the news of Darlan's defection to the Allies. The aged Pétain was no more than a figurehead: Darlan was the practical man who had been the real ruler of Vichy France, and the Nazis had believed him to be dependable. But he was a Frenchman, and seized the opportunity offered by the Allied capture of Algiers to return to his original side.

Hitler was furious. He ordered the immediate occupation of Vichy France—and the seizure of the French fleet at Toulon. In the latter objective he failed. The sailors obeyed Darlan, and the ships which could not escape scuttled themselves.

"What can we do with this traitor Darlan?" Hitler savagely hissed to Himmler, hastily summoned to the Führer's presence.

"We can remove him—he does not deserve to live."

The decision was made without argument. But a few hours later Hitler's natural cunning reasserted itself.

"It must not appear that we dealt with him," he said. "Make it seem to be the work of the Gaullists. Then the French will quarrel among themselves once more."

"That is a brilliant idea, *mein Führer*. I will see to it."

The following day Himmler's Algiers agent received a signal via Italy. It was brief, and without argument. It merely ordered the assassination of Darlan, with the blame to be thrown on de Gaulle.

Algiers at the time was a confused madhouse. The city and province were under Vichy control, but most of the junior officers of the garrison favoured General de Gaulle. Political as well as military factions wrangled, and in the confusion the Allied landing was made without serious loss.

A German resident agent in Algiers had an inappropriate name, Douce. He was Italian, but passed himself off as Maltese. Before he settled down in an import-export business a few years before the war, he had been a hypnotist touring Italian small towns and villages in one-night stands, earning his keep by inducing mesmerised provincials to make fools of themselves.

He received Himmler's order without enthusiasm. He was more at home with intrigue than with murder. But he knew that the order must be obeyed. He appreciated that the Germans must not appear to be concerned with the death of Darlan— and he was quite determined that Xavier Douce should not be implicated either.

He deputed two of his sub-agents to discover a suitable candidate. The process could not be rushed. So he began to receive almost daily reminders—he did not know it at the time, but Hitler was grumbling impatiently to Himmler about the delay.

But one evening a sub-agent reported. "There's a youth named Bonnier de la Chappelle. He's a hysterical type, and very anti-Darlan. I think you could work on him."

"Me?"

"Yes. I'm not going to do it. There'll be a big stink after this —I intend to keep clear of it."

The man was emphatic. Later, he escaped trial because his part in the affair—by his own account—had been trivial.

Prompted by the urgent messages from Berlin, Douce reluctantly prepared for action. Yet again the affair could not be hurried. He had to make the youth's acquaintance and gain his confidence, which would take a little time. Douce hoped that his interim report would calm Himmler's impatience.

But at last the opportunity arrived. Douce offered de la Chapelle a lift in his car—old, but well supplied with Black Market petrol. (The Black Market price at that time was one bottle of Scotch whisky for one four-gallon jerrycan of petrol.) He halted at a wooden hut along the coast. Before the Allied landing he had used it for amorous adventures: he had a possessive and jealous wife.

He produced drinks, with which he plied his visitor. He was studying the youth intently; the boy was certainly of an unstable type, easily influenced. It should be easy to dominate him. But would he fail at the critical moment?

Douce had become an Algerian Frenchman for the purpose of the enterprise. He offered a cigarette to de la Chapelle, and handed him a box of matches.

"Keep them. I've got plenty more."

After a few minutes of desultory talk about Algiers, Douce began to lead the conversation deftly from the Allied invasion to the sorrows of France.

"And now the Germans have occupied the rest of France!" he went on bitterly. "All because of that traitor Darlan! He collaborated with the Nazis, and now he brings this tragedy to France. He is a devil!"

"Yes!"

"Surely the Americans and British do not trust him! Now, de Gaulle—there is a patriot, for you! He loves France—he will restore her ancient glory——"

"But he has no authority!"

"The people of France——"

"*They* have no authority!" the youth persisted. "All authority is vested in the King!"

So the fellow was a Royalist! Douce changed his line of argument abruptly.

"But did you not hear?" he cried. "De Gaulle is a secret Royalist! Once the Germans are beaten he will restore the monarchy!"

"You don't mean that!"

"I do! I *know* it!" He was gazing at de la Chapelle with the staring eyes which had once hypnotised Italian yokels. "This is the whole purpose of his stand. He dare not announce it yet, for we have opponents. Is not our King of the House of Lorraine—and was it an accident that de Gaulle chose the cross of Lorraine as his standard?"

"Of course! I never thought of that!"

"Never fear. In the moment of victory King Jean will be crowned in Rheims Cathedral. What glory for France! What grandeur! France again the leader of Europe! And what a future for us who have foreseen these things!"

"You are a Royalist?" the youth enquired.

"Of course. And you?"

"Of course."

"We must seize the moment. Darlan must die—that is the first step, absolutely essential. Then de Gaulle will step into his place—as a potemrary viceroy for the King! I would manage the affair myself, but I am too well known—I would never be able to get near Darlan. But—do you know why I made your acquaintance?"

"No."

"Do you believe in the occult?"

"Well, I hardly know."

"I do." Douce launched himself into one of his professional expositions, filled with long words and learned names. It may have been meaningless, but it sounded impressive. Before the force of his personality and the piercing gaze of his eyes, young Bonnier was immensely affected, listening avidly.

"And then I had a dream," Douce was saying. "My messages often came to me in dreams. I saw the coronation of Charles VII in the cathedral of Rheims. There were the nobles and the knights, the archbishops, the people, and all the panoply of power. And beside the king stood a slight figure in silver armour——"

"Joan of Arc!" The youth's eyes shone almost as fiercely as those of his companion.

"Yes. And in that moment it was revealed to me that a new Joan of Arc would arise—but this time the saviour of France would not be a girl, but a youth! *You* Bonnier!"

"Me? *Mon Dieu!*"

"Yes. The scene changed. Our own King Jean stood by the altar. All about was glorious colour, and the people wept in their joy. And you, Bonnier, were the one who stood beside the King, supporting his right arm. You, Bonnier! Then the King went out to the cheers of the populace. But the cheers for Bonnier de la Chapelle were just as prolonged. Statues were planned all over France to the honour of the young man who had struck the vital blow—had laid the foundation for the recovery of the grandeur of France. The King announced the grant of nobility to his saviour—to you! All this I saw—all this I learned from supernatural sources. So I come to you, Bonnier—will you keep your appointment with destiny?"

"But how—how?" The youth was confused with thoughts of glory, his face flushed with the tremendous prospects Douce had outlined.

"Darlan must die—we have agreed that; the first step. You are not known—you could easily get into the Palais d'Été——"

"I have a friend who works there."

"Did I not tell you that this was ordained?" Douce cried

excitedly. "You will go to see your friend—and encounter Darlan instead. Then you will strike the fateful blow—for France."

"How?"

"Here is a pistol. I have long preserved it for this moment. It was blessed for this holy deed before the altar of Rheims."

He had won: he knew that he had won. Bonnier was intoxicated by the vision of glory. But Douce's years on tour had made him a practical psychologist. The exuberance of the moment might subside. Bonnier might revert to very practical considerations.

"My dream grew confused," Douce went on. "You escaped, of course—did you not stand beside the King in the cathedral of Rheims? But I could not see—maybe you did not escape immediately, but were rescued by your friends later. For the death of Darlan was greeted with intense joy. The people rose instinctively to clear out all Darlan's friends. De Gaulle assumed temporary power—on behalf of the King. And Bonnier was the hero of the hour! He had braved danger. Yes. I saw one episode..." Douce's imagination had served him well, but now he borrowed an item from the legend of Mata Hari. "A young man is led out to execution. But his face is wild with ecstasy. He has not failed his destiny. He stands by a post. When they try to blindfold him, he shakes his head with a proud smile. The soldiers raise their rifles: he faces them bravely—even happily. The command: 'Fire!' Twelve rifles bark—but the youth does not fall. His friends have been active—the rifles were loaded with blank cartridges. The soldiers see the youth's escape as an omen from Heaven. Wild with joy they rush to release him. Without the prison yard, a great throng awaits him, cheering and praying to God. And, I tell you, the youth who saved France—who served the King—was you, Bonnier de la Chapelle!"

The youth stood up, his eyes bright with ecstatic emotion. "Give me the pistol," he said.

TWENTY-THREE

The Death of General Sikorski

"What's the time, Flight?" asked an R.A.F. air mechanic.

"23.07."

"They'll be off soon."

"Yes. The engines are running very sweetly. These Liberators are good kites."

"But isn't the runway a bit on the short side for them?"

"Oh, plenty of others have got off."

True though this was, the airman's query was justified. Flat land is at a premium in Gibraltar. The racecourse had been commandeered as an airfield, and a runway had been formed across the narrow isthmus connecting the Rock with the Spanish mainland, and prolonged over an artificial dyke into the Bay.

"Lot of V.I.P.'s on board, aren't there?"

"Yes," said the Flight Sergeant. "General Sikorski, the Polish leader, and his staff. They're on their way back from the Middle East, and—look, they're ready. Clear the chocks."

A minute later the Liberator began to move forward. It gained speed rapidly, and took off from the runway with ample room to spare. Its navigation lights showed clearly in the darkness as it flew out over the Bay.

"Well, that's O.K. Is it, though? She's not climbing—hell, she's going down. Why doesn't—he's switched the engines off! God, she's crashed! Sound the alarm!"

He shouted another order, and searchlights began to play on the water. By the time he had gained the end of the runway, there was enough light to show the wrecked aircraft about half a mile out to sea.

A lifeboat was already on its way. By some freak of chance the pilot had been flung clear of the wreck. Although he was unconscious, his Mae West supported him until he was picked up. All the other occupants of the aircraft were dead.

This was a major disaster. General Sikorski was perhaps the one man who might have saved Poland from its unhappy fate. He had succeeded in making an arrangement with Stalin and, had he lived, he might even have persuaded Stalin to keep his promises. "A great Polish patriot and staunch ally," said Winston Churchill. "His death in the air crash at Gibraltar was one of the heaviest strokes we have sustained . . . He was the symbol and the embodiment of that spirit which has borne the Polish nation through centuries of sorrow and is unquenchable by agony."

An official enquiry was held into the tragedy. The pilot, an experienced Czech serving with the R.A.F., explained that the take-off had been normal, but that when he sought to gain height the elevator control had jammed. Such mishaps were rare, but were not entirely unknown already. Realising that he faced a crash, the pilot had shouted a warning and switched off the engines so as to lessen the impact when the aircraft struck the sea.

The enquiry dismissed the suggestion of sabotage, which was naturally raised, but in the absence of the wreck—which had sunk in deep water—if was unable to decide on the exact cause of the crash. It must have been an accident, the commission decided.

The Nazis proclaimed a different story to the world. The

crash had been engineered by the British Secret Service! Churchill had found Sikorski 'inconvenient,' and he had ordered his elimination.

Evidently one of our allies was prepared to believe Dr Goebbels's absurdities. Squadron Leader E. Prchal, the pilot of the doomed Liberator, has explained how after the war he was approached by a Communist agent who had been instructed to get direct evidence from him—to prove that the crash was an act of sabotage by the British Intelligence Service.

"I realised that a Communist cannot understand that an eminent personality could die a natural death or as a result of a real accident. In the People's Democracies such a death is very unusual."

But after the war innumerable German secrets were revealed. Major-General Erwin von Lahousen, deputy chief of the Abwehr, and second to Admiral Canaris, had kept a diary. Certain notes suggest that Sikorski had been killed as a result of the activities of Nazi agents, who managed to put sugar into the aircraft's petrol.

But this disagrees with the known facts. All four engines had functioned perfectly, and it was clear from the pilot's evidence that the trouble lay in the elevator control, which had jammed at a critical moment.

Yet this does not dispose of the whole of Lahousen's claims. It is quite possible that when he ordered the sabotage of the aircraft—for General Sikorski was certainly 'inconvenient' to the Germans—he suggested the well-known device of putting sugar in the petrol-tank. Later evidence, however, suggests that his agents had ideas of their own.

The headquarters of the German Abwehr in Spain was actually next door to the British Embassy in Madrid. There Dr Hans Höberlein sat at his desk in communication by radio telephone with his agents in eight listening centres. Two of these were in La Linea and Algeciras, adjacent to Gibraltar.

Höberlein happened to be away when an urgent message

came from Berlin on July the 1st, 1943. General Sikorski was to fly from Cairo to London, calling at Gibraltar on the way. It was believed that his Middle Eastern visit had revealed the possibilities of much wider activities by the Polish forces, and he would advance far-reaching proposals when he got to London. He must be prevented from doing so.

A German officer named Weber flew south to an air-strip near Algeciras. He had already summoned his agent at La Linea by radio telephone.

La Linea is a peculiar town. It is Spanish—but is economically dependent on Gibraltar! Every day thousands of men cross over to the Rock, most of them to work in the Naval Dockyard.

It was not difficult for the Germans to find a few dedicated Falangists among them, and to convert them into Nazi spies. Some of these had already been unmasked. The British Secret Service does not sleep. Some of the foremen in the Naval Dockyard were actually British counter-espionage officers.

Weber outlined the task to his subordinate from La Linea— there is some reason to believe that the man's name was Brosch, but this has not been confirmed.

"Now, who have you got?" Weber asked. "In a previous report you mentioned a man named Cuenca."

"Yes. But he's already booked. He's working on the project for blowing up the tunnel under the dockyard."

"Oh, yes, I remember. How is that going?"

"Very well. Cuenca works in a Gibraltar fruitshop which gets its supplies from a wholesaler in La Linea. Cuenca fetches them, and he hides our small but powerful time-bombs in bunches of bananas. He's never been stopped at the frontier—he's already got a good supply of bombs stored at the shop. After another dozen journeys we expect that he will have enough to blow up the tunnel."

(He did. But his chief did not know that Señor Luiz Lopez Cordon Cuenca was already under observation by British spy-catchers. A month later he was arrested, and on August the 31st

1943, he was condemned to death. The English hangman had to be flown out to Gibraltar for the execution.)

"Right," said Weber. "No, you mustn't take Cuenca off that operation. Who else have you got?"

"Well, I wonder—I was grooming the fellow for another job—to blow up the airfield control tower."

"This is more urgent. Who is the man?"

"His name is Gredos. He lives in La Linea, but works in Gibraltar. So does his sister, who is a sort of amateur prostitute. I thought of the idea when Gredos told me that she had become entangled with an American airman—a Private First-class who fancies himself as a great lover. He goes round to the girl's room on every night off. Apparently, after making love he is very sleepy."

"I begin to see!"

"Looking ahead, I instructed Gredos to make a trial. This he did. While the American was snoring in the girl's bed, Gredos borrowed his uniform and walked the streets of Gibraltar for an hour. The trial was very successful, and has given him confidence."

"He speaks English?"

"He speaks a language that will pass for American. It was after dark, and he ran into a picket patrolling the streets. He talked as little as possible, showed the American's papers, and aroused no suspicion whatever."

"Good. I see possibilities."

"There is only one snag. This Liberator bomber from Cairo may touch down only to refuel—an hour at the most. And the American may not be with the girl."

"She must inveigle him. I have had a signal that the Liberator will arrive at Gibraltar on July the 3rd, and will leave late the same night. So your girl must act—quickly."

"Right. I'll see to that. Now, what is Gredos to do?"

"I will brief him. I was an engineer before I took on my present job. And I was studying the plans of a Liberator as I flew down. We are quite well informed. Get hold of Gredos at once. Let him fix things with his sister, and then bring him here."

One part of the plan was excellent. With so small a space available, the airfield at Gibraltar could scarcely be enclosed—the main road to Spain runs straight through it! The airfield served the Americans as well as the British, and there was a maintenance company of American mechanics in the camp. Hence a man in American uniform would attract no attention.

Weber was pleased with his briefing of Gredos. The man was intelligent and confident. He went into Gibraltar to warn his sister, and returned to Weber near La Linea.

"Now the method," Weber began. "In American uniform you will have no difficulty in getting into the airfield."

"None whatever."

"As soon as the Liberator lands, it will be refuelled and serviced."

"Yes."

"The suggestion was that you should put sugar in the petrol-tanks, but that would be impossible—there would be half a dozen men about at the time. But during the servicing things should be easier. Now the servicing crew will be R.A.F."

"I suppose so."

"It will. So your first task is to acquire an R.A.F. uniform."

"Steal one?"

"No! Buy one—in Gibraltar. You can buy anything there. Dirty it. Then, once you are in the camp, put it on. If you are challenged, it is not impossible that the R.A.F. should ask American advice about a Liberator."

"No. I see."

"But I doubt if that will arise. In the servicing process there is a lot of coming and going—each man is a specialist, and looks over only one part. You should be able to slip in among them—and be the last to enter the aircraft. Have your story all ready."

"Right. I will rehearse it."

"Do so. In English! Now, look at this plan. This is the elevator control. It fits into a steel socket, rather like the gear lever of a car."

"I see."

"Around its base is a tiny space for leverage—it moves in its socket backwards and forwards."

"Yes."

"Here are some tiny pieces of metal. All you have to do is to ram one of these firmly between the control rod and its socket. A mechanic has made a mock-up of the elevator control—in tin, for quickness. But it will do for you to practice on."

He gave Gredos a two-hour rehearsal. By that time he was confident that the man could identify the elevator control and jam it within thirty seconds of entering the aircraft.

Considering the short notice, Weber thought that he had done very well. True, the fact that an agent like Gredos was on the spot was very helpful—and the fact that he had a sister was even more so!

But next day he got a shock. Gredos's sister had had a message from her lover that he would be with her on Sunday evening. By that time the Liberator would be in England.

She could not get into touch with the American to invite him for the Saturday—to his astonishment, Weber found that the girl did not know her lover's surname! She knew him only as Dixie.

Very well. Gredos was expendable, after all. He must wear R.A.F. overalls over his own clothes. True, if he were caught he would be unmasked, but that would not matter if he had completed his task.

"You can't appear in daylight out of uniform," Weber instructed Gredos. "Wait till after dark—within an hour of take-off there will be plenty of people coming and going— baggage men, and the like. Slip into the aircraft then."

For the first time Gredos seemed somewhat dubious. But later came news which restored his confidence—General Sikorski had decided to delay his departure by twenty-four hours. He wished to despatch a series of signals to the Polish units he had visited in the Middle East.

So the original plan was now possible. It worked perfectly. While the American slumbered in the arms of his lover, Gredos borrowed his uniform, entered the airfield, and donned R.A.F. overalls. The Liberator was one of half-a-dozen aircraft on the tarmac. There was an armed guard, but Gredos's disguise was most convincing.

Sure enough, there was much coming and going. A British officer—Colonel Cazalet, M.P., Liaison officer between the British and Polish forces, entered the Liberator to give it a final look over. As he left, for the moment accompanied by a Polish officer, Gredos ran up the steps confidently. His briefing served him well. In little more than the estimated time he had rammed a thin strip of metal into the socket of the elevator control, hammering it home with a pair of pliers. Then he hurried back into the town to hand back the borrowed uniform to his sister. He had neither been challenged nor spoken a word during the whole of his mission.

Weber watched the take-off through night-glasses from the Spanish side of the Gibraltar frontier. He saw the crash, but waited until he had seen the bodies brought ashore. His subsequent signal reporting success was relayed to Berlin. Major-General von Lahousen had no more details, and assumed that his own suggestion has been adopted.

Yet a little consideration should have shown him that he was wrong. Sugared petrol would have needed some time to take effect, and the Liberator had crashed immediately on take-off.

The experienced pilot was quite certain. "The take-off was normal. The plane reacted as usual. At 300 feet, with the under-carriage up, I straightened the plane. Then I felt a sudden jar—the elevator control was completely jammed ... There was no doubt that we must crash in a few seconds. I shouted 'Attention! Crashing!' and switched off the engines. Then I felt a terrific impact, and lost consciousness."

The vital parts of the controls were never recovered from the sea.[1] The official enquiry decided that the tragedy was an accident simply because no contrary evidence was available. The enquiry was only technical. A statesman would have been more difficult to persuade. He would have argued that the death of Sikorski was just *too* convenient to the Nazis. So the true story has lain for twenty years embedded in the mud off Gibraltar until today when information from German and Spanish sources makes this reconstruction possible.

[1] Though Commander "Buster" Crabb did manage to retrieve Sikorski's secret papers from the wrecked aircraft.

TWENTY-FOUR

The Other Side of Cicero

"OPERATION CICERO" has become one of the best known spy stories of the war.

It was related in a book by L. C. Moyzisch an attaché at the German Embassy in Ankara, the Turkish capital, and caused an immediate sensation. Later it achieved celluloid immortality. The case was outside my own province, but I heard about it from friends who were involved in it. It had several features of remarkable interest.

The British Ambassador in Ankara had a valet, an Albanian named Elyesa Basna, a very competent servant. In October, 1943, Basna established contact with Moyzisch through Herr Jenke, Counsellor at the German Embassy, and brother-in-law of Ribbentrop. Basna had once been Jenke's valet: he now offered to sell documents from the British Embassy safe—at a price. He asked £20,000 for a specimen batch he had brought with him.

These documents startled Moyzisch and the German Ambassador, von Papen. Coded cables flowed to and from Berlin, and the purchase was authorised. The Albanian's name was not known, and he was given the code name Cicero.

At least there would be no difficulty about paying the

large sums he demanded. The Germans had collected a number
of suitable men from their concentration camps and had set them
to making forged English notes. The idea was to drop them over
Britain in such quantities as to induce inflation. Some of this
money could now be used to pay Cicero: he might be a useful
spy, but he did not know a genuine British note from a forgery.

Cicero's method was simple. Evidently a skilled burglar, he
had been able to secure access to the safe in the British Ambassador's bedroom, where confidential papers were often kept.
He stole nothing: he simply took out certain documents,
photographed them, put them back in the safe, and took the
film to Moyzisch.

The Germans would certainly have got value for their
money—even if the notes had been genuine. Cicero supplied
copies of directives from the Foreign Office to the Ambassador,
of a report on a conference between Eden, Cordell Hull, and
Molotov in Moscow, and many other important subjects.

Yet all this precious information was wasted. The Nazis,
like the Russians, had too many espionage organisations: they
quarrelled, and spied on one another.[1]

Cicero's photographs were of great value to the German
Secret Service, providing as they did lengthy and invaluable
specimens from which they could break the British diplomatic
code. But because of the internecine quarrel, the vital political
information they contained was scarcely used: one group held
that the information was genuine, the other, that it could not
be trusted.

---

[1] The German Foreign Office had its own Intelligence Service run by
Ribbentrop. Then there was (a) the *Abwehr*, the Army spy and counter-
spy organisation, under Admiral Canaris, (b) the *Nachrichtendienst* (literally
Information Service) run by the notorious S.S. General Kaltenbrunner.
This eventually took over Himmler's private Secret Service. Goebbels had
another private organisation of his own. Rosenberg was in charge of the
Ostministerium, or Ministry of the East, a vast organisation which did
nothing but interfere in the work of others and enrich its leaders. As if these
rival bodies were not enough, the fanatic Nazi Bohle organised the *Auslands-
organisation der Partei*.

With such confusion and jealous—and zealous—rivalry, it was amazing
that German Intelligence achieved anything at all.

Moyzisch, a very intelligent man, was naturally annoyed that his remarkable coup was not used to the full. But he continued to receive the spools of exposed film from Cicero: at first he developed them himself, and more than once he was amazed at the secrets they revealed. He did not know, by the way, that the money he used to pay Cicero was forged: it was cleverly done, quite well enough to satisfy anyone but a bank expert.

But for the internecine Nazi quarrels, Operation Cicero could have been the most far-reaching espionage feat of the war.

A director of the Foreign Division of the Ministry of Economic Warfare was talking to one of his staff in his London office.

"About £5000, you say?"

"Yes. This Swiss is a genuine businessman. I see no reason to disbelieve what he said."

"What did he say? It isn't easy to pick up £5000 in British notes these days. It ought to be damned-near impossible."

"This Swiss businessman says that he bought the notes from an Armenian—also a well-known international trader, who lives in Ankara. We followed this up, of course. One of my men saw the Armenian—you'll find his name in my report. He is a very reputable man. He told us that he got the money from a bank in Ankara—he had plenty of dollars, but wanted sterling for a special deal."

"But how did the bank get hold of it?"

"That proved to be more difficult to answer. Our man had to resort to bribery—a clerk in the bank. He traced the transaction. The Armenian had produced dollars, as he said, and wanted £5000 in English money. This the bank was able to provide—and it got the sterling from a man named Moyzisch —an attaché at the German Embassy."

"The German Embassy!"

"Yes."

"So they have British currency!"

"Yes. Evidently in plenty."

"Is anything known of this man Moyzisch?"

"Yes. He is believed to be an Intelligence officer—and he has recently been in Berlin."

"This smells! I'd better have a word with M.I.6."

M.I.6. specialises in foreign affairs. Although it is officially Military Intelligence, Section 6, it works closely with the Foreign Office—and its head is a civilian.

One of its senior officers called at the Ministry of Economic Warfare. There he listened with great interest to the story of the British currency bought in Ankara.

"Very interesting!" said M.I.6. "How did you get on the track of the case?"

"Almost by accident," said M.E.W. "The London bank where the Swiss businessman paid it in—the manager came to see me."

"He was suspicious?"

"He had good reason to be! The money was in ten- and twenty-pound notes—*all of them forged!*"

"I wonder if there is any connection between your case and mine?" said another M.I.6 man later in the day. "It seems almost certain that the Germans have broken our diplomatic code. And the signs seem to place the break in Turkey."

"I wonder if there is any connection between your case and mine," said a senior official at the Foreign Office. "I've just had a disturbing report from Ankara. Look at the last sentence: 'Papen evidently knows more than is good for him.'"

For part of the explanation we had to wait for Moyzisch's story. He belonged to Kaltenbrunner's organisation but one day he disobeyed orders and showed one of Cicero's documentary photographs to his Ambassador, von Papen. This was reasonable, for the report showed that Turkey was yielding to British pressure to admit naval, military and R.A.F. personnel

—ostensibly to train Turkish forces, but actually to establish Allied bases. Even the detailed strength of the personnel was quoted. Other results of Anglo-Turkish staff talks were just as disturbing.

Von Papen acted with his usual thoughtless haste. He went to see the Turkish Foreign Minister, Numan Menemencioglu, who attempted to dispel the German's fears. To prove that the situation was much more serious than the Turk pretended, von Papen actually quoted from the secret report which Cicero had supplied.

The moment he had gone, Menemencioglu sent for Sir Hughe Knatchbull-Hugesson, the British Ambassador, and related his conversation with von Papen in full. The two men agreed that there must be a leakage at high level: the Ambassador reported accordingly to London, as we have seen.

The first reactions were commonplace. British Secret Service men—and locksmiths—were sent to Ankara. The security arrangements at the Embassy were checked and improved. New and complicated locks and other devices were fitted to all the safes.

"Locking the stable door after the horse has gone," one man grumbled.

"But are we locking it? We don't know that. We're only making things more difficult, not impossible."

"How can we find out?"

"Well, there *is* a way!"

There was no time for finesse. A senior secretary drew up an official report for London. It stated that the Turkish Government was now prepared to move rapidly to implement recent discussions. British submarines could be disguised as Turkish for the moment—a pseudo-sale could be arranged—ready for action. More in the same vein followed.

The report was *not* despatched to London. But a copy was deposited in the Ambassador's safe.

Sure enough, a few days later von Papen made another complaint to the Turkish Foreign Minister. But this only confirmed what the British Security Officer already knew. When he had put the copy of the report in the Ambassador's safe, a tiny hair had attached it to the next file. The following morning the hair was broken.

"At least we know which stable the horse was stolen from," he said grimly, as he thought over the next step.

"My valet?" snapped the Ambassador.

"Yes. I could have caught him in the act. He is an Albanian——"

"I know that."

"He hates the British because his father was once acting as beater for a shooting party and was killed—by an unlucky shot from one of the British guns."

(This was the spy's second effort. His first story was that his father had become involved in an unpleasant quarrel over Cicero's sister in Istanbul, where he had been shot. No one in the case ever doubted Cicero's powers of imagination. Later he gave as his reason for becoming a spy (*a*) that Britain was trying to drag Turkey into the war—though his conduct might easily have provoked a German attack on Turkey, (*b*) "I was sour and bitter with the realisation that at 39 I was a failure, doomed never to be anything better than a servant." Our old friend the inferiority complex is quoted to excuse a wide variety of conduct.)

"And because of that——"

"Much smaller things than that decide a man's course of action. And I gather that the compensation paid to the dead man's family was rather miserly."

"This is fantastic! You will arrest the man and hand him over to the Turks, of course."

"No."

"What?"

"No. On the contrary, I propose to build him up with his

German employers. They know about the check on Security precautions here—Bazna 'borrowed' one of our reports. So they may be suspicious that their spy has lost his value. I shall prove that he hasn't."

Moyzisch relates one of Cicero's triumphs—a full report of the Teheran Conference between Stalin, Churchill and Roosevelt, and their staffs. One of the military decisions was that a beginning should be made to soften up the satellite countries in the Balkans. As a first move, their capitals would be heavily bombed. Sofia would be the first, in the middle of January.

It was. With practically no air defences—a fact known to the man who selected the target—the city was devastated, and 4000 people perished. Cicero was completely justified and re-established.

But the Germans were not very clever. Because a phase of the military report had been fulfilled to the letter, it did not follow automatically that the remainder of the documents were accurate—or even genuine!

Allen Dulles is somewhat in the shadows these days. As head of the C.I.A., he was held—perhaps without justification—to be at least partly responsible for the fiasco of the 'invasion' of Cuba.

In 1942 Dulles had been appointed head of the Office of Strategic Services in Switzerland. The O.S.S. concerned itself with espionage, sabotage, political warfare and many other activities. Dulles proved to be a most capable and effective organiser and operator. Among other exploits, he established contact with many highly placed anti-Hitler Germans.

It was from the German Foreign Ministry, in fact, that Dulles learned that the Germans had obtained a copy of the proceedings of the Teheran Conference: he even got a very clear hint as to how it had been done.

Dulles, like a good ally, passed on this information to London. But Ladilas Farago reports (in *Burn After Reading*): "The British did not seem to be highly pleased when Dulles tipped them off to the indiscretion of one of their top-ranking ambassadors."

Of course they were not pleased: they knew all about it already. But Farago made an inspired guess when he continued: "From their [the British] conspicuous lack of gratitude, it was deduced that maybe the leak was deliberate and that Dulles had plugged a hole that his colleagues at British Intelligence were eager to keep open."

Walther Schellenberg, who followed Canaris as head of the Abwehr, did not trust Cicero implicitly. The documents he photographed were passed by experts as authentic, but his explanations of his own activities varied too often to be credible.

He declared that he always worked alone. But soon after the Teheran Conference report the Germans noted that an imprint of two fingers appeared on Cicero's photographs. Photographic experts declared that it was impossible for him to hold the documents and to operate the camera at the same time. The Germans had long suspected that Cicero must have had an accomplice, and this seemed to confirm it. And the imprint gave no indication of the nationality of the two fingers!

But, so far as the Germans were concerned, Cicero continued to burgle the Ambassador's safe, and to be paid in forged money—in all, he drew more than £300,000.

The Operation ended early in April, 1944. Moyzisch had an incompetent and hysterical secretary—it is difficult to see how a trained Intelligence officer could have employed her for so much as twenty-four hours. On April 6th she defected—to the British.

It was significant that Moyzisch did not know this. He knew that his secretary was missing, but no more. It was Cicero who told him the truth!

The British Intelligence Service sometimes exhibits a sense of humour—and even a sense of honour, which is unusual in spy circles. Maybe they acknowledged that Moyzisch had unconsciously been helpful to them. Maybe they would have been glad to engage his services outright. He was recalled to Berlin—as an accomplice to the desertion of his secretary. And it was already quite clear that Germany was certain to lose the war. The British offered him asylum and guaranteed his safety! He declined, but was able to make his own escape.

Cicero also escaped—to Egypt, with £300,000 in forged notes! He lodged a legal claim with German Governments on the grounds that he had been cheated—which was true. But neither Federal nor Communist Government would admit Nazi debts. When his story was filmed, he is reported to have appeared in Hollywood, demanding to play the part himself. Now he has written a book on his exploits: for this, at least, he will not be paid in forged money.

TWENTY-FIVE

Was Admiral Canaris a British Agent?

THE YOUNG MAN standing by an open window swung round as someone entered the office behind him.

The newcomer wore the uniform of a major. "I'm sorry, sir," he apologised. "I didn't know you had arrived."

"Where is the little old Greek?" snapped the man at the window.

"The Admiral is in the Filing Department, sir. I'll let him know at once that you are in his office."

The major hastily withdrew. Left alone again, the young man turned back to the open window. He was tall, burly, handsome in a rather brutal way, with cold, cruel, inhuman eyes. Not an obvious bird-lover. But he now did a curious thing. From the deep pocket of his military greatcoat he fished out an improbable object—a slice of cake. He broke it up with powerful stubby fingers and spread crumbs along the windowsill.

The door of the rather shabby little office opened again and a second man entered. He was a short, slim, elderly man in the uniform of a naval officer. He had bright blue, smiling eyes and rosy cheeks. His hair and bushy eyebrows were white and silky. At his heels trotted a couple of long-haired dachshunds.

"Reinhard, my dear boy!" he exclaimed. "How nice to see you! Feeding my little birds again, eh? What a good fellow you are!"

"Good morning, Admiral," said the young man addressed as Reinhard. "I hope you are not tired this morning. We kept you up very late last night. Ten-thirty, wasn't it?"

"Yes! Terrible!" smiled the Admiral. "Everybody should be in bed by ten o'clock at the very latest."

"I have a message from my wife," Reinhard said. "She asks me to say how much she enjoyed that wonderful borsch you cooked for dinner."

"I'm so glad, my boy. Next time I will make you a very special goulash that I think will appeal to you. You know how fond I am of these foreign dishes."

Reinhard looked down at the little Admiral with a glance of mixed affection and nervous respect. His brutal features relaxed into what was almost a smile.

"We were very amused to see that even in the kitchen you wear the correct attire. One doesn't often see an admiral in a white apron and chef's cap carrying in a great dish of borsch!"

"One must do the job properly," the Admiral said modestly. "There is a certain pleasing formality in these things. And now —what can I do for you?"

This may seem an unlikely scene between two high-ranking officers in the capital of a country at war. But every detail is historically accurate. The identities of the two officers make the episode seem almost incredible.

For the little, smiling, white-haired admiral, who loved birds and dogs and liked to dress up and play at being a chef, was Admiral Wilhelm Canaris, head of the Abwehr—the Secret Service of the German armed forces. And the burly young visitor to his office was Reinhard Heydrich, deputy chief, under Heinrich Himmler, of the Nazi Gestapo.

Canaris has been described as the most enigmatic figure of the second World War. This is an incorrect assessment of his character. He was certainly un-Teutonic, and this made it difficult for other German officials to understand him when they compared him with their often unimaginative selves. He is more easily understood by British readers, to whom his sense of humour does not seem suspicious, nor his love of animals a sign of weakness.

He was widely but quite wrongly believed to have been a British agent. This is indeed ridiculous, and arose from the Nazi-inspired fallacy that anyone who was anti-Hitler must be pro-British. Canaris was merely, like many of his countrymen, anti-Hitler, but he was none the less pro-German. There seems little doubt that through Abwehr agents he 'leaked' vital items of information to the Allies. He saw no future for his tortured country until Hitler was defeated.

Another incorrect detail of the Canaris legend gained wide circulation from his nickname of "the little Greek." This was because Hitler believed him to be descended from the famous old Greek patriot Kanaris—a belief which for reasons of his own Canaris encouraged. Actually his family originated in Lombardy.

With regard to the positive features of his character, I think he can be aptly compared with our own famous Admiral Sir Reginald ("Blinker") Hall, Director of British Naval Intelligence during the first World War. Brought up in the traditions of the old Imperial German Navy—that creditable imitation of the British Royal Navy—Canaris learned strict discipline, unvarying efficiency and a nice code of honour. And from his fun-loving Italian forbears he inherited a sense of humour more common in British than in German wardrooms. He acquired that decent freemasonry of the seven seas—that respect for an honourable opponent—noticeable even in war-time between the Royal Navy and its wayward German offspring.

When Canaris was assigned to German Naval Intelligence during the first World War, he took to the work as a duck takes to water. His Latin blood gave him the vivid imagination essential in Intelligence work, but absent in most of his German contemporaries. He organised a secret Spanish base for supplying U-boats, a ring of agents who reported the movements of Allied shipping, and revolts by Moors and Arabs against British and French rule in North Africa. And he also began a lifelong friendship with a young Spanish officer, one Major Francisco Franco, which was to influence the course of European history twenty years later. Canaris was widely but erroneously believed to have been at that time one of the early lovers of Mata Hari. In a battle of wits she would not have stood a chance!

It is a regrettable but inescapable fact that Intelligence work saps all but the strongest characters. It is necessary to become what atom-spy Klaus Fuchs so aptly described as a "controlled schizophrenic." The successful Intelligence officer must combine a scrupulously honest attitude towards his own department with a completely unscrupulous treatment of the dupes and stooges in his world-wide network. This soon became apparent in the character of Canaris, an essentially decent and humane man, who is known to have deliberately sent numbers of agents to their deaths in what he believed to have been a good cause. To my former colleagues of the British Service I can only say, "He that is without sin among you, let him cast the first stone."

So Canaris emerges between the two world wars not as an enigmatical character at all, but as the prefectly logical product of his cosmopolitan blood and his training. Officially, he was a brilliant spy-master—knowledgeable, efficient, unscrupulous. In private life he was kindly, humane, fun-loving. My favourite story about Canaris—not very widely known—is of when he was in a fast car with other high-ranking Abwehr officers— tearing through the countryside at the terrific speed which seemed to act on him like a tonic—and they passed a flock of sheep. Canaris gravely saluted the flock. His colleagues were understandably puzzled.

"Who knows?" Canaris said, turning to the others with his gentle smile. "One of them may be one of our Abwehr agents in a baffling disguise!" British readers who have any knowledge of

German mentality will understand that such incidents, which we think amusing, made humourless colleagues regard him as 'enigmatical.'

It is a tribute to the German Intelligence talent-spotters that Canaris was eventually placed in control of the Abwehr—the combined Secret Service of the German armed forces.

At that time the Abwehr was organised in three divisions: Espionage, Counter-espionage, and Sabotage. This was a clear-cut workable combination comparable with the British M.I.6, M.I.5, and the war-time sabotage organisation, S.O.E. But when Hitler came to power and adopted the old Roman principle of 'Divide and Rule,' a clumsy system of parallel Intelligence organisations was built up, as mentioned in the previous chapter. And all these competing organisations were staffed by Nazi amateurs—the "muscle-men," as Canaris contemptuously called them—and fought for Hitler's favour even to the extent of betraying each other's agents to foreign Security services so that they could be first with the news at Berchtesgaden.

Hitler was no fool in these matters. He realised that the only really reliable source of information was the Abwehr, run not by political fanatics but by staunch old professional Intelligence officers. But what Hitler did not realise was that his most efficient and most trusted secret department was the bridge-head of all the irreconcilable groups which were working for the overthrow of the Nazis.

Despite numerous fervent post-war protestations, only a tiny minority of the German people actively opposed Hitler. There was the "Kreisau Circle" under Count Helmuth von Moltke, men of noble birth who would not condescend to associate with lowly born types. There were Army officers, split among themselves into the "Old Men" with monarchical traditions who wanted to see the Kaiser's son back on the throne, and the "Young Men" led by Klaus Count Stauffenberg who wanted a liberal Government. Poles apart from these groups was the *Rote Kapelle*—the notorious "Red Orchestra," which was a most competent espionage group, functioning with typical Communist efficiency. There was never any effective liaison between these groups; nor was there between any of them and the unorganised "Bomb Plot" officers, who included Henning von Tresckow and the famous General Erwin Rommel.

So Hitler had little to fear except from the most unlikely quarter—the high-ranking Inner Circle of the Abwehr. It was a situation almost impossible for British readers to grasp—as at the height of the second World War treason were being plotted by every political party separately and simultaneously, including the Communists and the House of Lords, whilst—quite unknown to the others—the heads of M.I.5, M.I.6 and S.O.E. were actively planning the murder of Winston Churchill!

Whole books can be—and have been—written about the career of Admiral Canaris. This chapter aims merely at presenting his character from a fresh but, I believe, an accurate angle. But readers may reasonably ask how, in view of his anti-Hitler activities, he managed to survive so long. There were two reasons.

It is no exaggeration to say that Hitler's personality had a hypnotic effect, not merely on vast crowds but on more intimate gatherings. An agent of mine who was a pre-war Professor of English at a famous German University told me of his first meeting with the Führer. It was at a crowded cocktail party, with a hundred or so guests drinking, laughing and chattering. Suddenly the atmosphere changed—became electrified. Hitler had entered the room unnoticed, but his physical presence sapped the wills—even sapped the inborn common sense—of those around him. "I felt," said my highly educated, highly intelligent professor, "as if I were about to undergo an experience to which I could not possibly offer any resistance. Some influence had come into the room which I would find it impossible to oppose or resist. I did not even know that Hitler had arrived."

Although he never addressed large audiences, Canaris had that same hypnotic influence. So in his private conferences with Hitler—to whom for years he was entitled to immediate access

—they started on equal terms. Much as Canaris hated Hitler, he was almost the only man who could soothe him when the Führer flew into a maniacal rage with a row of ashen-faced field-marshals trembling before him.

So, approaching on the same mesmeric plane, from what common point could they start? It may seem a staggering assertion, but—they were both pro-British! Canaris greatly admired the Royal Navy, in whose borrowed methods and traditions he had been reared. Hitler greatly admired the British Constitution with its political farsightedness. And whenever differences of opinion threatened to upset the harmony of their discussions, the shrewd Canaris would slyly introduce a subject on which they definitely saw eye to eye— their mutual fear and hatred of Communism.

But—it may well be asked—why was Hitler never informed that the trusted chief of his Secret Service was plotting against him? The answer lies in one of those personal relationships which throughout history have helped to shape the destiny of nations.

Years before Hitler came to power, officers of the staff of Admiral Canaris—then in the German Navy—included a young lieutenant named Reinhard Heydrich. He absorbed the naval traditions of loyalty to other men of the sea, and he conceived an affection for his commanding officer. Heydrich was cashiered for an offence against the strict naval code of morality, and turned up later as a zealous and efficient officer of the Gestapo. He rose to the rank of deputy to Heinrich Himmler, and found himself a neighbour in a Berlin suburb of his respected old chief Canaris.

It is impossible to say to what extent their renewed association —which developed into a close friendship—was genuine on the part of Canaris. It is on record that the families regularly dined together, and that the gourmet Canaris, an expert in exotic foreign foods, would wear his chef's cap as he carried in steaming dishes of goulash or borsch. And it is on record that Heydrich, and a number of other officers who were seeking the

favours of Canaris, would try to impress the Admiral by
spreading crumbs on his office windowsill for the hungry birds
the old man loved.

And although captured Gestapo records are understandably
silent on the subject, it seems quite clear that when rumours
that Canaris was disloyal to the Führer reached high Gestapo
levels, they were suppressed by Heydrich in the interests of his
former naval commander and close personal friend.

Canaris probably attained the height of his influence in
international affairs at the outbreak of the Spanish Civil War.
As a fanatical anti-Communist he naturally took the side of his
old friend Franco. Shuttling back and forth across Europe in
fast cars and faster planes, Canaris exerted all his persuasive
powers on both Hitler and Mussolini. And he was the pre-
dominant influence in securing the despatch of unwilling
Italian troops and first-rate German bomber squadrons to
reinforce Franco's motley force of Spaniards, Moors and
Spanish Foreign Legion riff-raff.

But Canaris looked much farther ahead than was possible to
the inferior intellects of the Italian and German dictators.
Canaris wanted an anti-Communist Spain, but he certainly did
not want a Fascist Europe. So with his breathless journeys to
and fro across Europe by road, rail and air, he created a false
atmosphere of urgency in which he stampeded Mussolini and
Hitler into sending essential armies and air forces to aid Franco
before the Italian and German dictators had had the time or the
foresight to reflect what future favours they might demand in
return for their help.

So the German and Italian intervention in the Spanish
Civil War was accordingly organised on the basis not of a
bargain but of a gift. Hence Franco could not be blamed when,
safely in power, he dodged and wriggled during the second
World War—under the subtle influence of Canaris—and managed to avoid taking sides.

The time came when Britain was fighting alone against most
of Continental Europe, but not the Iberian Peninsula. One

shudders to contemplate an Axis-dominated Spain which could easily have closed the Straits of Gibraltar and denied the Mediterranean to the Royal Navy. Malta could not have held out for long. Allied landings in North Africa which at last opened the way to the conquest of Italy would have been impossible. For that, among many other things, Britain can thank the shade of Admiral Canaris. It was not so much that he liked us—he just didn't like Hitler. And even now it may be news to many readers that the smiling little white-haired man so often seen at General Franco's headquarters and calling himself Señor Guillermo was really Abwehr chief Admiral Canaris.

It was inevitable that in the course of years the rumours that Canaris was working against Hitler could not be dismissed, time after time, as fabrications. And the old Admiral lost a powerful friend when Reinhard Heydrich, then 'Protector' of Bohemia and Moravia, was murdered by Czech agents of Britain near the village of Lidice, whose inhabitants were massacred and their homes levelled in revenge. For Canaris the sands were running out.

The beginning of the end came early in 1944, and it started in distant Ankara. The chief local Abwehr agent was a Dr Vermehren, whose wife, Countess Plettenberg, was a devout Catholic and therefore an anti-Nazi. They decided to desert their country and seek sanctuary with the British. And as a result we obtained accurate, up-to-date, first-hand details of the organisation and methods of the Abwehr. It is hardly necessary to add that Hitler was in a state of frenzied rage. The many enemies of the old Admiral blamed Canaris. And this episode triggered off an anti-Canaris movement for which the cunning and jealous ex-poultry-farmer Himmler, head of the Gestapo, had long been waiting. Canaris was removed from office, and Himmler incorporated the Abwehr in the Gestapo.

After a short period of 'retirement,' Canaris was arrested, and on the 7th of February, 1945, he reached the dreaded prison of Flossenberg, in the lonely Franconian countryside, where 'top-secret' prisoners and hostages awaited their end.

He was interrogated under torture, and what he admitted—if anything—is not on record. After two months of hell the old man was led out to execution at dawn on the 8th of April, 1945—with the end of the war so near, and yet so far.

There had been many stories of how Canaris escaped to South America, where he was said to be still living. But they are contradicted by a reliable witness. He was Colonel Lunding, arrested as Director of the Danish Military Intelligence Service. Through the keyhole of his cell, Colonel Lunding saw Canaris taken from his adjoining cell, made to strip naked, and led out to the execution yard, with his nose broken during his last interrogation.

Canaris was not accorded the doubtful honour of being shot as an officer. He was hanged as a traitor. The S.S. thugs who carried out the execution were half drunk on extra rations of rum. And they killed Canaris with every possible refinement of cruelty. Another prisoner, Lieutenant Schlabrendorff, was told later by one of the drunken killers that Canaris was "hanged twice." He was slowly strangled with piano wire, taken down at the point of death and revived, then slowly hanged for the second and last time.

TWENTY-SIX

The Travelling Executioners

IT IS WELL KNOWN THAT UNDER THE REGIME OF STALIN political murders inside Russia took place in tens of thousands. It is less well known that even outside Russia murders and kidnappings were carried out on such a large scale that they required a separate department to organise them. This was Section OS2 of the Soviet Secret Service. It was known officially as the Department for Special Tasks. Its members were known unofficially as the Travelling Executioners.

Stories of the exploits of this dreadful department are so fantastic that many people simply refuse to believe them. Hence in this chapter I am going to avoid all speculation—I am going to omit stories of the elimination of nonentities. I propose to keep strictly to facts which are on record about OS2 plots involving well-known people. These can easily be checked by the incredulous.

In glancing briefly at a few of the numerous evil exploits of OS2, I must class kidnapping with murder. It might seem, indeed, that causing swift death by a bullet is a lesser crime than taking a victim back to Russia to die only after prolonged questioning under torture.

But I have space to deal with only a few major cases. The

minor cases number many hundreds. A West Berlin Security officer told me that during 1953 alone some four hundred people had been kidnapped and taken behind the Iron Curtain.

The use of stolen police uniforms, as in the first attack on Trotsky's house in Mexico, is an old device of OS2. It was being successfully used as far back as 1930.

On the 26th of January in that year, a Sunday, an ex-General of the Russian Imperial Army left his Paris flat to attend morning service at the near-by Russian Orthodox Church. He kissed his wife good-bye and said he would be home early for lunch.

The officer was General Kutyepov, and he was on the OS2 Black List. He was, like most of his caste and background, a violently anti-Communist exile, and was leader of an organisation called the Union of Russian ex-Combatants, whose anti-Soviet propaganda made it very unpopular in Moscow.

Not far from his home a passing pedestrian saw General Kutyepov having some sort of argument with two men who wore gendarmes' uniforms. They eventually hustled the General into a waiting car and were driven away at great speed. Later investigations showed that on that winter Sunday morning not a single arrest was made by gendarmes in any part of Paris. Nothing more was ever heard of General Kutyepov.

There was another notorious OS2 kidnapping in Paris, that of seventy-year-old General Miller, another prominent official of the Union of Russian ex-Combatants. The date was the 22nd of September, 1937, when the Union was considering co-operating in anti-Communist activities with the German Nazi Party. General Miller and another Russian, Lieut.-General Skoblin, were supposed to be meeting two Nazi agents in a Bois de Boulogne café. According to a statement made later by Skoblin, Miller did not turn up for the meeting.

Sûreté detectives later traced Miller's movements as far as Le Havre, whence the Soviet ship *Marya Ulyanova* sailed that night for a Russian port. He was never seen again.

As a sinister aftermath of the Miller kidnapping, Skoblin

was accused by his comrades in the Union of being a Soviet agent, and of having organised the kidnapping of Miller. He hotly denied having made any appointment to meet Miller, stormed out of the meeting in apparent rage—and he too disappeared for ever.

The Miller case was one of the few of OS2 crimes which resulted in a trial. A Paris court decided that Miller had been kidnapped and that Mme Skoblin was guilty as an accessory. She was sentenced to twenty years' imprisonment—one of the heaviest sentences ever passed on a woman in France.

The Bois de Boulogne was the scene of an even more brazen OS2 crime during the same year. Dimitri Navachine had been a Soviet diplomat; shocked by Stalin's 'Purge' trials, he had foolishly announced that he was going to reveal all that he knew about the methods of the Russian dictator. He left home during the morning of the 21st of January, 1937, to take his usual walk in the Bois. Two men were following him and, within sight of a number of pedestrians, they shot their victim dead, jumped into a waiting car and escaped. They were never traced.

It was the Navachine murder which caused Trotsky to warn his followers in France that any of them who possessed inside information about the 'Purge' trials might suffer the same fate. He became worried about the safety of a great quantity of irreplaceable records which he had stored with the Paris Institute of Political Science. And, as we have seen, his nervousness was justified.

Later that year Trotsky's son, who called himself Leon Sedov, was murdered in a Paris hospital, as I have described in my account of the later murder of the old Red Army organiser himself.

The Travelling Executioners struck yet again that year, this time in peaceful Switzerland. Early in the morning of the 5th of September a body was found in a car which had been parked during the night in a Lausanne shopping centre. The OS2 squad had acted with unusual savagery, as the wounds included seven bullets in the torso and five in the head.

The body was identified as that of Ignace Reiss, who had formerly held an important post as Resident Director of the Soviet Secret Service. He was another of the many Russians who disagreed with Stalin's 'Purge' policy, as a result of which in July he had been summoned to Moscow for trial and punishment. He wisely declined the invitation. A first plan to kill him and his family with poisoned chocolates failed when the woman agent concerned lost her nerve at the last moment. The OS2 gunmen got him a few weeks later.

That year, 1937, was certainly a busy one for the Travelling Executioners. Even inside Madrid, where during the Spanish Civil War Franco's forces were besieging Republican troops, death-squad leader Salas was organising the murders of Trotskyists. And "General Kotov," alias Leonid Eitingon, Chief of the Spanish Department of OS2, was doing the same in Barcelona, assisted by his murderous mistress, Caridad Mercader, whose own son murdered Trotsky three years later.

The chaotic conditions of the Spanish Civil War made things easy for OS2, especially as there was only superficial unity among the Republican Militia, which included every shade of Left-wing opinion from moderate Republican to violent Anarchist. It was not difficult for OS2 agents to provoke arguments which led to actual fighting between companies of Government troops. Afterwards the agents would explain that the trouble had been provoked by Trotskyists, which was some sort of excuse for rounding up a few more whose names were on the death-lists.

Thus perished Robles, Rein, Landau, Berneri, Wolf, Moulin and many others, and the Trotskyist leader Nin was kidnapped. There were British victims, too. Hamilton Gold of the International Brigade was kidnapped and never heard of again.

In the rest of Europe, outside Spain, the Travelling Executioners rested for a few months. Then, on the 16th of July, 1938, Rudolf Klement disappeared. He had been living in France and carrying out liaison duties between Trotsky and his

European followers. His headless corpse was found some weeks later in the river Marne.

The outbreak of the second World War produced a situation in Europe which offered to OS2 both advantages and disadvantages. An example of the latter was that victims with whom OS2 were just about to catch up were sometimes at the last moment whisked off to internment camps. One of these was the German Communist Willi Munzenberg.

Munzenberg had formerly been so trusted by Moscow that he had been in charge of all Communist Party publications in the whole of Germany. Then, like so many others, the 'Purges' disillusioned him. He quarrelled with Stalin and fled to France. Stalin labelled him as a 'deviationist' and passed his name to OS2. But before the Travelling Executioners could deal with him France had fallen, and the Vichy Government had interned him.

But OS2 were not baffled for long. They adopted the simple and obvious expedient of instructing a couple of their agents to behave so as to get themselves interned. Inside the camp they made friends with Munzenberg and were surprised and delighted to find that he had managed to smuggle in with him a large sum of money. "That's fine!" said Munzenberg's new friends. "We've got an absolutely safe escape-route to America fixed. We'd have been over there by now if only we'd had enough cash. If the three of us escape from the camp together, we'll guarantee to get you to the United States if you'll provide the necessary bribes."

It seemed a sound plan to Munzenberg, for escape from the camp was not very difficult. Many minor Vichy officials had lost heart when their country surrendered and felt no particular loyalty to the Pétain regime. They felt that it might even be a good thing if a few Communists got away to start stirring up trouble for the hated Germans in Occupied France.

So Munzenberg and his friends broke out of the camp one day without being stopped. Within a couple of hours Munzenberg's body was hanging from a tree in a near-by forest. It is

known that his murderers were smuggled out of France—
though not to America—by the notorious OS2 leader Otto
Katz. Munzenberg's substantial funds, as might be expected,
were never traced.

In 1941 a mysterious death in the United States bore all
the hallmarks of one of OS2's more artistic jobs. The victim
was Walter Krivitsky. He had been one of Stalin's favourites,
with the high rank of General in the N.K.V.D. As one of the
most trusted Resident Directors of the Soviet Secret Service,
he had been closely concerned in collecting evidence, true or
false, against victims marked down for purging, including the
transit from Germany of the forged documents which sent the
famous Marshal Tukachevsky to the firing-squad.

Krivitsky had been in France at the time of the Reiss
murder, shortly after which he had been recalled to Moscow
'for consultations.' But so many of his former colleagues had
received similar invitations and had disappeared without
trace immediately they set foot on Soviet soil that Krivitsky took
fright. He fled to America, where hitherto OS2 had not been
very active.

It was bad enough for Krivitsky to have disobeyed an order
to return to Moscow. But what he did next was worse. He
published a book entitled *I was Stalin's Agent*, which caused a
very irritated Stalin to place his name at the top of the OS2
death-list.

With his lengthy first-hand knowledge of OS2 methods,
Krivitsky was fully aware of his perilous position. He said to
American friends, "If they ever try to prove that I committed
suicide, you mustn't believe them." And who "they" were is
anybody's guess. Shortly afterwards he was found dead in a
Washington hotel (on the 10th of February, 1941). Beside the
body was a farewell letter to the effect that he had killed himself.

There was no conceivable reason why Krivitsky should have
committed suicide, but at the inquest there was only one possible
verdict. The letter was undoubtedly in his handwriting, but why
should he have written it? The theory in Intelligence circles was

that when the Travelling Executioners caught up with him and he knew that death was inevitable he agreed to write the suicide note on the condition that his wife and children were not molested.

If I am to keep to a roughly chronological account of OS2 crimes, I should now switch to Turkey and the story of an attempt which failed—one of the very few. But I dealt with this more fully in my account of the world's luckiest failure, Franz von Papen. I refer to it here merely as an example of the completeness and unscrupulousness of OS2 murder plans. The Macedonian agent who was to have committed the murder was given a device which he was told was a smoke-bomb that would enable him to escape in an artificial fog. When he set it off he certainly disappeared—but not into a smoke-screen. It was a high-explosive bomb, and he disappeared into unrecognisable shreds of mangled flesh. He had served his purpose and was expendable.

To return to the United States, some other OS2 crimes in that country concerned less well-known figures, such as the teacher Juliet Poyntz. She had been a Communist secret agent but changed sides, and planned to write an exposure of her former comrades. She disappeared from a New York street and was not seen again. One of the men questioned by the police in connection with her disappearance was the labour leader Carlo Tresca, who made a statement that her killer was OS2 operative George Mink, a Philadelphia taxi-driver. This was very indiscreet on Tresca's part, so OS2 murdered him on New York's Fifth Avenue in 1943.

A case in which OS2 displayed, for once, some degree of patience was that of the American author, Louis Adamic. He was a friend and admirer of Marshal Tito of Yugoslavia, and was writing a book extolling the virtues of Titoism. Stalin, of course, could not admit that any brand of Communism was any good except his own. To him Titoism was as much anathema as Trotskyism, for different types of Communists fight among themselves almost as fiercely as different types of Christians used to do. OS2 were told that something simply must be done about Adamic and his book.

OS2 behaved at first with most uncharacteristic restraint. Adamic told a friend that he had been repeatedly threatened with trouble unless he destroyed the manuscript of his book. During 1949 he received several visits and warnings at his New Jersey home from an OS2 agent. In 1950 a squad of four agents came to his house and demanded to be given the manuscript, but fled when some unexpected visitors arrived.

Adamic became understandably worried by these visits and threats and moved to California. But OS2 has a long arm, and late one night he was approached in the street by two OS2 agents who demanded to know where he kept the manuscript. When he refused to tell them, they produced blackjacks, beat him unconscious and left him in the gutter. California did not seem, after all, to be a very safe hiding-place.

Back again at his New Jersey home, Adamic continued doggedly to work on his book. But not for long. At dawn one morning in September, 1951, neighbours saw that his house was on fire. Firemen rushed to the blaze and found that the house had been drenched with oil before the fire started. In the bedroom was the body of Louis Adamic, holding a rifle in his dead hands. He had died from a bullet which had entered his head just above the right ear.

There is not the slightest doubt that this was an OS2 murder, but it was an amateurish effort compared with such well-planned killings as that of Krivitsky. If the object was to suggest that Adamic had shot himself, why was it necessary to set fire to the house? And suicide with a rifle is not merely unusual—it is extremely difficult. It involves arrangements of strings, because, with the muzzle against one's body or head, the human arm is not long enough to reach the trigger. Even with a pistol it is an awkward and chancy business to shoot oneself above the ear. With a rifle the shot is a physical impossibility.

It can be safely assumed that this rather feeble attempt to fake a suicide brought a reprimand for the OS2 operative responsible. And in OS2 a reprimand is invariably in the conical shape of a bullet.

During more than a quarter-century of OS2 killings, ordinary citizens whose only sources of information were newspapers mostly refused to believe that the Government of one of the greatest countries in the world had a special department of trained criminals who, month by month, steadily went on committing political assassinations in which none of the killers involved were ever brought to justice. But something very important happened in 1954.

Early in 1954 a visitor from Russia arrived in West Germany. He was OS2 Captain Nicolai Evgenyevitch Khokhlov. He was a murder-planner of long experience—as far back as 1942 he had been assigned to murder Franz von Papen, the German Ambassador to Turkey, but had refused to do so. His reasons must have been sound, for it does not appear that the refusal had any adverse effect on his career for the next twelve years.

His latest assignment was another liquidation—that of Georgi Okolovich, chairman of an anti-Communist organisation in Frankfurt which was annoying Stalin. For this purpose Khokhlov had been issued with ingenious weapons specially invented in the research laboratories of OS2 in Moscow.

These special weapons were the sort of things which writers of cheap spy fiction long ago gave up writing about—as being too fantastic for sophisticated readers to swallow. One was a miniature pistol, about four inches by three, which could be concealed in the palm of the hand and, being electrically fired, was almost noiseless. The other was a cigarette-case containing what appeared to be cigarettes. But each cigarette was a miniature gun, firing through its tip a small but fatal expanding dumdum bullet treated with a deadly poison.

It is fortunate for the Western world in general, and for Georgi Okolovich in particular, that Captain Khokhlov once again refused to carry out his assignment. Instead of completing his mission he traced the local headquarters of the United States Secret Service, handed over his weapons and made a statement, asking for political asylum from a regime of murderous tyranny which he had found to be, at long last, insupportable. His story is a matter of history, and was released to the world, if any reader should wish to check it, on the 23rd of April, 1954.

TWENTY-SEVEN

The Katyn Murders

THE TRAVELLING EXECUTIONERS always got their man—or woman. But their activities were scarcely popular in other countries—no small part of the suspicion felt towards Russia was due to their murders. If Stalin 'liquidates' a few thousand of his supporters, that may be passed off as an aspect of Russian internal politics, but if he orders the murder of even one London resident, he is certain to arouse real indignation.

The 'executions' were never announced in Russia itself. Nevertheless, they led to such angry comment abroad that OS2 decided on a change of method. Their victims should not be assassinated. If they committed suicide, then the fangs of critics would be drawn.

I have already mentioned the cases of Krivitsky and Louis Adamic. Not all the victims were well known, however: nor was the method always direct. Oksana Kasenkina was a humble teacher in the school for children of Soviet officials in New York. When ordered to return to Moscow, she sought sanctuary with a friend, Countess Alexandra Tolstoi. The Russians removed her forcibly, and claimed that she was returning to Russia of her own free will—whereupon she threw herself from a third-storey window.

As it happened, she had a remarkable escape and was not

killed. Had she died, the verdict would have been obvious. But when, in an American hospital, she told the full story of her persecution, it became obvious that driving persons to suicide is a form of murder.

This was confirmed by Captain Nicolai Khokhlov, who has already been mentioned; he revealed dozens of cases of assassination or 'suicide,' with full details of training given to the murderers.

He was an intelligent man, and knew the risks he ran in his flight to the West. It is not surprising that he was taken seriously ill—his illness due to a rare irradiated metallic poison, skilfully administered.

The victims of the planned 'suicides' ranged from those who sought political asylum in the West to political suspects or opponents and 'expendable' or unwanted secret agents. But one case, nearer home, came into a different category.

When Stalin made his pact with Hitler in August, 1939, his price was the eastern half of Poland. Russia had an ethnic claim to part of the territory, but the northern and southern regions were indubitably Polish. With Poland shattered by the Nazi attack, Stalin marched in to occupy his share of the booty. The bulk of the Polish army was engaged in the west. No resistance to the Russian advance was possible—indeed, some Polish units even thought that the Russians were marching to aid them against the Nazis!

181,000 Poles were carried off to P.O.W. camps in Russia. The 9369 officers were housed in camps around Smolensk, Kharkov and Kalinin.

When, in June, 1941, Hitler turned on his partner, General Sikorski, the Polish leader, hurried to Moscow. He was welcomed by Stalin, for he proposed to create a new Polish army from the Polish prisoners of war. But there was an immediate difficulty—most of the Polish officers could not be traced. Stalin gave a different 'explanation' at each interview. But the officers were not forthcoming.

Then, in April, 1943, the Germans announced the discovery of mass graves at Katyn, near Smolensk. I had known weeks earlier, for the graves had been discovered by local peasants. The Poles were shocked. More than 8000 officers had disappeared without trace—and more than 4000 bodies were found in the graves at Katyn. The Russians blamed the Germans, but all the evidence suggested that they themselves had been responsible. Until April, 1940, relatives of the officers had received letters: then they all ceased suddenly, at the same moment. In an unusual flash of candour Stalin muttered to a Polish Minister, "We made a terrible mistake."

The Poles asked the International Red Cross to investigate. Stalin used the implied slur to break off relations with Poland and to prepare to impose a Communist Government upon her. It was a double tragedy.

Nor will it ever be forgotten in Poland. When, during the revolution of October, 1956, crowds gathered in Warsaw protesting against Russian rule, they raised a spontaneous shout: "Katyn! Katyn!"

The Russians still accused the Germans of this horrible crime, and duly charged the Nazi leaders at Nuremberg with being responsible for it. They did not pursue the case, however, for the 'evidence' was scanty and tended to incriminate Russia rather than Germany. But at least one witness was available whose evidence might have been decisive.

Ivan Kriwozercow (the name has also been spelled as Krivozhertzov) lived in a Russian hamlet not far from Smolensk, on the edge of the Katyn forest. He was a peasant farmer, working on the "Red Dawn" collective: he was physically unfit for military service.

In March, 1940, he and the other inhabitants of the village commented on the arrival of lorry loads of prisoners with picks and shovels: they were then marched into the Katyn forest. There, they told the local people, they were employed on digging long pits—they did not know their purpose.

In the following month the villagers noticed that the forest was heavily guarded by N.K.V.D. soldiers—no civilian was allowed within it. More lorries were arriving daily, loaded with Polish prisoners: but the lorries returned empty. In Stalin's Russia curiosity was not encouraged. The forest had already been used for executions: but surely these pits could not be graves? They would hold thousands of bodies.

By the end of July, 1941, the Germans had occupied the region. They were not opposed by the peasants—had Hitler not treated the Russian populace as beasts he might have won the war. But at least the people could once more gather wood in the forest of Katyn.

Kriwozercow was emphatic that the Germans knew nothing about the mass graves. He himself first heard of the massacre—apart from obvious suspicions at the time—from Polish prisoners brought by the Germans for forced labour. Some of them claimed that they had discovered the graves.

By the beginning of 1943 the tide of war had turned against the Germans. They now made attempts to win over the rural Russians. Ivan did not like the Germans—but neither did he like the Communists, who had murdered his father and appropriated his farm. But the truth appears to have slipped out casually. One of the German propaganda publications mentioned that General Sikorski had failed to find his officers in Russia.

"Of course," Ivan blurted out to a German. "They are still here, buried in the Kosogory wood, part of the Katyn forest."

"Whereabouts?"

"I don't know exactly. But Kisielev does."

Kisielev was a neighbour, "a very pious man." He pointed out the uneven edges of the pits—"I had long noticed them, but did not know what they were." There were also some rough crosses, made of timber. Kisielev explained that these had been put up the previous year by the Polish labourers. The pits had been dug and filled long before the Nazi invasion.

The Germans began to dig, and revealed the bodies of more

than four thousand Polish officers. They were all from the camp near Smolensk. (The bodies of the officers from the other two camps have never been found.)

Ivan, Kisielev and many others gave their evidence on oath to a German judge. The Germans at once exploited this gruesome revelation. Deputations were invited from all over Occupied Europe. British prisoners of war, including medical officers, were sent to view the bodies—and to talk to the local peasants if they so wished.

But now the witnesses were getting perturbed. Every week the Red Army advanced closer to Smolensk—and Katyn. The massacre had become a world sensation, and Stalin was furious. What would happen to the men who had revealed the facts?

Local Communists assured the witnesses that they had nothing to fear, but some did not trust their word, and fled to the West. Ivan Kriwozercow was among them. His was a serious responsibility—he was the man who had first told the Germans about the graves. So he decided to leave, and made his way to Germany, where he worked as a labourer until the German collapse. Then, fearful of Russian vengeance, he left Berlin for Bremen. Movement was easy in the utter confusion of those days. Hundreds of thousands of prisoners and forced labourers were trying to get home.

In Bremen Ivan went to a local American headquarters. A tired G.I. received him casually.

"What's on your mind?" he asked, through an interpreter.

"I have something important to report."

"Such as?"

"I can tell you the full story of the Katyn massacres. I am a Russian, and lived near by——"

But the American had never heard of the Katyn massacres. "So you're a Russian? Then I'd better send you over to the Russians. They'll know what to do with you."

Ivan fled precipitately.

It is strange how vital news is so often declined. When

Igor Gouzenko defected from the Russian Embassy in Ottawa in 1945, he carried with him full documentary evidence of one of the outstanding spy-plots in history. He wandered all day round newspaper offices, but no one would listen to his story. When at last he was able to report it to official circles, the reaction of the Canadian Prime Minister was startling—he proposed to send Gouzenko back to the Russian Embassy!

Ivan Kriwozercow got clear of Germany. At length he reached England, in company with a friend named Chomiak, also from his village near Smolensk.

In London he gave evidence before a Polish judge—the entire interrogation was recorded on tape.

"You ought to go to Nuremberg," said a Polish official. "The Russians have charged the Germans with the Katyn murders—you ought to give your evidence there."

"What? And commit suicide? Evidently you don't know the Russians!" said Ivan—and promptly disappeared.

"Now listen carefully," said the Director of OS2 in Moscow to one of his agents. "We have never yet operated successfully in England, but this case is vital."

"Who is the objective?"

"A Russian."

"A Russian?"

"Yes. He is a defector. He should never have been allowed to escape from Russia—but that weakness has already been dealt with. He is now in England."

"His name?"

"Ivan Kriwozercow."

"And his address?"

"I don't know. You will have to find him. Our people in England will help you, of course."

"And when I find him?"

"He will kill himself. It must be very neatly done—there must be no suspicion. No brutality—he must die, that is all."

"How long have I got?"

"It is urgent. I am watching the Nuremberg end. There is a possibility that he may be sent there."

"Nuremberg! Why?"

"That is not your affair. All you have to do is to eliminate him—very gently."

Ivan and Chomiak lived in fear—when I saw the latter, years later, he still trembled at the mention of Katyn and the thought of what could so easily happen if the Travelling Executioners traced him.

It soon became evident that their fears were not unfounded. A public-house row began one night in Slough. It did not concern Kriwozercow—but someone struck him over the head with a beer-bottle. It might have been a 'mistake' in the confusion of the fight, but he read it as a warning—and disappeared!

He changed his name to Michel Loboda, and went to the West Country, moving from one district to another. But the arms of the OS2 are long. He lodged in Pill Camp, but disappeared at Christmas, 1947. Two days later the body of Ivan Kriwozercow alias Michel Loboda was found hanging from a beam in a barn near Bristol.

The verdict was inevitably suicide. There was no evidence to suggest anything else. As the man was unknown save as a casual worker, no one was available to tell his story to the coroner. It is doubtful if the few people who knew him had ever heard of Katyn—save Chomiak, and he was afraid. If he talked too freely, he would almost certainly share Ivan's fate.

And in Moscow an agent was congratulated on his neat accomplishment of a very delicate mission without arousing the suspicion of the British police.

Postscript

JACK SOBLE DID NOT SPY FOR MONEY. His father, a refugee from Lithuania, had done well in the U.S.A. as a pig-bristle manufacturer, and had handed over a prosperous business to his son.

The Russians recruited Soble as an agent. It was reported later that they made threats that unpleasant things could happen to members of his family still in Lithuania. His subsequent conduct suggests that he had no family loyalty whatsoever. The fact is that Soble had a neurotic and vacillating character, and was flattered when the Russians offered him a position of some authority.

He was ordered to build up a spy ring in New York, and did this very successfully. Two of his recruits were Maurice and Lorna Cohen—who later appeared in the Lonsdale case in England, when, their name changed to Kroger, they operated Lonsdale's communications centre at Ruislip. But later Soble failed to satisfy his employers. He spent a lot of money with very little practical result. And he did not know that one of his agents had been infiltrated into his organisation by the F.B.I.

Early in 1957 he and his wife were arrested. It was a relief to the American authorities when they pleaded guilty, for an

espionage trial could reveal secrets it was designed to protect.
In the U.S.A. it was widely believed that Soble deliberately
pleaded guilty in the hope of a lighter sentence.

Maybe the same objective prompted the freedom with which
he talked about his associates—including his brother, Dr
Robert A. Soblen.[1] This man was of more determined character,
and emphatically denied that he had ever been a Russian agent.

However, he was found guilty after a trial in August, 1961.
There was some sympathy for him even in America: he was
sixty-one, and a victim of lymphatic leukemia—the doctors gave
him only a year to live; his offence, if any, had been committed
fifteen years earlier, and the evidence against him was supplied by
his own brother, already shown to be undependable. The trial
was in secret, and the charge was not espionage but conspiracy.
This did not provoke confidence—it is easier to prove a charge
of conspiracy than one of spying.

He was sentenced to life imprisonment, appealed, and was
astonishingly released on bail. True, the figure was large—
seventy-five thousand dollars, but any bail was amazing in
such a serious case.

Soblen promptly fled to Israel. The laws of extradition did
not apply, but the Israel Government was persuaded to return
him to the U.S.A. On his way home under guard, he attempted
to kill himself before the aircraft reached London. Then, after
acrimonious discussion, the British Government decided that
he must continue his journey. This time he did not fail; he took
an overdose of drugs and died.

The case left many uneasy feelings. The man preferred to
die rather than face what he claimed was an unjust punishment.
And would he have been released on bail had there not been a
doubt about his guilt? This suspicion has been aggravated by the
fact that to this day it has never been revealed how he 'conspired'
to aid Russia, and what secrets he had revealed fifteen years

[1] It is not uncommon for emigrants to the U.S.A. to change their names
to something more pronounceable—and not all members of a family have
the same ideas.

before. Many American lawyers are uneasy about the whole matter.

1962 proved to be an unfortunate year for Britain: confidence in British naval security was shaken by the Lonsdale case, and then followed that of William John Vassall. It was a pitiful example of a well-known pattern. Vassall had allowed himself to be photographed in compromising circumstances, and was then blackmailed by the Russians into spying for them.

Homosexuals are a favourite target for such treatment. But in actual fact Britain—so often a pioneer in espionage methods —used homosexual agents many years before Russia. True, they were generally used as spy-catchers rather than spies. Soviet spy-masters are comparative newcomers to the old Secret Service game. They have certainly developed some new and rather unsavoury techniques, but they have learned a good deal from old-established British methods—to say nothing of devices favoured by Hitler's Gestapo.

Sex has been a factor in Secret Service ever since Samson succumbed to the wiles of Delilah. Perhaps the most intriguing story in this connection is that of the Chevalier d'Éon, that brilliant spy of Louis XV. According to the needs of the current assignment he (or she!) could pose as a gallant and cultured officer or as the fascinating "Mademoiselle Lia de Beaumont." As the latter the Chevalier was appointed a maid of honour to the Empress of Russia. Later, the Tsarina offered the Chevalier—now a man—a post in the Russian Imperial Army.

The Chevalier's ability to assume convincing disguises was due to the fact that he was of the unfortunate type of biological freak known as a hermaphrodite. He was one of a mercifully rare type—infinitesimal in numbers compared with the percentage of the population who are homosexuals, and promising material for the recruiting agents of the spy-masters.

Homosexuality is a far more common condition than most people realise. For obvious reasons it is impossible to compile figures, but it is probable that homosexuality is about as prevalent as left-handedness. Thirteen out of the first fourteen Roman emperors were homosexuals; so were many of Britain's most famous martial leaders.

The tragedy for homosexuals is that they are often and automatically classed as 'perverts' by people who don't know what they are talking about.

The subject is of vital importance to a Secret Service officer who employs homosexual agents. They, naturally, are wonderfully equipped to resist the wiles of beautiful women spies! The type known as 'inverts' can be and have been brilliantly successful. Those known as 'perverts' are always disastrous.

It is necessary to explain that, strictly speaking, a homosexual is anyone, man or woman, who is sexually attracted to a person of the same sex. In modern usage, however, a homosexual means a homosexual man; a homosexual woman is known as a Lesbian. Both homosexuals and Lesbians are included in the term 'sexual inverts,' which means an individual in whom normal sexual impulses are reversed, or inverted.

Poles apart from the 'inverts' are the unfortunate 'perverts,' in whom the sexual impulse is not necessarily inverted but is perverted—which implies that the impulse is twisted in some unnatural or evil manner.

Many years before the Wolfenden Committee sat, Military Intelligence officers were already studying the two types. The perverts were quickly judged to be useless for Intelligence work, and their files were marked 'P.U.'—Permanently Unemployable.

The others, the inverts, were more interesting. The exhibitionists—the rouged, mincing types who wore women's silk panties and nylon stockings—were promptly discarded. The residue included men and women of great intelligence, artistic sensibility, personal charm, and with qualities of leadership. Such people often find an outlet in public-spirited enterprise.

They were sorted out into 'natural' and 'synthetic' homosexuals. The 'natural' was almost invariably the son of a dominating mother and a rather feeble father—the offspring, in other words, of a family in which the normal roles of the masterful father and submissive mother have been reversed.

The 'synthetics' were more tragic. Some were men who had entered domestic service as boys—handsome young footmen who had been seduced into homosexual practices by a perverted employer. Selection was of course made with the utmost care.

Some of the homosexuals selected for service did a grand job for their country One such man, indeed, saved thousands of British lives. It was during Hitler's flying-bomb campaign. Patient counter-spy work established the fact that the Germans were getting vital weather reports via a young foreigner in London. He could of course have been dealt with drastically, but a cleverer course was pursued. Under observation, the young foreigner proved to be a homosexual. So an English invert made his acquaintance. Their common impulses soon made them fast friends—there was no suggestion of any physical connection. The Englishman soon exercised an influence over his friend, and used it cunningly. The result was a stream of *misleading* weather information to the Germans, with hundreds of flying bombs falling harmlessly into the North Sea!

A famous psychologist has said of the perverted homosexual: "He has a blunted moral sense—there is a defect in his conscience. He does not choose to be cured. He feels that he is a member of a third and misunderstood sex. To men like this, the loyalty oath means nothing."

In 1961 America was staggered by a case as startling as that of our own Burgess and Maclean—with which, indeed, it had close parallels.

William Martin and Bernon Mitchell held important posts in the National Security Agency. As skilled mathematicians, they were in charge of teams employed in breaking foreign codes. Suddenly they disappeared from their posts. They were next heard of in Moscow. There they talked. Their country, they declared, was "fighting dirty." They had defected because they knew that the United States Government was interfering in the internal affairs of other countries. (The Russians, of course, *never* interfere in the internal affairs of other countries!) They described how the United States had broken the codes not only of Russia but of allies of America. And they reported on hundreds of details the U.S.A. had learned from decoded messages.

The effects of their treachery dumbfounded their fellow-countrymen. A Pentagon authority declared that these were equivalent to the effects of the betrayal of atomic secrets by Dr Klaus Fuchs. All the countries named, of course, promptly issued new codes to their diplomatic and Intelligence staffs. The effects of one act of treachery can be considerably more disruptive than the activities of a dozen spies.

Why had Martin and Mitchell betrayed their country's carefully guarded secrets? The truth emerged. They were homosexuals. They supported the opinion of the famous psychologist—to them the loyalty oath meant nothing. They had an urge to rebel—to be different: this is often a feature of the homosexual's moral make-up.

Not one of their friends or members of their cryptanalyst staffs had ever suspected their homosexual tendencies. Nor had Security staffs.

But someone had. There was no question of blackmail in this case. Secret Service work often involves great mental strain, and may develop any latent tendency towards neuroticism. Russian agents would certainly have been assigned to mix socially with the N.S.A. cryptanalyst staff. One of them may have noticed signs of suppressed strain in these two men. If he knew his job—as he would need to do if he wished to survive—he would have ferreted out their secret. What machinery was then set in motion is not yet known. But—Mitchell and Martin were in Moscow.

Ordinary American citizens were worried. Why, they asked, did Security experts not make the same observations as those evidently made by a Russian agent?

The same question was asked, of course, at the time of the

defection of Burgess and Maclean. Here were two homosexuals whose failing *was* known to many of their acquaintances. Maclean, indeed, was a sexual freak—a happily married
husband and father when sober, but a homosexual when drunk.
Someone in Whitehall should have noticed this condition, with
its sinister possibilities. The Russians did.

It is important to note that Britain is one of the few countries
in Europe where Russian agents can exert pressure by blackmail on homosexuals. It is almost the only country where homosexuality is a crime. Some Security officers have recommended
the amendment of the law—Lesbians, not less culpable, are
not similarly punished.

The vast majority of homosexuals—born that way—are
honest and clean-living people. Their treatment arouses a
feeling of resentment, which in its turn could make them an
easier prey to Russian pressure. But it would be quite absurd to
suspect every homosexual of being a spy. All that can be said
is that he is more likely to be suborned than a normal man
because of the possibility of blackmail.